Y0-BED-190

THE AFRICAN IMAGE

by the same author

*

DOWN SECOND AVENUE

THE AFRICAN IMAGE

EZEKIEL MPHAHLELE

FREDERICK A. PRAEGER, *Publisher*

New York

BOOKS THAT MATTER

Published in the United States of America in 1962
by Frederick A. Praeger, Inc., Publisher
64 University Place, New York 3, N. Y.

Library of Congress Catalog Card Number: 62–19981

Printed in the United States of America

This book is dedicated

to

EDWARD DAVIS

for a stimulating and elevating association, but for which I should not have summoned the cheek to risk any more dangers after my early stutterings.

ACKNOWLEDGEMENTS

Acknowledgements are due to the University of South Africa for permission to use material from—*The Non-European Character in South African English Fiction*—a thesis the writer submitted in 1956 for a senior degree. This concerns essays on Olive Schreiner, Sarah Gertrude Millin, Alan Paton, William Plomer, Laurens van der Post, Peter Abrahams, Thomas Pringle, Percy Fitzpatrick, William Charles Scully, Nadine Gordimer, Joseph Conrad, E. M. Forster and William Faulkner. To this has been added entirely new material on Nadine Gordimer, Sarah Gertrude Millin, Doris Lessing, Elspeth Huxley, David Karp, Joyce Cary, Sylvester Stein, William Plomer, Uys Krige, Jack Cope, Ethelreda Lewis and the rest of the writing discussed in Part Two of this book. Thanks are also due to the publishers of the journals, *Africa South* and *Drum*; of *Africa in Transition* and the journal, *The Twentieth Century* for permission to incorporate the writer's articles in Chapter 3; of *Encounter* for the article that constitutes Chapter 6. Details of these and other obligations are indicated either in footnotes or in the Bibliography.

Soon will the earth cover us all: then the earth, too, will change, and the things also which result from change will continue to change forever, and these again forever. For if man reflects on the changes and transformations which follow one another like wave after wave and their rapidity, he will despise everything which is perishable.

MARCUS AURELIUS

There are no fixtures in nature. The universe is fluid and volatile. Permanence is but a word of degrees.

RALPH WALDO EMERSON

CONTENTS

PREFACE

In the summer of 1959 I went to Britain on a four-and-a-half months' leave. I was going out of Africa for the very first time in my thirty-nine years of life. In July 1960 I attended the annual conference of the American Society of African Culture at Philadelphia, where I sat on the 'Negritude and Culture' committee. With three other African delegates I was taken on a ten days' tour of Philadelphia, Washington, Chicago and New York.

On both these excursions I was continually being required, often to an annoying degree, to put myself across. I found it necessary often to change my stance, to overhaul my attitudes, consolidate my dislike for British conventionalism and American smugness and *naïveté* in thinking that the African's mind is so undeveloped that you need only stuff dollar bills into his pockets and he won't think of socialism. On the other hand I found myself warming up to British courtesy in public places and that easy manner of the American that helps a stranger glide into a comfortable if sometimes superficial relationship, as distinct from having to dynamite his way through before he can be accommodated by the British.

The week I spent in Paris *en route* back to Nigeria after the summer vacation in Britain was enough to give me a glimpse into the fiction concocted so glibly by complacent middle-class Africans about 'the colour-blindness' of the French. Yes, the white world is still a pretty dark one for the man of colour, especially in the so-called 'Free World'.

It was my impressions in Britain that threw up into relief my thoughts on what I choose to call the African image, and I yielded to the inner compulsion to put them down on paper.

In September 1957 I exiled myself in Nigeria. I was one of the two hundred or so non-whites who had been banned from teaching by the South African Government because we had criticized its 'Bantu education' policy. Other repressive laws were mounting, and I had to get out or shrivel up with bitterness. So here I am, with my wife and children, an extra-mural lecturer of the University College, Ibadan.

Since I came here, I have been chafing and trying to readjust my underdog mentality—in short, to live with freedom. I have also run full tilt into political and social argument and discussion which would hardly ever arise where I come from, but some of which is just another aspect of contemporary thinking among our angry black men throughout the continent. I now see my personal problem of coming to terms with this new setting as part of the much larger one that finds considerable comment in all this discussion and argument.

My purpose in raising it all in this book is as much to try to clear my own mind about things as to try to evaluate the sense and nonsense that is often said and thought by whites and blacks, top dogs and underdogs about each other and about themselves.

E. M.

University College, Ibadan

Part One

POLITICAL IMAGES

Chapter 1

THE AFRICAN PERSONALITY

The African personality. A charming phrase. When Dr. Kwame Nkrumah uttered it at a plenary session of the All-African People's Conference in December 1958, it did mean something. Within the four walls of that packed hall in Accra, the whole of Africa, except for the Gambia and Sudan, sat and listened, waiting for something to unify her peoples. And as the applause shook that Community Hall, I felt elevated. A thrilling sensation shot up to my head, and the roots of my hair caught it.

I was sure that I was speaking the same language—I, a South African exile—with my fellow-Negroes from East, Central and West and North Africa. In a sense I was right. And this idea of an African personality took on a palpable shape: something that could express the longings and ambitions, aches and torments, the anger and hunger of our people and shout them out to the outside world.

During committee discussion and subsequent plenary sessions the African personality began to recede, to become vaguer and vaguer, and even to seem unreal. But at the same time we were reaching out for each other in order to understand one another's peculiar problems. And we found a unifying factor in this one thing: the aching desire to be free and, as Kwame Nkrumah said, to attain the political kingdom. This bond cuts across cultural, ethnic and other cleavages.

I came away from that conference, as most of the Africans must have, with renewed courage and zip. And now I know why the idea of the African personality can remain but a glorious myth, which had nothing to do with the success of the Accra Conference.

At best, it can be but a focus, a coming into consciousness. It's no use pretending that it means anything in any practical terms.

The Muslim-Arab north is closed to the African culturally. For the Nigerian, Ghanaian, the Sierra Leonean, the Ugandian, the Nyasa, and the Northern Rhodesian, the issue seems pretty clear. They are not faced with a white settler community that has any claim to equality of place in government. Only 4 per cent of land in Nyasaland is occupied by Europeans and 2·5 per cent in Northern Rhodesia. With the formation of the Central African Federation, the small white settler groups have been made to feel strong and eager to make concerted claims they would not have had the numbers to sustain in their respective territories. And, proportionately, African interests have been undermined. That is why the Federation had to be rammed down the throats of the unwilling Africans. In French West Africa—or should one use that inflated phrase, 'the African states of the former French Community'?—there are strong and influential pockets of French commercial enterprise, but here also whites can be 'put in their place'. French administrators can still be given a choice by the African authorities to stay or go.

In Kenya, Tanganyika, Southern Rhodesia, South Africa, there are multi-racial communities, where each racial group wants to be adequately represented in government. In these territories, as in Algeria, it would be plain madness to tell the whites, Indians, Arabs or Coloured people to quit, or even to occupy a status of sufferance.

In the Portuguese territories of Angola and Mozambique, where there are now rumblings of political resistance, the Portuguese feudal lords simply consider themselves as being in a part of Portugal, virtually.

So, when West Africans say they want freedom, they mean they want an entirely African government. Ugandians must still face up to the presence of Asians; they can't ignore them, and they have no moral right to boycott internal Indian trade, apart from the fact that such an act is not practical politics. Some parties in Kenya mean 'majority rule'. This in turn implies a government by Africans as a majority race. Other parties, on the other hand, say they have their doors open to all races. For them freedom will mean a mixed majority party in government, representing non-racial groups, the hope being probably that the Africans will always be in the majority in a mixed party. In South Africa, by 'freedom' we of the banned African National Congress, mean a state of life in which there will be a non-racial society in which I can vote for any man, black or white, who speaks my language; in which all parties will be mixed and there won't be any need to talk of minorities. The Congolese wanted and have been granted independence. The Africans will rule. But even within this framework there are conflicting interests among the tribes which it has profited Belgian and American investors to keep apart over the years. It remains to be seen what the white man's place will be in the Congo when the present strife is over. In the British Protectorate of Basutoland, although the blacks will dominate the National Council, there is a common voters' roll for black and white.

On the political plane, therefore, all these different meanings we attach to freedom make nonsense of the African Personality. To add to this, with the exception of Guinea, and perhaps Ghana, none of the countries in Africa which have been or still are under white rule have deviated from the party system of parliamentary democracy. And apart from talk of dispensing with the opposition, there is no sign of future change. How is the African Personality expressed in all this imitation? Capitalist economy has for a long time now been battering on African traditions. Our traditional forms of communism and communal responsibility in which the land belongs to the people under the chief's trusteeship, co-operative farming, and so on, are fast going. Private enterprise is setting in. Africans have amassed capital and have enormous interests in property, for all the talk of Socialism in certain parts of West Africa. Programmes for redistribution of land and other social reforms do not exist in such parts.

Beyond the focus on freedom from colonialism in certain countries and fascist white rule in others, and the emergence into nationhood of others, the only thing that can really be said to be capable of expressing an African Personality lies in those areas of cultural activity that are concerned with education and the arts. And this requires no slogan at all. Guinea and Mali are already turning away from the educational system of French orientation. Nigeria and Ghana have begun to realize that an educational system modelled purely along British lines does not necessarily supply the needs of free emergent countries.

Throughout Negro Africa the content of education will have to outgrow colonial origins of whatever brand. The African artist, because he must needs deal with African themes, rhythms and idiom cannot but express an African personality. There need be no *mystique* about it. The experiences that his art is about and his perspective are peculiarly African—if his art has authenticity—as distinct from a European's or American's or a Chinaman's. Perhaps a Pan-African conference of sociologists, artists, writers and educationists need to meet and talk about these things.

But even here, it is no use pretending that we are talking about anything absolute. The artist must keep searching for this African Personality. He can't help doing so because after all it is really a search for his own personality, for the truth about himself. But if he thinks of the African Personality as a battle-cry, it's bound to throw him into a stance, an attitude, and his art will suffer. The paradox is that the only reasonable area where this personality can be looked for is apt to negate it very often, simply because of the individuality of every artist.

It is the few artists and writers who have been trained overseas who are most anxious to remind themselves that they are African and to reorientate their art. They get irritated when others fail to see the need for an 'African Personality' slogan. Not so long ago I had occasion to speak to William Conton, the Sierra Leonean author of *The African*, and some Ghanaian artists at a conference on African culture in Ibadan. They thought I was minimizing the problem of reorientation for the African who finds himself soaked in European tradition and back among his people. Maybe because I haven't had an overseas education.

Mr. Conton's novel, *The African*, is a beautifully written and highly polished book and it shows a keen sensitivity. It is also a good example of how political slogans, if made a principle of art, can destroy the impact a work of art might have had. He is all the time advertising the African way of life to the foreign reader, with an air of discovery. His hero does say he is rediscovering the

African in himself. The purity and innocence of Africa . . . naked feet . . . a girl soaping her body and laughing in the rain. The damnable old *cliché* that we have come to associate with the colonial or the European who comes to Africa with that back-to-the-womb expression on his face. A number of experiences Mr. Conton's hero goes through in order to rediscover his Africa, to 'project the African Personality', are contrived, and this is the stance that spoils the author's good writing. Must the educated African from abroad come back to re-colonize us? Must he walk about with his mouth open, startled by the beauty of African women, by the black man's 'heightened sensitivity'? It's all so embarrassing.

The number of African artists and writers who have not been discovered because they are locked up in their ghettoes in multi-racial communities, and who cannot speak to a world audience because of brutal white rule and racial prejudice, is much too large compared with the few who go abroad—too large for us to worry excessively about the latter. We are going to confuse the majority group with such slogans as the 'African Personality'. The problem of the African who wants to readjust himself to a country he has long left is not an inherently African dilemma. Everywhere else in the world there are artists who are battling to readjust themselves—as exiles or former exiles, and in several other roles.

We are not going to help our artist by rattling tin-cans of the African Personality about his ears. The dial of response inside him will quiver in the way the dial of a balance does when you throw a weighty object on it instead of placing it gently. And while it quivers like that it does not register anything at all. That's how slogans act on an artist. In the final analysis, the battle must be resolved inside himself as a result of his own effort. Every artist in the world, African or not, must go through the agony of purging his art of imitations and false notes before he strikes an individual medium. Leave the artist to this process of evolution; let him sweat it out and be emancipated by his own art. He is after all the sensitive point of his community and the cultural impacts about him must, if he has the make-up of an artist, teach him to express the longings, failings and successes of his people. He will also know that if he wants to list the good qualities of the African, a monograph is the place for that.

There is another aspect of the African Personality. This is *négritude*. I deal with this at length in the next two chapters. The two concepts often quarrel with each other, because *négritude* wants to peg things. 'Emotion is at the heart of *négritude*. Emotion is Negro.' So says Leopold Sédar Sénghor, an apostle of this creed. This is supposed to show in Negro writing, especially poetry. And here we have something biological. On the other hand, as Professor St. Clair Drake, formerly head of the department of sociology at the University College of Ghana, indicated in a speech at one time, African politicians vary their verbs when they talk about the African Personality. Some will say we must 'project' it; others want to 'assert' it; others again will 'establish' it; others want to 'promote' it.

Chapter 2

WHAT PRICE 'NÉGRITUDE'?

In 1955 the first conference of the Society of African Culture met in Paris, its place of birth. Negro artists and writers came together then to discuss the various problems attending the concept of *négritude*—a word coined to embrace all Negro art, or the negroness of artistic activity. The term was created by the great Negro poet of Martinique (West Indies), Aimé Césaire, to denote a certain quality which is common to the thought and behaviour of Negroes. African and Afro-American Negroes were present at that conference. The Society was conceived by the men who publish the journal, *Présence Africaine*.

One of the most important figures who inspired it was Leopold Sédar Sénghor, poet and politician and President of Senegal. The editor of *Présence Africaine* is Alioune Diop, a most devoted apostle of *négritude* and a man with drive. The editorial board includes such other men as Thomas Diop, the Senegalese, and Jacques Rabemananjara, the poet who was exiled from Madagascar.

The journal is devoted to putting across to a largely ignorant world the various aspects of African culture. It is significant that it is not the African in British-settled territories—a product of 'indirect rule' and one that has been left in his cultural habitat—who readily reaches out for his traditional past. It is rather the assimilated African, who has absorbed French culture, who is now passionately wanting to recapture his past. In his poetry he extols his ancestors, ancestral masks, African wood carvings and bronze art and tries to recover the moorings of his oral literature; he clearly feels he has come to a dead-end in European culture, and is still not really accepted as an organic part of French society, for all the assimilation he has been through. As a result, French-speaking African nationalists have become a personification of this strong revulsion, even although some of them have married French women.

Says Leopold Sédar Sénghor in his *Prayer to Masks:*

> You purify the air of eternity, here where I breathe air of my fathers.
> Masks of maskless faces, free from dimples and wrinkles.
>
> Say, who else could return the memory of life to men with a torn hope?

In his beautiful poem, *New York,* he contrasts Manhattan with Harlem, the Negro quarter. Of the former, he says:

> No mother's breast, but only nylon legs. Legs and breasts that have no sweat nor smell.
> No tender word for there are no lips, only artificial hearts paid for in hard cash.
>
> Nights of insomnia or nights of Manhattan! So agitated by flickering lights, while motor horns howl of empty hours
> And while dark waters carry away hygienic loves, like rivers flooded with corpses of children.

Of Harlem?:

> Harlem! Harlem! Harlem! Now I saw Harlem! A green breeze of corn springs up from the pavements ploughed by the naked feet of dancers,
> Bottoms waves of silk and sword blade breasts, water-lily ballets and fabulous masks.

Manhattan women are just 'scented crocodiles' to Sénghor.

Leon Damas, from French Guiana, writes in his *Black Dolls*:

> Give me my black dolls
> to disperse
> the image of pallid wenches, vendors of love,
> going and coming
> on the boulevard of my boredom.

In *Balance Sheet*, Damas says:

> I feel ridiculous
> in their shoes, in their dinner jackets,
> in their stiff shirts, their paper collars,
> with their monocles and their bowler hats
> I feel ridiculous,
> with my toes that were not made
> to sweat from morning to evening
> in their swaddling clothes that weaken my limbs
> and deprive my body of its beauty.

Jacques Romain from Guinea (he died recently) writes in *When the Tam-tam Beats*:

> Your heart trembles in the shadows
> like a face reflected in troubled waters.
> An old picture rises from the tomb of the night,
> You feel the sweet magic of yore;
> A river carries you away from the shore,
> Carries you away into ancestral fields.

Much of the poetry is sheer romanticism, often it is mawkish and strikes a pose. But it *does* show a revulsion on the part of these poets, most of whom lived in France, Negro as they are.

Lately, *Présence Africaine* has, unfortunately, been too preoccupied with anthropological creepy-crawlies to devote enough attention to the problems of the artist in his present predicament. It worried me a lot that such a useful institution did not seem to be aware of cultural crosscurrents that characterize artistic expression in multi-racial societies. They seemed to think that the only culture worth exhibiting was traditional or indigenous. And so they concentrated on countries where interaction of streams of consciousness between black and white has not taken place to any significant or obvious degree, or doesn't so much as touch the cultural subsoil. A number of these enthusiasts even became apologetic about the Western elements in their own art. So on my way back to Nigeria from Britain, in November 1959, I stopped in Paris to exchange ideas with the men of *Présence Africaine*. Where do *we* come in—we, who are detribalized and are producing a proletarian art? Has the Society of African Culture no room for us? This is what I wanted to know. Gerard Sekoto, the Pretoria painter, accompanied me. During the ten years that he has been in Paris, he has been trying to come to terms with himself about his art and jostling with no fewer than 4,000 painters in Paris alone for attention. (He still uses African themes even in his present social climate. His 'Mother and Child' works are to me the most fascinating things Sekoto has ever created. They exude, as do his other creations of the Paris period, a wonderful spirit of freedom and display a universality which could only result from an impact of cultures in the artist.)

We met Thomas Diop, Rabemananjara, Paul Niger from Guadeloupe, and Dr. Misipo, the Cameroonian scholar. During our talk Sekoto and I tried to bring home to our friends the problems facing culture in multi-racial communities like those in South Africa. I shall try to make myself clear presently in this chapter. Our choral and jazz music, literature, dancing in South Africa have taken on a distinctive content and form which clearly indicate a merging of cultures. And we are not ashamed of it. Particularly is this so in our serious music. They couldn't understand why our classical music should not be purely indigenous. Rabemananjara argued that there could be no conscious merging of cultures until we had attained political independence. But then the artist never waits for that kingdom to come: our vernacular and English writers had been producing work since about 1870—long before organized political resistance took shape in 1912. And we in South Africa are poised between the two main cultural currents. We have got to do something about it, as we indeed are doing, more than the whites with blinkers on are prepared to admit. That is why our music will always be more vital, vibrant and meaningful than *boere-musiek* (Afrikaans music), which is a monument to a dead past, full of a false posturing, hemmed in as it is by a frontier laager.

After we had given an account of our social and political history, as best as we could in two hours, our French-speaking friends indicated that only then did they realize how both real and unreal the African Personality can be in terms of cultural expression. In fact it was already clear that the artist at work and the nationalist who blabbers all this political jargon are not one and the same person: something happens in one's art which does not support, and is not supported by, another man's platform theories. They admitted that while we try to re-establish our past, such a function can only find proper focus if it is going to help us know ourselves better in the context of present-day cultural activity. When I am engaged in creative writing, for instance, my characters interest me in so far as they are in a so-called mixed society. What they were and what they did before the white man came interests me only as far as it throws light on their present behaviour and human relationships. And then I don't want to depict African characters only. I first came to know the white man at the point of a boot and then at the point of an index finger—as a servant to him. I know there is much more to him than his fear of me, and I want to explore this other side. But then he won't let me!

At the end of our talk, our friends asked me to convey a message of solidarity to the oppressed people of South Africa. And how do these people respond to their situation?

We are in a small dingy room, in the heart of an African township. Alexandra, to be precise—a sprawling collection of dusty houses and filthy narrow streets. A bachelor's room, maybe, in a tenement. Everything about the interior is drab. A flickering candle stands on a corner table, burning as if it would never stop. A combo of six are grinding out a jazz arrangement, noisy but robust. The trumpets neigh; the alto-sax moans unashamedly and whimpers; the rickety old piano tries valiantly to surrender to the player who is reconciling a few false keys. But the show must go on; the drummer beats it out as he stoops over his instruments, head tilted one side, the mouth drooping, open like a safety valve to let out all the emotions that pulsate inside. It's a tableau of excruciating concentration.

Excruciating? Yes. There is a certain divine compulsion to play, and it's a kind of sacrifice, an assertion. You see, these lads have been sweating in the city during the day, absorbing all the hurts and insults from the white man, in a city where they are not allowed to live among whites. They have had to stand in bus queues for long weary hours each way. They must do something to fortify themselves for the next day's demands. And so on the cycle goes. Tomorrow and other days they will be playing in a hall for people to jive. Again it will be hot jazz, coming straight from the anvil on which human emotions come under the endless hammering of the day's experiences.

In every South African town, big and small, there are jazz bands and troupes. Some disband and new ones come up and some of the old ones go on, mellowing with time. It must go on like this because it is an escape as well as an assertion. If there is no escape, someone will crack up somewhere, someone will be trampled down and the human mind doesn't give in so easily. You may be arrested for not having a pass or for protesting against certain laws, but no one can arrest you for singing or performing on an instrument. It's one of the last strongholds of human dignity and self-respect.

What is produced is the kind of music one often hears on gramophone records peddled under meaningless labels like 'Zulu jive' or 'Bantu jive' or some such romanticized thing. It's most of the time an imitation of American jazz with vernacular lyrics. A number of our shops and restaurants have juke boxes. Out on the street, and on the veranda, where no European comes to tell you that you're making noise for him, boys and girls are to be seen jiving as if nothing else in the whole world mattered.

It may be startling to a non-South African to notice how much of our cultural life is American. It won't be so startling when one considers that 5,000,000 Africans are urbanized and therefore detribalized. The 3,000,000 working on European farms are at least detribalized, owing no allegiance to a chief. The 3,000,000 under chiefs move constantly between the city and the Reserves, and already jazz troupes are to be found in the villages. But why should it be the American and not the British way of doing things? The simple reason is that the British are not as demonstrative and extrovert as the Americans. The black man is naturally demonstrative, and in the south he will look for the most intensive, as well as the nearest, medium of expressing himself.

There is another aspect of the music of the south: the more serious and meaningful, because more creative, aspect. We have a large crop of African composers who use European notation and infuse into the vernacular lyrics, librettos and rhythms an African idiom. These composers have given choral music a great push during the last half-century. Go anywhere in South Africa and you will hear a countless number of male-voice and mixed choirs, in the most outlandish places. They sing both European and African compositions. Eisteddfod festivals are supported by enthusiastic choirs in and out of school. It has been said that some African choirs in South Africa easily rank with the best in Russia or the British Isles.

Escapist music, like escapist art in general, is only a temporary phase in the cultural life of any people; temporary in the sense that it cannot substitute more creative art. It is our serious music that tells, and will continue to tell, more and more eloquently the story of Africa, her longings, sufferings, apathy, her strength, her weakness.

The Negroes are the largest cinema-going group in South Africa and they have until recently been confined to Jewish- and Indian-owned cinemas, not being allowed to enter European cinemas. A new law is being introduced to prevent Negroes from entering Indian-owned cinemas, so that Indians, Coloureds and Africans do not mix. And a number of films are banned for Negroes, but can be shown to Coloureds and Indians of all ages, to say nothing about whites.

Women, whether they be literate or not, soon find themselves in one cultural club or another: cookery, sewing and knitting clubs; self-help clubs where housewifery and other aspects of domestic life are predominant topics of study; mothers' welfare clubs which collect money and build and manage nursery schools; food and vegetable clubs which buy groceries and sell to club members at reduced prices; ballroom dance clubs. Women who do not enter the teaching, nursing and medical professions go into domestic service, factory and clerical work for the small number of non-white employers or for white agencies relying on non-white patronage. Because of the terrific sweep of industrialization and urbanization and repressive measures, the gap between the uneducated and educated man or woman is very narrow.

The white man's policy of apartheid has the effect of creating a double stream of cultural life in South Africa. The whites with their own schools, universities, cinemas, theatres, sports teams and stadiums, concert halls and so on, and the Africans, Coloureds and Indians with their own inferior institutions. If the white ruling class could make a law to stop us listening to or performing Bach, Mozart, Beethoven, Chopin and the like, they would do so. The reason why the Government won't introduce television is the fear that non-whites will—even more than the radio and cinema make it possible at present—form part of an ever-growing world audience; an audience that is absorbing more and more entertainment and becoming more and more involved in a cross-breeding of ideas. A dangerous antidote to apartheid!

Recently, the non-white South African Federation of Football Associations applied for affiliation to FIFA, the international soccer federation, on the grounds that its European counterpart in South Africa is an apartheid body and theirs not. The international body has decided to keep the white soccer federation as a member and reject the non-whites' application. Not so the world table tennis federation, which has kicked out the European body and affiliated the non-white group. Other favourite sports among non-whites are rugby, boxing, golf and cycling.

Whenever celebrated artists have come to South Africa on contract, we have asked them to come and perform to non-Europeans in our own segregated halls. Violinist Yehudi Menuhin; pianists Eileen Joyce, Louis Kentner, Julius Katchen; singer Isobel Baillie; actors Sir Lewis Casson and Dame Sybil Thorndyke and Emlyn Williams did accept our invitations. Dozens of others decided to sacrifice art for the colour bar. Like the late Gigli and all the other Italian operatic stars, pianists like Claudio Arrau, singers like Elisabeth Schumann, Erna Sack, Victoria de Los Angeles—all these have come and gone like mere names without performing for the millions of non-whites eager to hear them.

Since Father Trevor Huddleston asked British artists three years ago to boycott South Africa by refusing to perform there because of her racial policy, the British Musicians' Union and Equity, the theatre union, have been up to all sorts of mental and verbal gymnastics to avoid straightforward action against South Africa. Band-leader Johnny Dankworth was the first and so far the only musician to turn down an engagement in our country. Equity has decided to allow its members to perform in South

Africa only on condition that they are allowed to give a certain proportion of their engagements to non-whites. This means, needless to say, an acceptance by such artists of the poor segregated halls that non-whites use. And still we stand in front of His Majesty's or Colosseum or Empire theatres in Johannesburg and gaze with envy at the placards and read big names in the entertainment world, knowing that we shall never enter. . . .

Two English-speaking universities, that in Cape Town and that in Johannesburg, have for many years been admitting hundreds of non-white students on the basis of academic equality and social apartheid, i.e. in sport and residential halls. Here our doctors and lawyers have been trained. Natal Province has two parallel universities with the staff overlapping in several departments. Here there is also academic equality. Natal has also a medical school for non-whites only, who must undertake never to treat white patients. Fort Hare University College, exclusively for non-whites, has produced most of our graduates and political leaders. Outside Fort Hare, there are eight independent universities with an average population of 4,000 white students. Among them is the University of South Africa which caters for about 4,000, about 1,000 of whom are non-whites, all taught through correspondence lectures as external students. The Government has now passed an Act in Parliament preventing non-whites from entering the two 'open' universities and placing higher education for Africans directly under the Department of Bantu Administration and setting up machinery to create inferior colleges that will serve separate ethnic groups.

Three things emerge from the segregationist policies of the white Government which prevent the non-white from becoming either a stable peasant or a stable urban worker, and creates in him a haunting sense of insecurity. First, the South African white has come to accept a double stream of cultural life, which the African hates because he knows that he can never be independent even in the dream-state the white man says he can make for the black man. Second, cultural development is seriously hampered in an unsettled black community and can only reach pigmy stature among the privileged and sheltered white community. Third, traditional culture, much of which the missionary destroyed, has come to be associated by the Negro with an inferior political status and ethnic grouping which will destroy all the work that has been done by the educated Negro to unify all the tribes. Just as the primary and secondary school curricula are designed for African Coloureds and Indians and whites separately, so is the syllabus for African crafts meant for Africans only and therefore highly suspect. A gramophone record company which has been recording indigenous music throughout Africa purely as a commercial venture tries to sell its wares by telling us that Duke Ellington, Louis Armstrong, Beethoven, Mozart and so on are foreign and so we should love and stick to our own music.

In spite of these setbacks, a proletarian culture is in the making. To this the average white man is completely blind. He himself doesn't even realize that he has been influenced by Africans. You only need to see a South African white abroad and outside his social setting to notice how deep that influence has gone. And in spite of the Mixed Marriages and Immorality Acts that prevent marital and sex relations between black and white, intermarriage between races in South Africa would have a better chance of success than anywhere else on this continent—more so than the white ruling class are prepared to admit. Three hundred years is a long time in terms of cultural impacts. Escapist music, like the flood of escapist short stories now being produced, is a passing phase. Composers like Mohapeloa (Basutoland), Matshikiza, Masiza, Motsepe, Tyamzashe, Moerane, Sidyiyo, Marivate, Mamabolo, are names that will last because theirs is the choral music, mentioned earlier, which blends the West and Africa.

A good deal of this is protest music; about the black man's sufferings, police terror, the sinking of the *Mendi* during World War I, great epidemics and so on. Some of it extols certain memorable mission stations, the impact of Christianity. Some of it again is pastoral and some contains themes of love, homesickness and the innocence of childhood. Yes, it is a music composed against the background of unsettled communities, perpetual refugees who keep moving to the tune of Government proclamations and the cycle of migrant labour. It derives its power from the black man's sense of insecurity.

In February 1959 a great jazz opera was produced in South

Africa—*King Kong*. Even the Afrikaans press was ecstatic about it. The story was written by Harry Bloom, author of the prize-winning novel, *Episode*, and the music composed by Todd Matshikiza. The choreography was by a white man. The music reveals influences of Gershwin, Cole Porter and other composers of American musical comedy. But there are also vigorous, earthy African rhythms which are typical of the composer's earlier four-part music.

The body of music that Mr. Hugh Tracey of the African Music Society has recorded as African indigenous art will be of interest only to historians or at best to composers who feel disposed to use it as a basis for contemporary themes and forms. By itself, it belongs to the museum. And it is inane for anybody to say, as Mr. Tracey has often said, that this is the music from which we shouldn't ever deviate, or neglect in favour of Mozart and Duke Ellington.

I was first introduced to the enchantment and power of European classical music by a friend of mine, Simon Ngubane, twelve years ago. He is one of the best music critics in South Africa and is music supervisor in African schools in Natal Province. We were listening to a broadcast performance of Wagner's *Overture to Tannhäuser*. In a moment of sheer ecstasy that often makes him burst out into a spirited stammer, Simon pinpointed the portion depicting Tannhäuser's conflict and war against temptation. He knew I had for months been struggling to penetrate the meaning, or rather the poetry, of this form. I had grown fat on jazz—raw, ripe and rotten, and suddenly I had been seized by the desire to explore and understand the classics. That was the beginning of my awakening in this direction. Ever since I have found classical music immensely elevating and satisfying: Mozart, Beethoven, Chopin, Dvořák, Vivaldi stand high on my scale outside opera. Later, when I turned to jazz again for diversion to fit the mood I was in at the moment, I discovered how much veneration I have for Duke Ellington's music. For me, he and Gershwin—in that order—are still the greatest of the greats in jazz, and they have ceased to be just an excuse for diversion or background for conversation.

Village and location arts and crafts are continuing, but both artist and craftsman are poised between the forces that harass their security on the one hand and those that inspire them to retain their dignity and self-respect on the other. It may be said that these very forces should create the content of artistic effort. But the enlightened Negro whose responsibility it is to harness the creative forces of his people and give them direction is also in a conflict: to call a march back to indigenous culture and thereby help the Government to reconstruct ethnic groups and help work the repressive machinery, or leave things to drift as they do at the moment, leaving it to individual cultural activity to go the way creative genius guides it.

In the field of writing, the problems are no less acute. Vernacular writing has developed remarkably in its hundred years or so of existence. Earlier, it was restricted by a strong religious and moral content in the narrowest sense because it was published by missionary presses and written by enthusiastic converts. There was no kind of protest writing until a few Africans broke off from a missionary venture and started their own newspaper, *Imvo Zabantsunde* (*Negro Opinion*), now eighty years old. Book production continued in the hands of missionary presses, and the fiction was sickly, sentimental, romantic and semi-religious, and meant mostly for school readership, subject to the censorship of European school inspectors. Only in later years have books succeeded in their adult appeal like Thomas Mofolo's *Chaka* (in Sesotho) and a new Xhosa classic by A. C. Jordan and poetry written in Zulu, Sotho and Xhosa. Many of the recent works have been published by university presses as well as progressive missionary presses like Lovedale in the Cape Province, Morija in Basutoland. These presses have produced poetry by Mqhayi, Jolobe, Vilakazi, and plays by Khaketla, Dhlomo and so on, more about which later. The introduction of the study of three main Bantu languages at the universities of the Witwatersrand (Johannesburg), Cape Town, Natal and South Africa and Fort Hare College has over the last twenty years caused a spurt in vernacular writing.

A new stage has been reached in this development of vernacular literature. One that marks the beginning of disaster. An Afrikaans press in Johannesburg has recently come into existence backed by Afrikaans capital in which the white Government has both political and material interests. The fiction this press is promoting and consciously boosting for publication, whenever it portrays a non-white character who comes to the city, shows him up as a wretched picture of frustration. The hero must return to the rural areas. The reason for this? The white Government is consciously organizing legal machinery to control the influx of Africans into the towns and cities. Town folk are regarded as obstinate, intractable and too politically conscious as they become absorbed by city life, and this makes them demand voting rights: something the white man cannot tolerate. And yet frustration does not really drive the African back to the rural areas: what is there to go back to?—desert soil, eroded lands, overpopulated land, malnutrition. But if a black writer can portray a character who goes back, it is regarded as a vindication of the white man's policies. No other perspective will be published by this press. And it has created a mighty empire because it enjoys the largest circulation in African schools which are all under the Government now. White education officers in charge of African schools must recommend Bantu books for use in our schools: this is the sort of filter that is intended to keep "pure" the mind of the African child. How does an adult literature grow in such conditions?

South African Negroes writing in English write short stories today. It is not easy for the oppressed African to organize himself for the writing of a novel unless he produces the kind that panders to European 'supremacy'. The short story strikes swiftly and drives home a point with economy of language and time. The short story in such a multi-racial setting, in my own experience, goes through three stages: the romantic-escapist; the protest short story; and the ironic, which is the meeting point between protest and acceptance.

Imagine that you lived in an African or Coloured location. You had to travel fifteen miles each way between the location and the town where you worked. Each way you were among hundreds of other workers and you all poured into the electric train coaches until some sat on ledges of windows and the doors couldn't even shut. You were among the many who didn't need any effort to keep upright because you were crushed on all sides and to the point where your feet were literally suspended above the floor. Or you might be in the long, long bus queues which stay long from

4.30 to 8 p.m. Every day of your working life you had to go through this.

Out of the train, you had to look for the exit meant for *you* as a non-white person. As you converged with the whites in the city streets again, you ran into another sharp reminder: police stopping Africans for passes and queues of people who had already fallen foul of the pass law. You got through because by a stroke of luck you had remembered to take your pass with you. Once work had started, you didn't know what might happen between you and a white boss or foreman or the shop assistant or the post office clerk, whose presence hovered over you like some monstrous explosive thing.

When you reached home the same way you had left in the morning, maybe at 9 p.m., you felt physically tired and spiritually flat. You tried to settle down to writing. Your whole being quivered with latent anger; words, words, words spilled on to the pages, and you found yourself caught up in the artistic difficulty of making a parochial experience available to the bigger world on terms that may very well be possible. For then you had to give an account of your bitterness. Blinded by it, in addition to other things, you had to grope for the truth. Somewhere in this dark alley, you felt it was a hopeless fight because so much of your energy went into the effort to adjust yourself to the conditions which threaten every moment to crush you. You had to abdicate, as so many others had done and were doing, or write escapist stuff, or get out of your native habitat.

The white writer is in a privileged class. He is not physically harassed in the way his counterpart on the other side of the tracks is, and his spiritual battles are of a different set and order. Of this later, when I shall talk about African writing.

What kind of Negro readership would you be addressing yourself to? A varied one, whose tastes range from Peter Cheyney and James Hadley Chase to Dickens and Shakespeare. You are dealing with masses of people who left school after Standard IV, i.e. who spent five to six years in primary school. On their own, while working, they have cultivated a reading habit. Newspapers and periodicals, detective fiction are lapped up in enormous quantities. You also have masses of people who did three years of secondary schooling and dropped out while others were climbing up. Their tastes cover detective fiction, adventure with a love interest, pure love stories and plenty of Dickens and fiction that is set in South Africa. The pyramid tapers up quite gradually into the clerical and professional occupations where interest in fiction and non-fiction evens up, and fiction reading is much more wholesomely selective. Non-fiction taken out of libraries consists mostly of technical and academic handbooks.

And their other interests? In trains and buses lively bits of conversation, including controversy, can be heard every morning and evening about local politics and events in Ghana, Nigeria, Central Africa and East Africa, Asia, and about East-West tensions. The average townsman and secondary-school pupil are always curious to know what is happening outside South Africa. They identify themselves with the American Negro who appears in films and with the black man who is being granted independence in other parts of Africa.

Here is a country where paradoxes overlap most painfully: the ideal meeting point of indigenous character and idiom and the modern, as indicated by the modern Negro composer; the refusal of the white man to be taught anything by the African; the resistance offered by the whites to the impact of the Negro's culture such as still survives in his social relationships and communal responsibility, in his music. (So far, I know of only one white composer who has used an African theme and tune in composing a suite. This is Stewart Hylton Edwards.) Then there is the fear of focusing the Negro's attention specifically on his indigenous culture in a situation where two sets of uncompromising political aspirations are locked in a life-and-death struggle; the dynamics of culture which are always urging people to assimilate and reject an environment. We dare not now look backwards, or fight a rear-guard action, no matter how much ethnic grouping white authority wants to impose on us. Even if it were desirable for us to piece together the shattered remnants of 'Bantu culture', the artist, the musician, the writer wouldn't wait for that day. He must go on creating. Let us see who will win in the end—the written law that is intended to order people's lives about or the unfettered mind of the artist. The law can't stop Todd Matshkiza's *King Kong*; it can't tell those young men and women what wedding songs to sing.

To us in multi-racial communities, then, *négritude* is just so much intellectual talk, a cult. Of course, we have not had the misfortune of being educated abroad and being assimilated like our French-speaking friends. But *Présence Africaine* would do better, while preserving African culture where something of value still lives, to help the African artist in his present predicament; to seek out those of us who write or paint or compose in dark ghettoes and bring them to a world audience.

Chapter 3

ROOTS

I was invited to a Trinidadian party in London during my leave in Britain. The host and hostess were a charming couple. As far as I could judge, the bulk of the twenty or so guests present were working class. There were a nurse and a teacher. Throughout, West Indian music boomed from the radio; I introduced myself to about five of the guests and even engaged them in conversation. But it was very brief each time. They were very reticent, even among themselves.

Here was a group of people who seemed to be trapped, trying to counter the embarrassment of finding themselves thrown together in the same cage. And so they danced and danced, probably only too glad to make conversation unnecessary. I too threw myself into their earthy and hot 'road march'. For a while I forgot that I was in a small little island.

Andrew Salkey, the West Indian writer, told me that West Indians feel ashamed to be identified with Africans. Their African past as it were is still burning round their wrists, ankles and necks. I am not asking them to identify themselves with us: after all, it isn't their fault if they were taught some nasty things about us by their colonial masters and pseudo-historians; same as American Negroes were. One can only regret that West Indians do not seem to have caught up on the considerable body of progressive literature on Africa that has been turned out during the last twenty years.

What I resented in Britain were the superior airs of the West Indians, except in the case of their intellectuals. But at the same time I realized how frightfully insecure they are in Britain. Insecure people don't like other insecure people crashing into their little world and threatening to compete with them for a secure state. One can understand full well how there come about to be small islands of aliens in Britain, but one is depressed by it. Nigerians keep very much to themselves in the best of worlds. The South Africans, a negligible proportion of the 250,000 coloured people in Britain, come of the most cosmopolitan of African nations. But contacts between black and black and between black and white are slender and few. Yes, the white man's world is still a very tough and cruel one for the dark-skinned man. It is a painful paradox which Mr. Michael Banton poses in his most revealing book, *White and Coloured*: 'Why should Britons be strongly opposed to any discrimination in the public treatment of coloured people and at the same time be so hesitant about treating them equally in private relations?' It *is* difficult to reconcile the willingness on the part of the British to accept a group and not the individuals in the group. Look at the brutal group attitudes that have worsened rather than improved with the years in East and Central Africa. The Afrikaner can, in very paternalistic fashion, treat his servant very well as long as the latter 'keeps his place'. But the Afrikaner loathes the black people as a group. The Englishman can say quite glibly, 'A wonderful tribe those people are—so well behaved, so humble'; or 'I've given my boys a holiday today—let them have their fun, poor bastards'. And yet he is a difficult man to get at from my side of the colour line and keeps up a tacitly superior pose in his dealings with me as an individual. I think he despises and distrusts me.

The American Negro, as distinct from the West Indian, has begun, if mainly as an intellectual activity, to do research into African cultures and history. In this activity the intellectual hopes to bring to the doorstep of other Negroes the facts about Africa and its peoples. It is also an act of identification, a projection into one's African origins and therefore a placement of one's sentiments in alignment with those that we see in the African's political and cultural aspirations. A remarkable instrument for this projection is the American Society of African Culture (AMSAC), the United States counterpart of the Paris-oriented Society of African Culture, and affiliated to it. The Society has thus taken over from where intellectual giants like the 90-year-old Dr. W. E. B. Du Bois have left off. As early as 1915 Du Bois was already studying and writing on African affairs. At home in the 1920's he was waging an intellectual war against Booker T. Washington because the latter was urging his people to justify themselves and prove themselves worthy before the white man could give them political freedom (dip the bucket where you are and you'll find water). But at the same time Du Bois was working hard to draw the Negro's attention to Africa.

Marcus Garvey's Back-to-Africa movement of the 1920's was bound to fail. The Negroes were still fighting desperately hard to consolidate their freedom for which the Civil War had been fought. A symbol of this freedom and the Negro's commitment to an American existence was to be found in the manner in which New Orleans jazz burst at the seams, as it was bound to sooner or later. It was wrenched from its plantation origins as a result of the contact with whites, and it was thus made available to the rest of the world.

In the years following the first World War there was a conscious effort on the part of United States writers to discover the 'New Negro' and in the process the values of Negro folklore were reasserted, and Africa was also 'rediscovered'. Soon Harlem poets were hankering for old Africa and its kraals and jungles and tom-toms. They came to be known half-sarcastically as the 'Rhythm Boys'. One of the most typical works of the 'Roaring Twenties' was Carl Van Vechten's novel, *Nigger Heaven.* In it he explored the exotic life of Harlem which he depicted as something approaching animalism. Van Vechten was intrigued by the cabaret life of this black ghetto, and painted a romantic picture of Negroes intoxicated by jazz and the tom-tom beat of its drums; of Negroes lost in the savage rhythm of their dancing, a rhythm that recalled the dances of the Hottentots and Bushmen and African Negroes, 'swaying under the moon'. Harlem, in a Negro poet's words, was a veritable new African colony. Dr. Du Bois blasted Van Vechten for romanticizing Harlem life. Professor Stirling Brown, the poet of Howard University (Washington), says this passionate longing of the 'Rhythm Boys' for Africa was a 'cheap faddism':

'Wa-wa trumpets, trap drums (doubling for tom-toms) and

shapely dancers with bunches of bananas girdling their middles in Bamboo Inns and jungle cabarets nurtured tourists' illusions of "the Congo cutting through the black". . . .'

Even in angry protest, Claude McKay could say to the white man:

> Be not deceived, for every deed you do
> I could match—out-match: am I not Afric's son,
> Black of that black land where black deeds are done?

Nostalgically he says in his sonnet, *Outcast*:

> For the dim regions whence my fathers came
> My spirit, bondaged by the body, longs.
> Words felt, but never heard, my lips would frame;
> My soul would sing forgotten jungle songs.
> I would go back to darkness and to peace.
> But the great western world holds me in fee,
> And I may never hope for full release
> While to its alien gods I bend my knee. . . .

Countee Cullen's poem, *The Shroud of Color*, another of these mawkish poems couched in passionate words:

> Now suddenly a strange wild music smote
> A chord long impotent in me; a note
> Of jungles, primitive and subtle, throbbed
> Against my echoing breast, and tom-toms sobbed
> In every pulse beat of my frame. . . .

This phase of the 1920's passed. More and more Negro writers began to vindicate themselves as Americans.

In a brilliant paper read to the third annual conference of AMSAC in Philadelphia, June 1960, Professor Harold Isaacs of the International Studies Centre, Massachusetts Institute of Technology, discussed five Negro writers and their ancestors. He surveyed the attitude of each to his African ancestry. First, there is Langston Hughes (born 1902) whose writing life began in 1921, and has stretched over to our time. Of him Professor Isaacs says: 'Langston Hughes has proved to be the hardiest of all these literary figures (of the 1920's). He was among those yearning after the ancestral home way back then, and he is helping to exult in its new eminence now. . . . With Hughes this was more than a device or a literary style; it was a way of functioning, of coping with life.'

On his first visit to Africa Hughes exclaimed (something taking hold of him inside): 'My Africa, Motherland of the Negro peoples! And me a Negro! Africa! The real thing, to be touched and seen, not merely read about in a book.'

And then there is that famous poem of his, 'The Negro Speaks of Rivers' (1921), which first appeared in Du Bois's *Crisis*.[1]

> I've known rivers;
> I've known rivers as ancient as the world and older than
> the flow of human blood in human veins.
> My soul has grown deep like the rivers.
> I bathed in the Euphrates when dawns were young.
> I built my hut near the Congo and it lulled me to sleep.
> I looked upon the Nile and raised the Pyramids above it. . . .

Hughes was also one of the 'Rhythm Boys':

> The low beating of the tomtoms
> The slow beating of the tomtoms,
> Low . . . slow
> Slow . . . low
> Stirs your blood. . . .

He showed, in the poems that assert his blackness, a vigorous identification with Africa. 'But in the end he was badly tripped himself by the vogue for primitivism'. During the depression years, Hughes had a patron, a rich old lady. He gives an account of this in his autobiography, *The Big Sea*: 'She wanted me to be primitive, and know and feel the intuitions of the primitive. But, unfortunately, I did not feel the rhythms of the primitive surging through me, and so I could not live and write as though I did. I was only an American Negro—who had loved the surface of Africa and the rhythms of Africa—but I was not Africa. I was Chicago and Kansas City and Broadway and Harlem. And I was not what she wanted me to be.' He parted with his patron.

[1] Langston Hughes: *Selected Poems* (Alfred A. Knopf, New York, 1959).

A man of deep sincerity and a beautiful mind, and a warmth one finds only in very few people as successful as he, Hughes has arrived where he is by sheer industry and many soul-searching years. In recent years, he has sung of Africa in different tones:

> Africa,
> Sleepy giant,
> You've been resting awhile
> Now I see the thunder
> And the lightning
> In your smile.

He is preoccupied more than ever before with the Negro's commitment in his present condition:[1] 'Advice to Negro writers: step outside yourself, then look back and you will see how human, yet how beautiful and black you are. How very black—even when you're integrated.'

Richard Wright (born 1909), best known for his novel, *Native Son,* died in November, 1960 in France. He was more concerned with his place as a world citizen, and this concern had involved him in ideological conflicts. He had felt it important that he should reject the Communist movement, of which he had long been a member. As to his roots, he says in his lectures, *White Man, Listen*: 'I'm a rootless man, but I'm neither psychologically distraught nor in any wise disturbed because of it. Personally I do not hanker after, and seem not to need, as many emotional attachments, sustaining roots, or idealistic allegiances as most people. I declare unabashedly that I like and even cherish the state of abandonment, of aloneness; it does not bother me.'

When first the idea occurred that he might visit Africa, Wright thought: 'Africa! Being of African descent, would I be able to feel and know something about Africa on the basis of a common "racial" heritage? Africa was a vast continent full of "my people". . . . Or had three hundred years imposed a psychological distance between me and the "racial stock" from which I had sprung? . . . My emotions seemed to be touching a dark and dank wall. . . . Am I African? . . . What would my feelings be when I looked into

[1] American Society of African Culture, *The American Negro and his Roots* (New York 1960).

the black face of an African, feeling that maybe his great-great-great-grandfather had sold my great-great-great-grandfather into slavery?'

This suggestion that he might discover an emotional attachment to the people of Africa, of course, was bound to mar and distort his subsequent impressions of Ghanaians. Another thing he kept harping indignantly on was the possible role the blacks might have played in the slave trade. Throughout his journey he resisted the African way of life and judged it by Western standards. When he failed to fathom African beliefs and customs, he came out with some annoying generalizations: 'I found the African an oblique, hard-to-know man who seems to take a kind of childish pride in trying to create a state of bewilderment in the minds of strangers.'

And: 'I found that the African almost invariably underestimated the person with whom he was dealing; he always placed too much confidence in an evasive reply, thinking that if he denied something, then that something ceased to exist. It was childlike.'

(How condescending 'childlike' sounds.)

He also felt distrusted and so he thought he was face to face with the 'African's doubt of strangers . . . lodged deep in the heart of African culture'. How a man is able to assess a culture which, on his own admission, he cannot feel part of and which he resists, and fails to find *rapport* with, only Wright knew: 'I had understood nothing. I was black and they were black, but my blackness did not help me.' And then he was startled by the evidence of African survivals in American Negro culture!

Ralph Ellison (born 1914) has hardly any visible sentiment about his African roots. To the question, What am I? Ellison says, 'I answer that I am a Negro American. . . . For me, the Negro is a member of an American-bound cultural group with its own idiom, its own psychology. The American Negro stock is *here*, a synthesis of various African cultures, then of slavery, and of all the experience of Negroes since.'

But in an effort to correct much of the *mystique* of *négritude* Ellison goes to extremes when he asserts: 'The African content of American Negro life is more fanciful than actual.' The fact is that there *are* African survivals in American Negro life. You see them in the Negro's gait; in his bodily rhythm in a dance; in his 'separatist' religious worship where he is not ashamed to surrender himself to the emotional intensity of the devotional moment; in the abundance of his laughter when he is really tickled. For the Negro writer to admit this is not necessarily to deny that he is the synthesis of historical processes and present-day experience.

James Baldwin (born 1924), like Richard Wright, in desperation and with a sense of suffocation went to France in 1948. He came back to his fatherland in 1958 for good, determined that his struggle was right there where he had left it: to help the Negro, by means of his writing, to outlive his sense of inferiority. Baldwin found the Africans he met in Paris difficult to get on with. He felt that in spite of the African's privations, he had never 'endured the utter alienation of himself from his people and his past. His mother did not sing *Sometimes I feel like a Motherless Child*. . . . They face each other, the Negro and the African, over a gulf of three hundred years—an alienation too vast to be conquered in an evening's goodwill. . . .'

Professor Isaacs records a conversation he had with James Baldwin, in which the Negro writer said: 'Sénghor (the apostle of *négritude* and its theoretician) frightened me because of his extraordinary way of being civilized and primitive at the same time . . . I was committed to Western Society in a way he could not be . . . I couldn't really hate America the way they did. They (Africans he met in Paris) hated America, were full of racial stories, held their attitudes largely on racial grounds. . . . Whenever I was with an African, we would both be uneasy. On what level to talk? The terms of our life were so different, we almost needed a dictionary to talk. . . .'

Elsewhere, Baldwin says: 'This depthless alienation from oneself and one's people is, in sum, the American experience.' In effect, it is the search for an identity that makes all Americans kin, as Professor Isaacs remarks.

Lorraine Hansberry (born 1930), in whose play, *a raisin in the sun*, the Nigerian character and the image he represents of his people are so beautifully drawn without a condescending or patronizing tone, feels she is not Africa or Mexico, but Chicago and New York. 'Africans', she thinks, 'have their own identities, and American Negroes have—or must shape—their own.'

At tne conference of the American Society of African Culture held at Philadelphia I hit upon a vague desire among some Negroes, to dislodge themselves culturally and seek a reorientation in African values. Mr. Samuel Allen, the Negro poet who writes under the name of Paul Vesey, presented a paper analysing *négritude* as seen and felt by Aimé Césaire, Leopold Sédar Sénghor, and interpreted by Sartre. Briefly, here are Mr. Allen's signposts: Mr. Alioune Diop, secretary of the Paris-born Society of African Culture, gives as the *raison d'être* of a *négritude* the fact that the world has been taught there is no culture other than the West's, no universal values which are not hers. The effort to determine the common elements of Negro African culture is but one phase of an historic renaissance which has only begun to reshape the image of man upon the earth. *Négritude*, then, is the complete ensemble of values of African culture, and the vindication of the dignity of persons of African descent.

Jacques Rabemananjara, the Malagassy poet, says the unity of Negro culture is an act of faith. Aimé Césaire is said to be reflecting the essence of *négritude* when he says in a poem:

> Hail the royal Kailcedrat!
> Hail those who have invented nothing!
> Who have explored nothing!
> But they abandon themselves, possessed, to the essence of all things,
> Heedless of taming, but playing the game of the world. . . .

Sénghor finds the African's heightened sensibility and his strong emotional quality as his chief psychic traits. Two sources, he says, explain the origin of the psychic profile of the Negro African: the milleniums of his tropical experience and the agricultural nature of his existence; the heat and humidity of tropical regions and a pastoral closeness to the earth and the rhythms of its seasons. Emotion, he finds, is at the heart of *négritude*: 'emotion is Negro'.

Ranged against these opinions, Mr. Allen records, are those of the late Richard Wright (on American Negro poetry): its common characteristics, its rebelliousness, its intensity, its despair, can be attributed to the common social factor of oppression. Sénghor, on the other hand, finds in a poem by Wright an intensity which he considers as peculiarly African. George Lamming (Jamaican writer): politics is the only ground for a universal Negro sympathy. Peter Abrahams (South African born and now living in Jamaica): any singularities in the Negro's creative art can be attributed to the social fact of his rejection by the West.

Although Mr. Allen objectively reports these views, he himself asserts that Africa is looked to by many for a 'new humanism, for new psychic ways, for a vital force'. Earlier, in a paper included in a publication of AMSAC, *The American Negro Writer and his Roots*, Mr. Allen had said: 'Let us consider briefly the possible relevance of this concept (*négritude*) to the work of the American Negro writer or, to put it differently, its validity for a writer in our cultural situation. I think it has a role. This is not necessarily so for all of us, the writer not being a soldier marching to command. He writes, when he writes most creatively, pursuant to his own individual and most deeply felt need. The racial accident of his birth may have little influence or only indirect influence on the purpose of his writing. . . .

'It is probably true also that it was not by chance that this concept, negritude, originated among the poets rather than among those working in prose. Except for certain highly imaginative works, the novelist writes within a framework of what we term reality. He must in part concern himself with Plato's shadows—with plot and setting. His characters must grow up. He is constrained to a certain degree of reasonableness. The poet has probably a greater chance to penetrate, at once without apology and without a setting of the worldly stage, to the deepest levels of his creative concern. And so, perhaps what we are saying may have greater applicability to poetry than to prose.'

Mr. Allen had also observed that for Sénghor the *négritude* of a poem was *less the theme than the style* (my italics); 'its characteristic manner, the intensity of its passion, its rhythmic flow or the quality of its imagery, whether he writes of a ritual dance in Dahomey, of the Brittany sea coast, or of the nature of God and Man.'

Look at this poem by Aimé Césaire, of which Mr. Allen renders a translation in order to demonstrate how Césaire emphasizes the 'dynamic quality' of *négritude*:

> My negritude is not a rock, its deafness hurled against the clamour of the day
> My negritude is not a film of dead water on the dead eye of the earth
> My negritude is neither a tower nor a cathedral
> It plunges into the red flesh of the earth
> It plunges into the burning flesh of the sky
> It pierces the opaque prostration by its upright patience.

The theme is, of course, clearly *négritude*. Because the poem is a passionate outcry, a self-vindication, it has an intensity of style, of imagery: 'its deafness hurled against the clamour of the day'; 'the burning flesh of the sky'; 'upright patience'. Abstract ideas are given a concrete meaning. What have we proved? An intensely conceived subject begets—or calls for—intensity of style; so that it becomes irrelevant to talk about theme and style separately. What is so distinctively *négritude* about that? One could find in Baudelaire an intensity to match this. The difference would be that Baudelaire wouldn't talk *négritude*, but Césaire does, because he *is* Negro. So we go back to the theme, the subject of all this talk.

The main reason why *négritude* has enchanted a few American Negro writers consists in their resistance against the tendency on the part of the outside world and their fellow-Americans to regard their work as a tributary to some major American stream, or against the desire among other writers to join the mainstream of American culture, 'a desire for obliteration and passive absorption by the majority'.

The American Negro has the right to seek his roots in Africa if he wishes to, for all the good it might do his art. We must realize that he is living through a series of crises. Mr. Arthur Davis, another Negro writer, lays bare the predicament of his people most ably in his essay in the AMSAC publication referred to above. He says now that the lynching days are all but over, the enemy that gave Negro writers a common purpose is capitulating, and integration is taking place, the most fruitful literary tradition of Negro writing has been shattered: the protest element is being destroyed; the spiritual climate for integration exists, he says, and 'it becomes almost a tragic experience because it means (especially for the writer in his middle years) giving up a tradition in which he has done his apprentice and journeyman work, giving it up when he is prepared to make use of that tradition as a master craftsman'. Some writers have tried to shift the emphasis from the protest aspect to the problems and conflicts within their Negro group itself, while retaining the Negro character and background. Some even write about whites. Frank Yerby, for instance, with ten or more best-selling novels in succession, has never used a Negro background or Negro principal characters. Mr. Davis says that he hopes from the integration crisis his people 'will move permanently into full participation in American life—social, economic, political, and literary. . . . He (the Negro artist) will discover what we all know in our objective moments, that there are many facets of Negro living—humorous, pathetic and tragic—which are not directly touched by the outside world.

It seems to me, an outsider, that the Negro's commitment is so huge in his country that he will probably find it more profitable to concern himself with producing good art inside his social climate, as a 'native son'. If he finds the American civilization frustrating, he should realize that it is not a parochial malady. Everywhere, especially in Africa, we are up against this invasion by the white world upon our sense of values. It was a healthy thing to discover that the Negro's image of the African was changing to the good. Until President Nkrumah, Dr. Nnamdi Azikiwe, Tom Mboya, Julius Nyerere, Dr. Hastings Banda went to the United States, the Negro thought of the African as a primitive man whose jungle existence had largely outlived the processes of education. The Americans saw these men on TV and heard especially Nyerere and Mboya brilliantly weather the storm of pressmen's questions and often make them look silly. Both middle-class and working-class Negroes told us how revealing these pictures were. I still cannot explain the ignorance of some of the literate Negroes, when United States publishers tell us the book market is glutted with books on Africa, many of them quite good. Negro porters, taxi-drivers, spontaneously revealed their pride in Africa. One old man stopped three of us visiting Africans in Harlem to ask who we were. Then he told us, quite emotionally, how stunned he was by the articulateness of the African leaders he saw on television. On the other hand, we were told, French-speaking Africans who were coming to the United States on and off despised what they regarded as the Negro's lack of fight in response to so much discrimination aimed at them. It reminded me that our French-speaking brothers need a heavy course on African affairs. They just don't seem to know the social forces at work in African countries south of the Equator. They are too often apt to bring a philosophical mind to political and cultural questions in a changing continent.

How similar the American Negro's cultural predicament is to ours in South Africa and in other multi-racial communities. The needle that registers your response as a writer swings between protest and romantic writing, and then, when you are spiritually emancipated, the needle quivers around the central point—the meeting point between rejection and acceptance. Then you know both how excruciating and exciting it is to be the meeting point of two streams of consciousness and the paradoxes they pose. That is what makes our art. If there is any *négritude* in the black man's art in South Africa, it is because we *are* African. If a writer's tone is healthy, he is bound to express the African in him. Stripped of Sénghor's philosophic musings, the African traits he speaks of can be taken for granted: they are social anthropology. We who grew up and were educated in Africa do not find anything new in them. Simply because we respond intensely to situations is no reason why we should think non-Africans are incapable of doing so, or that we are the only section of the human race who are full of passionate intensity. These traits are not anything we need make slogans about, in terms of art. Or are we supposed to dig up the bones of Victorian aesthetes and start beating our drums with them? In my struggle to overcome the artistic difficulty that arises when one is angry most of the time and when one's sense of values is continually being challenged by the ruling class, I have never thought of calling my *négritude* to my aid, except when writing protest material. But is not this elementary—shall I call it 'underdoggery'?—that Sénghor is talking about? Even he must know, however, that his philosophy will contain his art only up to a point: it won't chain his art for long. He must know that his *négritude* can at best be an attitude, a pose, where his art is concerned, just as it was a pose in my protest writing. Excessive protest poisons one's system, and thank goodness I'm emancipated from that. The anger is there, but I can harness it.

For the rest, I must expose myself to cultural impacts around me, trusting in the truth expressed by Professor J. Newton Hill of Lincoln University at the opening of his paper, 'The Idiom in African Art', read at the AMSAC conference:

'It is probably well for us to admit at the very beginning of this study that an artist may express, and frequently with remarkable ability, the sentiments of the race to which he belongs. This is not subscribing to any philosophy regarding environmental influences on the artist, nor is this an admission that the artist is inescapably controlled by ethnological factors. What we mean is rather, that an artist by the simple relationship which he bears to the persons and things all about him, can seldom speak absolutely for himself—as if a being in isolation.

It seems that the two societies of African culture would be more profitably employed if while they preserved traditional works of art in Africa, they sponsored the great amount of talent that is to be found in Africa, artistic talent that has so long been bottled up in countries like South Africa, East and Central Africa. There is plenty of literary art waiting to be published and needs to be encouraged. In effect, these societies must concern themselves with the artist in his present dilemma. Then, of course, the American Society can continue keeping watch over Negro attitudes towards Africa. I cannot ask much more than this of the Americans, because they are not, like the French-speaking Negro, committed to come back to Africa and lead a movement.

What about identification from the African side? The South African non-white is always looking for symbols of freedom and advancement, as one of his responses to white domination. The magazines *Ebony* (now banned because it highlights Negro achievement and is therefore apt to 'mislead' non-whites), *Sepia* and *Bandstand* have done much to project an admirable image of the American Negro in South Africa. Hollywood has done the most in its portrayal of the Negro. The image was automatically transferred in our minds to the West Indian. He too became a symbol. The early American films merely caricatured the Negro in such idiot-looking, clumsy figures as Stepin Fetchit, in the frightened male servant and fat mammy, in the silent, non-committal taxi-driver, the large and menacing black man, the jazz artiste who was always brought in edgeways. But it was enough, to our immature minds, that the Negro was hitting the screen, which we could never hope to do except in shots advertising tea and Vim scouring powder.

Chapter 4

THESE CHEEKY KAFFIRS, THOSE IMPERTINENT NATIVES

The wider setting against which the African intellectual must be understood—at any rate in the Union of South Africa—is almost precisely the same as that of the non-intellectual. In fact it may not differ very much from that of the non-literate. By 'setting' I mean broad and basic things such as his origins, family background, where he lives and how well he lives. His personal history differs of course, and his view of himself, and the view which others take of him. Sometimes, by no means always, his daily occupation differs.

First, his family background. There are many who come of families educated and established for two or more generations in towns; but if not he, then his father or grandfather was a man who came from a tribal community which had never experienced the need for formal school in the Western sense. In the process of time this man gets caught up in the stream of an industrial revolution or a European farming economy that goes beyond the ordinary subsistence level of his community. Because he is not allowed to buy land except from small released areas he finds himself compelled to leave the now arid and over-populated Reserves.

He drifts to the towns to seek work so that he may pay his taxes and levies and feed his dependants who remain scratching for a living on poor soil in the Reserves. He must understand his employer's instructions in English or Afrikaans, read names of streets and shops. He feels utterly inadequate in this respect, and he begins to realize how vital education is to the needs of his kind.

'You must go to college, my son, and come and look after me

and your brother and your sister. They must also go to school.' So said my mother when I went to high school. This kind of 'pep talk' has launched thousands of Africans into the uncharted seas of an insecure education in an insecure life.

When my mother sent me to school, she had been a town-dweller for over twenty-five years and owed no allegiance to tribal authority, except in a detached academic way. The only features that still identified her and her parents with the tribe were language and the behaviour patterns they still upheld at home.

The rural Reserves were contracting at a terrific rate, so that the soil was also deteriorating. If Africans tried to go back to their tribe, they would find no land to occupy. In a setting of ever-expanding industrialization all of us 'refugees' developed an ironic sense of permanence in city life, where the black man is not welcomed by the white man except as a labourer. If a stable peasantry *were* to be consciously established, how many would come to work for 3s. 6d. a day in the mines?

While guest speakers continue each year on school speech days to tell you that the African must make the best use of his opportunities so as 'to uplift' his fellow men, you know nothing could be farther from your intentions. You want to get a better job and earn a living and support your parents and their other children. You are dogged by a ghastly sense of insecurity. You must seek a short cut to a profession. Teaching is the nearest. It costs too much in time and money to become a doctor or a lawyer. Yes, you may learn a trade, too, if you're lucky enough to find a good industrial school. Anything you take up must be geared to this unsettled existence, which you are made to lead by socio-economic conditions that you have no voluntary part in shaping. You are being educated to fit into an environment, not to change it.

Those you live with demand very much of you. 'We have failed,' they keep saying to you. 'Now it's *your* turn to do something to save us.' On the family plane, it is economic power you are expected to win; on a community level it is political power. The technical skills that produce engines, tall buildings, good roads and bridges, the cure of diseases and modern conveniences have taken on a symbol of power. And then there is the big stick which keeps prodding one's ribs: the power to govern.

But whatever the original impetus has been, in this process of being educated, one cannot stop there. Education has a way of acting on the personality like a stone that is thrown into standing water. The enlightened African looks around him, and according to the degree of his sensitivity perceives the meaning of his position in relation to the masses. He engages in certain intellectual and cultural pursuits in order to adjust himself and to remove whatever obstacles undermine his dignity. At a certain point the bare economic motive to survive merges into the political and cultural motives.

Except that I have academic interests and was to a certain extent able to pursue them, there are in South Africa many like me who come from the same kinds of home, and live now under the same uncertain conditions and in the same way as their fellow African townsmen. They are very much affected by the constant movement of their people, either by Government order, or force of economic circumstances, or the shortage of housing which compels people to move out of townships to squat on open land.

There are many ways, however, in which the intellectual is really worse off than others. Before industry started to employ a considerable number of Africans, the teacher's salary, low as it was —£6 10s. a month—was above that paid to unskilled workers. So was the clerk's. Today the workers have climbed up to skilled and semi-skilled jobs and their wages exceed those of the teacher and the clerk. Again, because most intellectuals are in Government employ or that of state-subsidized private agencies, they have not been able to do much for the masses for fear of victimization, and the loss of even the little they earn. And now the masses are disillusioned: even the village schoolmaster does not enjoy the wholesome respect that his predecessor did.

It is a lonely man who is not taken seriously by his own people, yet cannot keep aloof from them and their daily miseries.

The teaching profession is the most common among educated Africans. The teacher's course is not long—three years if one takes it after the primary school Standard 6; two years if one had done a three-year course in high school. It is a most expensive undertaking to study medicine.

One may be a traffic inspector. But only very few cities and towns employ African inspectors. There is also the job of assistant librarian. But municipal libraries are a negligible number. There are a few openings for social work, but the only school of social work for Africans in South Africa has been closed down by the Government.

What about the educated man's prospects of a job among Africans, in the locations? My people have been a reservoir for the white man's cheap labour for so long that all too few of them can become economically independent of the white employer. It is true that the authorities do not allow any other racial group than Africans to own shops in municipal locations. But they are mostly grocery shops, and butcheries. There are very few other trades, because it is difficult to start without capital or training. In a Johannesburg township, the largest African location in the Southern Hemisphere, with a population of 200,000, there is only one printer; there is one plumber; three African and six European medical doctors (who have a special licence to practise here). There are three high schools, one social centre; two post offices. There are only two small clinics. There are no bakeries, abattoir, or market, or department stores or factories, or life insurance or estate agents' offices; no commercial school. There are no chemist shops, no stationery or drapery shops; no cinema or beauty salon; no park, except for open spaces that are used by armoured cars against the blacks during riots.

Now all these essentials would provide skilled and semi-skilled as well as unskilled work in the African urban areas. But when the intellectual has been virtually forced out of the white man's town, he falls back on a poor community that cannot use his services.

Yes, the intellectual is clearly not wanted in the city. He is regarded as a creature that always gets in the way, if not a positive menace. The whites prefer illiterates or semi-literates, who accept their humble station; who can run down and buy sandwiches, or a bunch of flowers for the typist, and sometimes a packet of cigarettes for her boy-friend. It must be the humble sort who accepts a tickey or left-overs from the typist's lunch with a grateful grin, and who goes about the premises like a trained animal.

There are certain people who have been hardened by the necessity to keep a job. They may be called 'Jim' or 'boy' by a shop assistant and keep calm. They know that if they allowed themselves to lose their temper every time they were thus insulted life under the white man would be perpetual pain. But there are some of us whose pitch of sensitivity is always high and does not allow such a philosophical acceptance of the position.

It is not uncommon for an African university graduate to be without work for which he is qualified. If he does get such work, then in common with other educated men, graduate or non-graduate, he receives only two-thirds or even a half of the wages of the semi-skilled worker of his face in, say, the building industry, or in the factory or a driver's job. And naturally he wonders if all his study has been worth his while. Often he dares not reveal his educational qualifications to a prospective employer or his boss. He must remain tacitly apologetic about his educational status. Meantime, he owes it to his people and himself to acquit himself well.

Two factors baulk the educated African's efforts: his colour and what is known in South Africa as the 'civilized labour policy'. The African's rival in this country is the kind of white worker—of about 18 to 35 years of age—who comes from the country, usually without a high school certificate. His counterpart in the city, the poor white, is an equally serious rival. In each case it is the European youth who has made a failure of academic schooling—who is enabled to take up a job as a shop assistant, store-keeper, post-office clerk, municipal location or other Public Service clerk, laboratory assistant, foreman and so on—all the posts which, as things are, the African university graduate might get.

This is the road the educated African travels in Southern Africa and in Kenya, where the problems of co-existence between black and white are similar in most respects. Here, he is being resisted by the minority group which has entrenched itself economically and politically and which cannot bear the thought of competing against an overwhelming number of black people. He is regarded as a menace. He is victimized, banned, deported or confined to his home town. In many cases he abandons the struggle and leaves it to hardier ones. His people lose confidence in him. They know, however, that they require a leader who can read the newspapers, in order to interpret the laws and ways of white folk. But the glamour of the village schoolmaster has worn off. A good deal of the time is thus spent in trying to regain the confidence of the masses before he can even organize them against the unjust laws that harass them.

Let us focus our lens on the educated African in a colonial or semi-colonial territory, such as West Africa or Uganda. Here, the education of the black man is encouraged and promoted. He has the golden opportunity of going to a British, American or Continental university. The small group of whites in the colonial service and in business couldn't care less how many Africans were educated. They constitute no political or economic threat to expatriates.

It is precisely for this same reason that there is a much wider gap, socially and economically, between the educated and the illiterate in a colonial country than in South Africa. In the latter, the white settler fears and resists the educated African and goes out of his way to humiliate him, to deny him the things education gives him the aspirations for, to reduce him economically below the level of the illiterate, and politically to the same level. Thus in a multi-racial community the black man cannot be apprenticed as an artisan or dentist or pharmacist, because neither the law nor the white trade unions will let him. The African plumber, for instance, who works among his own people, has learned his trade in the employ of a white plumbing firm while the white artisans weren't looking.

The doctor would not be allowed to examine white patients in a hospital. The clerk who holds a matriculation or some commercial certificate becomes an ordinary messenger. At best, he is given a pencil and notebook to keep an account of the stock in a wholesale warehouse. Within a political system that reduces him to the position of a puppet and forbids him even to protest against his professional limitations on pain of summary dismissal, the teacher can manage to subsist among a poor community; he is paid by the State. He has to swallow a good deal of his professional pride. The doctor who is thrown on a poor community does manage also, but it is always with the painful knowledge that a man who consults him does so at great sacrifice.

A multi-racial society, it is easy to perceive, is always producing unsatisfied urges among its African communities; the privileged white section forges the barriers to African progress by the very means which create the conditions for the growth of an industrial proletariat; the privileged class is creating conditions for a nationalist revolt and its own ultimate destruction by the very means whereby it seeks to protect itself, because the enlightened black man has now been flung back to the level of the masses. This is how non-white political leadership has been fashioned on the anvil of desperate necessity.

Not so in the colonial world. Politics for the enlightened African here is a career, not a desperate necessity. Particularly is it so in West Africa, where colonialism is on the way out. On every front here the purpose of politics is for personal prestige and supremacy, or for that of a clique or clan. In Uganda, the educated man has fallen foul of the feudal sanctions of his own society. Because British colonial policy has always preserved tribal authority with its benevolent feudalism, the enlightened African in East and West Africa and in Nyasaland and Northern Rhodesia now suddenly finds himself in sharp conflict with chiefs. In Ghana and Uganda the battle between the politician and tribal authority has begun. In Nigeria the clash must come soon.

Two things stand out uppermost in this colonial pattern. First, is the fact that the British administration has a quiet way of according such special treatment to the educated African as to cut him off from the masses. And then there is the terrible legacy of the British class system. The second results from the first; this distance between the enlightened and the unenlightened makes it virtually impossible for the ignorant to remedy any defection among the ruling class, whom they idolize with the same reverence that they accord the chief.

The class distinction I intimate is felt subtly among the educated class. Occupational rank and income seem to determine this class consciousness. Since coming to Nigeria two years ago, I have sensed this, tried to ignore or excuse it. But it has kept imposing itself on me. Then I came to realize that the main concern of the average educated African in Nigeria is to get into Government service, which affords him civil servants' quarters, a car, at least two servants and a comfortable living. There is a mad rush to pass examinations as a gateway to this Eldorado. Anything offered that does not ensure a certificate in the end is avoided. Cultural activity becomes the business mainly of those in the lower strata who find their lives empty without some ritual or another. Extra-mural lectures and week-end schools organized by the university college have a bias for studies in government and economics.

In contrast to this, the Negro in Southern Africa, who is denied a share in government, finds an escape and self-expression in intensive cultural interests—music festivals, choral activity, jive sessions, jazz bands and troupes, writing.

The educated man in Nigeria and Ghana, for all his possessive pride in native dress, foods, and customary behaviour patterns, and years of indirect rule through chiefs notwithstanding, is Westernized. And although he often resists European ways, he is most grateful to Britain and speaks fondly about British institutions—a warmth I don't share. I must confess that, apart from a handful of Britishers who are my friends, I know the British only at their worst: in particular, in their historical role in the country of my birth, South Africa. I think of the British mostly in terms of Cecil Rhodes, the anti-Indian and anti-Negro tribalists of Natal, Lord Malvern, Sir Roy Welensky and the white tribes they speak for. I have not had the luck or ill fortune to be in British institutions. Yes, I was educated in institutions run by English-speaking people. But outside St. Peter's Secondary School in Johannesburg, which occupied a unique position under the Community of the Resurrection, my English-speaking mentors were for all practical purposes South African.

The educated African in a colonial context has thus merely stepped into the colonial administrator's shoes. In certain cases he will not like too many enlightened people near him and will like to keep the masses in the dark. Will he have the moral courage to resist this temptation to entrench himself?

For a long time the white man in Africa has taken up various positions in his attitude towards the black man, all aimed at propping up 'white supremacy'. These positions have so far differed only in accent. Earlier, there was talk of an evangelizing crusade and Christian trusteeship over a 'child race'. Now that he realizes or is ready to admit that he is not dealing with a child race, he blatantly holds forth that we have just 'emerged from primitive barbarism' and do not grasp the processes of government and political responsibility, or that our cultures are incompatible with the Western way of life. In all cases, whenever the white ruling class took a step forward with discriminatory legislation, white Christian leaders have taken three steps in retreat, both parties claiming that they were acting in the name of Christianity.

Thus we hear whites in South Africa talk of 'Bantu culture' and apartheid which is meant to give us an opportunity to 'develop along our own lines'. We are told that this will save us the frustration that results from trying to compete with the whites in spheres of life already preserved for them as a birthright! In the Rhodesias we hear echoed by Welensky the same elusive talk that Cecil Rhodes indulged in in the Cape: the vote is for those of us who reach a certain standard of civilization. They know all the time that both sides can talk civilization for centuries and never mean the same thing. Go farther south, east, west and north on this continent and you will find the theory of gradualism takes on a slightly different complexion according to the brand of liberalism the white man practises: the garden party liberalism as we find it in South Africa; the Rhodes-Malvern-Welensky policy of gradualism as we find it in the colonies, with French and Portuguese variations; and international liberalism such as the million-dollar Moral Re-armament foundation is prepared to invest in so as to break strikes here and maintain the *status quo* between employer and employee there. Is it any wonder that gradualism paralyses the African intelligentsia as a liberatory force? It is meant to isolate the virus—in this case, the educated black man.

The modern technique of oppression in Africa is to pose the myth that there is a clash of cultures, and then to pretend that partition can resolve the conflict or that gradualism can lead to partnership between black and white. From this the method is to proceed to legislate for the group, without asking what this clash of cultures means in terms of individual experience. If the white man were not trying to pull off a fraud, he would probe the question. He would then discover that education, by its very nature, obviates the earthquakes and volcanoes that are supposed to rock the African when faced with European systems of government.

The whites in South Africa continue to blabber to us: 'You do not belong in the city. This is white man's land. Of course if you have come to work for us, you're welcome. By all means rent a house in the location. But if you were not born here, or if you have not been working for at least fifteen years continuously in this district, you must go to the Reserves, where you were born, and where you really belong. Even if you're not redundant, you've got to get this clear in your mind: you can't get the municipal vote. Besides, there are no high-grade jobs for you here. That's the white man's field.

'Why don't you go back and serve your own people? We'll give you local councils to govern yourselves in your townships—under white supervision, of course, until you've mastered the tricks of the trade. You're wondering what you'll do in the Reserves? There's work there for everyone who wants to work. We know the land is in a bad state, but the Government is doing all it can to restore and conserve soil and water. But you must understand you must use properly the land you have first before more can be added to that. Tell your people they're in for a time of prosperity in the near future. They'll soon be getting industries brought right to their doorstep. You'll soon have your own cities, with cinemas, theatres, swimming pools, parks, technical colleges, doctors, engineers and whatever else you want. Just as the Europeans have in their own areas. These things take time, and you'll spoil everything from the start if you agitate the minds of your people by telling them to demand parliamentary or municipal government. You know most of them don't care for such big things anyhow. They're still backward. . . .'

That's what they tell us. But we know not only that the promised Eldorado in the Reserves is too good to be true, but that if it were feasible, it would amount to an incalculable loss to our own people. It would mean that they must forsake the cities to which their labour has contributed so much, and turn to building for a dream state. Apartheid is immoral. If people cannot live together in one country, how can they as a state live peacefully with the other countries of the world? The Negroes of Montgomery in the

United States have long come to realize that the white man's separate-but-equal policy is just a pipe-dream. We resent being told to cut our suits according to our cloth, when we have been given moth-eaten material or none whatever.

And so the white world still battles for the soul of the African. I think the educated black man, frustrations notwithstanding, will yet emerge tough as tried metal from all this debris of colonial systems the West has thought fit to dump in Africa. How much of all this the African will find of some use in the scrapyard, and how much of his past, is still a big question. The fervent hope of everyone is that, having once recognized each fraud for what it is, he will not try to use it to oppress his own people and others whose genuine goodwill he needs. I personally cannot think of the future of my people in South Africa as something in which the white man does not feature. Whether he liked it or not, our destinies are inseparable. I have seen too much that is good in Western culture —for example, its music, literature and theatre—to want to repudiate it. If the white man shuts his eyes to the good that is in my culture, he is the poorer for it and I am one up on him. There is nothing I can do to cure his malady. He has used the labour of my people for three centuries. To this extent he is deeply committed to a co-habitation with us—and that is reducing the relationship to its barest terms. He has no just reason to deny me the political rights many other workers in the world enjoy, and the other good things education creates an awareness of and desire for. The white man has detribalized me. He had better go the whole hog. He must know that I'm the personification of the African paradox, detribalized, Westernized, but still African—minus the conflicts.

Chapter 5

THE NATIONALIST

I

It's an awkward thing to be called a *moderate* or a *liberal* in South Africa, or in any situation that requires nothing less than militancy to redress wrongs done to any section of a people. I am neither a moderate nor a liberal. A liberal in an African context is a white man who believes in redressing political wrongs by constitutional means. More often than not he accommodates himself in the legislative machinery in the hope that he can use the concessions by which he has come to occupy a certain position inside the machinery to persuade the oppressor to change heart. A liberal will thus fight parliamentary elections so that he can advocate reforms from a constitutional platform. For several years now we have been told continually by liberals to make use of statutory bodies like urban advisory boards, so-called Bantu authorities, where black people can serve in an advisory capacity. The present Liberal Party in South Africa is an aggregate of the old Cape liberalism which spoke of the franchise for 'civilized' non-whites; the kind that has a keen nose for concessions and was noised abroad by the late Professor Hoernlé; and liberal gradualism. Even the latest scrapping of the qualified vote in favour of adult suffrage for non-whites does not rule out a constitutional struggle in the programme of the Liberal Party.

I am still not a nationalist either. At least a liberal is sincere in his own screwy fashion; the moderate or nationalist can't be—in a southern setting. Or should I say they cannot be logical in their sincerity? Maybe 'moderate' shouldn't be offensive after all, being a relative term. But this is an angry continent and innocent words take on terrible connotations.

Having been born into the dark side of a segregated existence, I've never been encouraged to think anything except that I'm black. For three hundred years this has been drummed into our heads; first by cannon fire, then by acts of parliament, proclamations and regulations. Our minds have been so conditioned that a number of our responses have become reflex: everywhere, instinctively, we look around for separate entrances, exits, reception counters, bank tellers, separate public lavatories, train coaches, platforms, hospitals. Instinctively, we make sure that wherever we are, we have permits in the form of passes to stay in a particular location, to work or look for work in a particular town, to leave a particular town, to leave a white man's farm, to look for work in a district. And these permits have definite time limits. Our minds have been so conditioned that, whether we like it or not, we have come to rate our qualifications lower, in terms of wages and salaries than the whites do who possess exactly the same qualifications.

Always we have been thwarted as a group—as blacks. The Coloured people[1] were brought up on the idea that they were an appendage of the white man. They were more or less treated as such. They did not carry passes or permits; they were not harassed by police raids; they could look for work or live anywhere they chose and were on the common voters' roll in the Cape Province; they received higher wages than us in all fields of occupation; they had better opportunities for a university education, although they did not make much use of them, being, like whites, sheltered already; they lived in separate townships. They still enjoy these privileges, apart from their removal from the voters' roll.

But since 1948, when the Nationalist Party came into power, it has been gradually but sharply brought home to the Coloureds that they are a separate racial group, not white, not black, not Indian. They can now only vote for white senators to represent them. They are also being reclassified. Overnight, some find themselves reclassified as 'natives'. This new identification brings with

[1] Those of mixed parentage—black and white, speaking mostly Afrikaans as their mother tongue.

it passes, lower wages, change of residence, humiliation and contempt from their fellow-Coloureds.

The Indians have been treated like Coloureds for the most part, except that, in freehold areas, the Indians live separate, and they have never had the vote, direct or indirect. Indian communities are now being moved out of towns and cities, where the merchants had acquired property, to live in segregated areas. Here they are expected to trade among themselves. Their cultural exclusiveness would defy anybody who dared regard them as an appendage.

During my early life in Pretoria we in our locations were physically close to the Indians. We were as interdependent as trader and customer can be expected to be. Being sticklers for tradition, they didn't make it easy for us to know them beyond the shop counter or the jingle of coin on it. But it was a very happy relationship. The Coloured folk in a nearby location were a very easy lot to live with, too. Their men came to us to drink, and our men went to them for liquor brews that their own women didn't have. As boys we met Coloured boys at the market to carry vegetables and fruits for the white people.

When I went to live in Johannesburg I found the Indian wholesale merchant class, whose businesses depended on whites rather than on blacks, too full of themselves, even hostile to Africans. The retailers, who served Africans mostly, were much more human. Even the curly-haired boys from merchant families, very much to the disgust of their parents, fraternized with Coloured girls. Between the two of them, they released enough arrogance to make sour the lives of Africans who found themselves thrown in their midst.

For instance, there are two Indian-owned cinemas in Johannesburg—the Lyric and the Majestic. For a long time Africans have been going to these houses and made to sit in front, near the screen. The back rows were for Indians and Coloured, and it didn't matter how much the African could afford to pay. I remember the burning hurt I felt on the two occasions I went to each of these cinemas. Then I stopped going there altogether. So did a number of other Africans. Those who continued to go must have done so simply because it was part of a huge segregation machine: they were so used to the noise it made that they had ceased to be startled by it. Only when it stopped, perhaps, would they become aware that they had been outraged.

A good few Indian fruiterers who were right in the centre of Johannesburg never made the 'mistake' of serving a black man, or even another Indian, before a white customer, no matter who had come first.

In Natal, because of a longer period of contact between Indians and Africans, there should have been a closer association between them than in any other province. But in fact the rift has been the widest. The 1948 brutal riots between Indians and Africans showed this. The tribalism of the English in Natal had, since the days of Shepstone, been driving into the heads of the Zulus a sense of superiority over the other African tribes—a feeling which they, the English, could not justify by their treatment of the blacks as a child race. They resented the Indian's increasing economic power earned by sheer industry. And so it was easy for them to project this resentment into the blacks. The English openly incited the Africans against the Indians in those riots.

Thus the white man, the Indian, and the Coloured, each in his peculiar compensatory response—often a neurotic one—has through the years driven the Africans into a defensive position. It made him very colour-conscious. In 1912, when the African National Congress was formed in South Africa, it was a national response to the challenge which the Act of Union constituted: the whites had ganged up against us. Once and for all it was made clear that the black man was to occupy an inferior place in the eyes of the law, in the legislature and in the social and economic life of the country. Every time an African became a doctor, a lawyer, a university graduate, he was made a symbol of *African* achievement by us. He had fought for every inch he gained. The more it became difficult for the black man to stay in primary school for more than six years (he was not allowed to begin until he was seven) the more spectacular it looked when batches of graduates came out of university.

The last war did a lot to jolt the youth. They saw men limping back from the war, broken and shell-shattered. They were coming back to serfdom. White ex-soldiers were receiving special concessions to complete their university education. Of course no black undergraduate could afford to join the war, more so when he was not going to be a combatant. A strong nationalist spirit was brewing at Fort Hare University College. A brilliant 30-year-old scholar and lawyer, Anton Lambede, rallied a large crowd of young Africans and thus was formed the Youth League of the African National Congress. His slogan was *Africa for the Africans.* About 1946, I was very strongly influenced by people who regarded Lembede as a mere tribalist and rabble-rouser, and who saw the only salvation for Africa in unity movements which would include whites, Indians and Coloureds and Africans of like democratic persuasion. I could not go so far as to call him a *tribalist*, because, after all, the most remarkable gain for nationalism, at any rate in Africa south of the Equator, has been to unite various tribes into a national unit. Having started off as a defensive attitude, Lembede's call was the first move in an offensive. For over forty years now in South Africa, Sotho, Xhosa Zulu and Shangana-Tsonga have been intermarrying and tribalism is no longer a problem.

And yet, although I could not condemn Lembede outright, I wasn't moved by his slogan. Sometimes I thought I was, especially when I thought of the apparently prosperous Indians and Coloureds and their treatment of us. Again, my childhood days came back to me, and I could not but pity the Indians and Coloureds: the whites have always refused to regard the Indian as an integral part of South African society—if they ever think of such a thing; so the Asiatics have sought refuge in economic security. The Coloureds have sought refuge in the illusion of the white man's protection.

The African National Congress realized this immediately after the Afrikaner Nationalists had taken over. Even after the Youth League had overthrown the Old Guard, epitomized by Dr. A. B. Xuma, they extended a hand of friendship and solidarity to the Indian and Coloured intellectuals and democratically-minded whites. And the Freedom Charter that came of this alliance in June 1955 lays down a basis for a non-racial society in South Africa. Lembede had died in 1948. Except for occasional echoes of what is supposed to have been his creed (of a doubtful pedigree), all has been quiet around his grave, until recently, when the Pan-Africanist Congress was formed. In 1959, then quite a small group, they broke away from the National Congress. The PAC precipitated the anti-pass campaign that led to the Sharpeville shootings of 21st March 1960, when 72 Africans were killed by police. Both the PAC and the ANC have been banned and the leaders arrested or detained. Until this time, the PAC still commanded a much smaller membership than the ANC.

The PAC claimed that it resented the ANC alliance with Indians Coloureds and Whites; that Africans should go it alone; that all whites are oppressors and that the issue is clearly between black and white; that the black man must rule the country because it is his; that the ANC is under a bourgeois leadership; that the Freedom Charter of the Congress Alliance, by stating that the land should belong to all, regardless of race or colour, was penning wolf and lamb together.

But there are inconsistencies in the PAC. First, it now regards Coloureds as Africans and Indians and whites not. Second, it claims that it is working for a non-racial society in South Africa—while it rejects a multi-racial struggle in organizational practice. Third, there is not a single liberatory movement in Africa which does not have a bourgeois leadership. In countries where so much nationalism is talked about, the leaders are educated men schooled in the tactics of the West. And the PAC claim that they are Socialists may be just so much cant, just like the socialism the Indian Congress in India pretends to. There, the land policy is so backward that the people have to depend on the philanthropy organized by the Bhoodan Movement. The PAC likes to identify itself with Nkrumah of Ghana, Azikiwe of Nigeria, Banda of Nyasaland, and Mboya of Kenya. Nasser was one of those people to whom the PAC often sent token invitations to its get-togethers.

It is in one way an easy and almost instinctive thing to be a nationalist. You find yourself with your back to the wall, first; then, like a hedgehog, you draw your head inside and underneath those bristles you manufacture a kind of venom as it were. Impotent at first. But without an outlet, it poisons your system. You may spit it out now and again, or gather around you some slogans and put on a mannerism, grow a beard and walk about with a stiff uncompromising neck. The Afrikaners have never been artists, generally: they do not know how to *look* nationalist. They have not half the art Africans have. Because it looks so instinctive to become a nationalist, being one looks more real than not being one, as real as it is that we have been oppressed as a group. (If I do not say 'African nationalist' it is because, in this context, I consider everyone born in Africa, who regards no other place as his home, as an African—be he black, white, Coloured, or Indian. Even the self-styled 'Afrikaners' in South Africa—for their own good, if not mine as well.)

It is a grave responsibility for a man to carry when he wants to be independent in a society built on the foundations of interdependence, even outside the master-servant relationships. Granted that we the blacks have reaped less out of the situation than the white rulers. But the gravity of your responsibility lies in the fact that you, as a nationalist, are associating your brand of nationalism with that of Banda, Nkrumah, Kaunda (Northern Rhodesia), Azikiwe, Awolowo and so on, which has thrived on a totally different social and political climate from yours. The gravity also lies in the fact that you are unwittingly joining the Afrikaans in their ambition to create parallel streams of legislative, political, economic and cultural growth: separate trade unions, places of entertainment—the lot.

Let's carry the thing to its logical conclusion. Suppose you do win your freedom. It is bound to be on the basis of black versus white, the latter being in power. And all your talk about not being anti-white—in a multi-racial setting—is just so much tongue-in-the-cheek stuff. In a Ghanaian or Nigerian setting, nationalism has taken the form of Africanism since the Colonial power abdicated: it is now simply a feeling of being African, and being anti-white is irrelevant.

Here, then, you have both the reality and unreality of the position of the Afrikaans and African nationalists (to go back to that awkward terminological distinction!). Paradoxically, the African nationalists do not really present a challenge to the Afrikaans. What does present a challenge is an organization that consists either in close association or in an alliance of black, white, Indian and Coloured. Such a body constitutes a negation of the Afrikaans' theory of separateness, their medieval clannishness.

What about the non-nationalist—like me? The apparent unreality of my position lies in what turns out now to be an endeavour on my part to civilize a large mob of white tribalists whose every act or attitude is motivated by the primitive instinct of fear; also it lies in the fact that non-nationalists accommodate the help of a small band of democratically-minded whites who belong to a privileged race and do not in fact suffer any humiliations directly. On the other hand, if we asked them to forgo their privileges, we should in effect be saying that our unprivileged position is a desirable one to be in.

The pain of not being nationalists lies in the cold realism of it. We are aiming at a common society and to prove that multi-racial societies can thrive and become a glorious reality in Africa. The black nationalist in a multi-racial context appeals not only to the most dangerous, because corroding, element of human nature among his people but also to the worst hedgehog qualities of those who would like to crush him. He, of all people, should know this because the Afrikaans nationalist has all through the years been evoking the same response among his own people and from our side. We have watched the Afrikaans and the Natal English shrink and shrivel up within their tribal cocoons; we have seen their minds grow pettier and pettier; we have seen them become more and more barbarous. Yes, they taught us violence, mental and physical, into the bargain. And the decay has not ceased.

We who look forward to a South Africa with a non-racial society where there won't be any need for minority fears, appeal to the nobler element of human nature, even when we know that the white ruling class is far gone. This is the test: if the white ruling class have any morals left to enable them to honour the democracy they shout so much about, let them fulfil its requirements without the rather old and mouldy qualifications that often drool from their mouths while they dine like the masters they are. Because of the ultimate goal we have in mind, it would not make sense to exclude like-minded Indians, Coloureds and whites at the organizational level. After all, there are still several of the others who continue mentally to live in their tribal enclaves, blacks included.

Whether one is a nationalist or not, one finds one's civilized sensibilities outraged by the mass arrest of over 500 African leaders and followers in Rhodesia and Nyasaland early in 1959. And I am using the epithet 'civilized' deliberately and in a sense Sir Roy Welensky is either incapable of appreciating or which scares him into such ridiculous postures as I shall demonstrate presently. The Devlin Report is now history, and so is the retreat of the former Colonial Secretary, Mr. Lennox Boyd. I find myself in full sympathy with the nationalism of Dr. Hastings Banda (Nyasaland) and Kenneth Kaunda (Northern Rhodesia) and their Congresses. Here are countries supposed to be under British protection, in which whites own a negligible percentage of the total land, and which could at least be treated like Basutoland, where very few white settlers are not discriminated against. This nationalism would have been allowed a healthier outlet if Federation had not been stuffed down the throats of the Nyasalanders and the Rhodesians. What, other than a militant response, could one expect in an atmosphere like that?

The British public and press have never sounded so progressive as on the Central African Federation incidents, or displayed such remarkable sensibility even while the British Government continued to be adamant in its show of force and total disregard of human lives. Militant and violent nationalism all over Africa, whether it be African or Arab, is the crop the white man must continue to reap from his dragon seed.

II

Let's listen to the words of a few notable men on their problems in Central and East Africa. Their posturings give us a clear if disturbing idea of the tug and tussle in which this extensive portion of Africa is entangled.

First, Sir Roy Welensky: 'We have set ourselves to build up a country in which there is opportunity for all regardless of race on the basis of partnership between the races . . . the coming years will see more and more attempts to get us to bargain away the standards we have set in return for political appeasement; I will oppose these with every legitimate means at my command.' (*Federal Newsletter*, 14th November 1958.)

This is aggressive talk. 'Partnership' has become a notorious word in African politics. The settler communities think of it in terms of superior and junior partners. The arrest of Mr. Clutton-Brock and Mr. John Mutasa at St. Faith's Mission in Southern Rhodesia during the 1959 crisis shows to what extent the whites regard partnership—the mission of St. Faith's—as a frightful heresy. Again, 'standards' is a stock subterfuge for white administrators in Africa. In any context, when they are justifying 'white supremacy', their 'standards' come down to mean their fat feudal comfort. Discrimination that is intended to benefit the victim is a strange creation of Southern Africa.

In reply to the demand by progressive opinion in the Federation that there should be an immediate smashing down of colour barriers, Sir Roy has said that the Government does not intend now, or in the future, to legislate for social admixture. Still aggressive! If, when people are left to their consciences, they discriminate against blacks as they do in Southern Africa and the Deep South of the United States, what should the Government do but legislate? No one would be so inane as to suggest that people be compelled to mix. But you can remove obstacles that prevent them from meeting socially when they *want* to, and create conditions in which they will meet without fear of public censure and the mental cruelty that goes with it. Residential segregation, serving Africans through small windows in shops, inequality in voting rights, can be put to a stop only by law. Only when human dignity and mutual respect are restored—and in Southern Africa they have reached low water mark—can people have any urge to mix socially. If Sir Roy is at all keen to see a country in which black and white are going to live together *as a nation*, why is he so timid about social mixing? How do you build a *nation* in which the act of mixing is ridden with a guilt complex or is regarded as too strenuous an effort to make it worth while?

Here is more fighting talk. Referring to nationalism, he says: 'I see no reason why this tidal wave should be considered irresistible, and no reason why nothing should be done about it if there are grounds for believing that its progress is damaging or if it does not leave in its wake benefits to the peoples concerned which are substantial enough to compensate and more for the destruction of the benefits of the old order. . . . The principle of one man one vote is inherent as much in Communism as in African Nationalism, but it is the special pride of African Nationalism.' (Speech in Federal Assembly, 7th April 1959.)

Oratory is not a strong point in Sir Roy: often he runs into awkward phraseology and long sentences which he cannot handle skilfully. The general idea one gathers from his speech is that if, for instance, you release a current of water from a tap by pressing a lever or knob, you can keep wondering why the water does not stop even though you maintain the pressure with your hand! The last sentence baffles all reasoning, to say the least.

Another piece of contempt: for Sir Roy 'there are some who find it difficult to believe that men who pay so much lip service to non-violence can have planned the violence they have, in fact, planned. These people who have not realized that primitive Africans—as has been shown in Kenya and elsewhere—easily turn to violence to settle matters which elsewhere are more naturally dealt with in the framework of law and order. Until the coming of Europeans, the whole history of Africa was one of violence and pillage. Respect for law and order is still something of a veneer and the primitive African can easily be inflamed—a fact which is, of course, well known to educated African leaders.' (*Central Examiner*, 25th April 1959.)

There was, of course, Hola Camp; atrocities in other Kenya detention camps in the early days of the Mau Mau; there were the 50,000 Africans who were moved by force of arms from the Gwembe Valley near the Kariba Dam in 1958, when eight blacks were killed; the shooting and loss of African life in Nyasaland in 1959. And what about the H bomb and the violence of Europe? In the early days of white conquest and settlement in Rhodesia, Arthur Shearly Cripps, missionary in Mashonaland (1907–52) and poet, could write this about the whites:

> O Mirthless liars of the market-place,
> Your sullen stamps thud dully night and day:
> Blood after blood you spill your bloodless way:
> Pow'r-dazed, doom-blind, you win your panting race. . . .

And of the Africans who were penned in small poor reservations:

> Dry breasts and wombs that miscarry.

He predicted in much the same way John White, the Apostle of Mashonaland, had protested, that the day Africa became politically conscious, the black man would sigh:

> The Lion of the state makes me his meat:
> Flesh gnawed from bones of mine Church Jackals eat—

It is common knowledge that immediately after the All-African People's Conference in Accra in December, 1958, the Rhodesian authorities prepared for a power demonstration. Sir Roy makes no bones about his interpretation of the Accra resolutions, which is that a plan of violence was decided on, a plan Rhodesian delegates were said to have brought back home with them. Now, who enjoys the monopoly of violent primitive passions? The Federal Prime Minister isn't going to tame an explosive situation by making such offensive remarks about Africans, partnership with whom he keeps harping on.

When the whites came to Africa, they were emerging from a war-ravaged Europe. The veneer of respect for law and order on them did not take long to peel off once they were faced with organized African communities. Exasperated by lack of response from people who had a completely different (not inferior) sense of values, the whites have never outgrown the colonial habit of projecting their own savagery into the underdog. Professor O. Mannoni throws considerable light on the settler mentality in his valuable book, *Prospero and Caliban*.[1] His view is that Shakespeare drew the colonial type in Prospero, who later becomes reluctant to abandon his magic and leave his desert island to return to a highly competitive society. Prospero despises Caliban (the aborigine) and complains that Ariel (the good native whom he rescued) does not show gratitude and in effect takes the master's promise of independence too seriously.

Professor Mannoni writes:

'What the colonial in common with Prospero lacks, is awareness of the world of others, a world in which others have to be respected. This is the world from which the colonial has fled because he cannot accept men as they are. Rejection of that world is combined with an urge to dominate, an urge which is infantile in

[1] Frederick A. Praeger, New York 1956.

origin and which social adaptation has failed to discipline. The reason the colonial himself gives for his flight—whether he says it was the desire to travel, or the desire to escape from the cradle or from the "ancient parapets", or whether he says that he simply wanted a freer life—is of no consequence, for whatever the variant offered, the real reason is still what I have called very loosely the colonial vocation. It is always a question of compromising with the desire for a world without men. As for the man who chooses a colonial career by chance and without specific vocation, there is nevertheless every possibility that he too has a "Prospero complex".' This complex prompts the colonial to go out and seek, in infantile fashion, the African's habitat which he identifies with some lost paradise.

Finally, Sir Roy Welensky writes in the *Federal Newsletter*, 25th September 1959:

'What now disturbs me is an apparent reluctance on the part of some to accept the emerged African as a full member of society—and let me add that I am not referring to social integration, because whom a man entertains in his home is his own business. I am referring, however, to the need to remove barriers between men of equal ability and equal standing, wherever such barriers exist. . . . I am not advocating throwing away the standing or the achievements of the white man in the Federation. On the contrary, I intend to preserve them, for this is the only way. . . . Nor do I see any particular merit or value in liberalism out of control, or out of touch with reality. . . .'

This time it is not the aggressive Prime Minister speaking. It is a politician who has worked up his electorate into an attitude which he now wants to unbend—not too much, though. He is pleading, trying to persuade, to reassure. The timid dentist is apologizing to the patient for having to extract the rotten tooth. The same man had this to say later, after apologizing for the refusal of a Rhodesian coffee house to admit Sir Francis Ibiam, then chairman of the Council of the University College, Ibadan, Nigeria: 'We cannot expect the world to treat us with any great respect so long as we hand out this kind of treatment to our visitors.' But perhaps the world will appreciate it if we treat our own African people in the same way. . . .

So much for Sir Roy. Now for fighting talk from the other side—this time in Kenya. Mr. Oginga Odinga, then president of the Kenya Independence Movement, said recently:

'As an African country, Kenya's political, social, economic development must also bear the brand of African nationalism. Most immigrants and the few Africans whom they have misled, condemn and treat African nationalism as a threat to their stay here. But as nationalism is an inherent right of the indigenous people of any particular country, we know that no force on this earth will ever manage to suppress African nationalism in Africa. Our message to the immigrant races in Kenya is that by advocating African nationalism, the Kenya Independent Movement does not intend to drive them away. In a free Kenya under democratic government, we assure them that all will enjoy equal rights and human dignity, irrespective of race, colour or creed. That Kenya will be ruled by the African majority is inevitable and it will be to the advantage of the immigrants to accept this now and not later. As to the constitutional development, the K.I.M. rejects the concept of multi-racialism and instead offers to establish a true democratic system based on universal adult suffrage on Common Voters' Roll. The advocates of multi-racialism seek to delay the date of Kenya's freedom under a purely democratic government. The immigrants need to be told that without the natural resources and indigenous man-power in Kenya, no amount of capital and skill would have achieved anything. Otherwise, why did they not go to settle and invest capital in the Sahara Desert?'

The whites, who have been enjoying glorious privileges all the way, should not be startled by this kind of talk. Nor should Mr. Michael Blundell, former Minister of Agriculture, be surprised that his multi-racial New Kenya Group does not stand high in the esteem of the majority of Africans. All the years he was an executive in the legislature, he has represented to the Africans the power of white rule in Kenya and all that is associated with it. During that time he has not come out with any land reforms that could endear him to the people. Land hunger drove the Mau Mau to desperation.

There are, however, flaws in Mr. Odinga's argument. When we talk about a multi-racial society or government we should really only be referring to the *physical* composition of it, the pattern of it.

In our dealings with one another, we should then speak of a *non-racial* society or government: one in which a political party may consist of blacks, whites, Indians, Arabs. Evidently, Mr. Odinga is not thinking of this. For he speaks of Kenya being ruled by the *African majority*, which seems to preclude the participation of the minority groups. Otherwise he would not find it necessary to re-assure them by saying: 'By advocating African nationalism, the Kenya Independence Movement does not intend to drive them away.' It is difficult to reconcile 'in a free Kenya under democratic government, we assure them that all enjoy equal rights and human dignity, irrespective of race, colour or creed' with 'As an African country, Kenya's political, social, economic and cultural development must also bear the brand of African nationalism.' I think you must either tell people to quit or let them stay in a non-racial relationship to yourself. You cannot tell them you are not driving them away and then give them an inferior status purely on grounds of colour. The whites, on the other hand, will have to purge themselves of their high-and-mighty and defensive attitude and submit to revolutionary changes in land ownership. They have had a good start ahead of the Africans and Asians in everything, and it is not right for them to ask the African to wait or move slowly towards the ideal state.

One is rather inclined to agree with Mr. Iain Macleod, the Colonial Secretary, if only on his basis for an independent Kenya: '. . . With developments in the franchise African influence will necessarily and significantly increase. But I do not approach this in terms of majority rule by a particular race. Africans will attain their position not just because they are Africans but because the majority of those who will come to play a part in the government of their country will be Africans.' But of course Mr. Odinga is an underdog right inside the Kenya situation, and I may be wrong in assessing his situation through a pair of South African spectacles, not being, by nature, political myself.

Mr. Blundell has made this demand that the African should wait before he can exercise an unqualified vote—in the true style of liberal gradualism. In reply to Tom Mboya's 'undiluted democracy', he says that his New Kenya Group is not prepared to enter into discussions for constitutional changes based on a universal franchise on a common electoral roll for all the people of Kenya in the conditions of today. Everywhere in this angry continent, whenever blacks have been made to wait until they are 'educated and civilized', whites have entrenched themselves in a way in which no law could ever dislodge them later.

Finally, here is an extract from an article by Dr. Bernard Chidzero, a Rhodesian. The University College of Rhodesia and Nyasaland would not admit this man on its staff because he has a Canadian wife, and Southern Rhodesian whites do not like mixed marriages. He has had to go to England and wait until he can attempt to re-enter his country. The article represents the kind of progressive thinking among Africans which the whites in Africa had better heed before it is too late. The whites have to make the next move now.

'The grim reality which must never be lost sight of is that until the African has constitutionally-recognized political power adequate to safeguard whatever gains he makes, there is no guarantee that the present process will not be reversed or frozen. The imperatives of the European electorate are such that liberalization can only reach a certain point.

'Partnership, as "equality for civilized people and government in civilized hands", means government on European terms and under European domination for as long as the European minority can deploy its economic power, educational superiority, and administrative know-how, while employing subtle and crude shock-absorbers—such as limited African participation in government and limited inter-racial social amenities—to accommodate the interests of a small number of Africans.

'On the other hand, by partnership the African and the progressive understand individual equality and a non-racial society. It is a partnership based on the concept of non-racialism. It inevitably means government by majority consent, and a majority which, though it is predominantly African because of numerical preponderance of the African, will none the less disregard racial difference. . . . The emphasis is on the individual regardless of race or colour, and implication that the whole society must permit to individuals freedom of movement and association and participation in government.

'The British people and Government must make a clear choice between these two policies. No aimless drifting will do. . . . The lack of intercourse between the racial groups, a product of history and the legal structure as well as convention, constitute a most serious obstacle to mutual understanding and confidence—the foundations of unity. Inter-racial amity and the establishment of government by consent demand the dismantling of the present social and political structure.'

There have been the Devlin and Monckton commissions, and they have said a lot to bear out Dr. Chidzero's words. And yet Sir Roy, full of himself as cock of the walk, continues to crow in his wildest manner because he is sure of support from the Tory establishment in Britain.

If nationalism is the antithesis of tribalism, then I am a nationalist. But if, in a multi-racial society, a nationalist's object is to replace a white dictatorship with black fascism, to replace, say, Afrikaner tribalism with black chauvinism, then I can't go along with him. Nor is it healthy or constructive for the leaders of the Pan-Africanist Congress to say: 'There is no room for Europeans in Africa. We do not want to chase whites away from here. If we chase them from here we will have no servants. Their wives will work for our wives. The days of the whites are numbered. We shall apply the pass laws to control them. If the whites accept Africanism, that is good. Let them stay. If not, they must pack up and go. If any European or Coloured wants to join us he must first see the native commissioner and declare himself as a native and pay the £1 15s. tax. Let him rub out his name as a European. The Coloured or European can join the PAC providing that he admits that he is an African and not a European.' If we reject the pass laws, the South African concept of master-servant relations, native commissioners and the poll tax, why should we think others will like them, unless we want to oppress them?

Surely this is chauvinism. The PAC's secretary for education writes: 'Nationalism demands that the interests of indigenous peoples should dominate over those of aliens, because the country belongs to the indigenous peoples. . . . Democracy demands that those of the majority should dominate over those of the minority, because they are a majority. In Africa in general, and South Africa in particular, the African people are indigenous to the soil, are the real workers and are the majority. Their right to the effective control of their own interests is, therefore, unchallengeable.'[1] As the secretary speaks often of 'white domination' in his article, it is quite clear that in his thinking no other race is indigenous to Africa except the African (the black man in this context). The Africans also have 'their own interests', separate from those of the Indians, Coloureds and whites. So we know what he means by 'those of the majority should dominate over those of the minority': the African must dominate over the other races.

In his article, the PAC man attacks the African National Congress's Freedom Charter of 1955 which seeks equality of opportunity, redistribution of land, a government by both black and white, no matter who have elected them, universal adult suffrage: in effect, a non-racial society. The article does not tie up with what the PAC president says—that by 'Africans' in the slogan, AFRICA FOR THE AFRICANS, he means all those, black or white, who believe in majority rule. Or else someone is playing around with words and phrases for his own amusement.

The coming together into a United National Front of exiles from the African National Congress, the Pan-Africanist Congress, the South African Indian Congress, and the democratically-minded whites operating from Accra, London, Cairo and New York, is an excellent thing. Only good can come of it.

III

In his essay, *African Nationalism*, Mr. Ndabaningi Sithole gives an analysis of this historical phenomenon. He tries to be fair to all sides, even to colonialism and its 'positive role' and to missionary endeavour which, with colonialism, forged the weapons that destroyed the latter.

When Mr. Sithole[1] speaks about African nationalism and its alleged incompatibility with communism, I fail to follow him. His thesis is that African nationalism has always sought to drive out

[1] 'The Africanist Case' in *Africa South,* Vol. 4, No. 3, 1960.

European imperialism and therefore cannot reasonably exchange this for Communist imperialism. 'The Communist Party', he affirms the words of a Ghanaian student, 'represents foreign rule that aims at world subjection.' The author cites the examples of Egypt, Morocco, Tunisia and British colonies in Africa to show that African peoples have always been against foreign domination. This is of course history, and there's no point arguing against it.

And then his final analysis: 'Africa as a whole seems well fortified against communism since both the European powers and the African people have been conditioned against it. Africa as a whole has been predominantly Westernized economically, politically, socially, ideologically, and educationally. Practically all highly educated Africans have been Western-educated.'

Mr. Sithole, who up to now has been logical, lucid and objective in his analysis, falls foul of the clichés of the Western world here. The trouble is that he doesn't speak of communism as an *ideology* but as *foreign domination*. To him, to be a Communist is to be dominated by Russia. Shouldn't we, on his premise, say that the 'Westernization of Africa'—this 'common ground between the West and Africa', free enterprise and all that—is a submission to foreign rule? Can he sincerely tell us that Guinea, or even Cuba, is dominated by Russia? Mr. Sithole might have told us why he thinks communism, as an ideology, is unhealthy for Africa. To suggest, as he does, that communism is bad because there is no common ground between Africa and Russia is illogical. Is it inconceivable to him, especially in view of what has happened in the Middle East, for an African nationalist to be a Communist?

I must see communism in action in Russia before I can pass judgment. So far I have only the Western leaders and press to go by, and that's not reliable, for obvious reasons. But I do know the evils of capitalism because I was born and bred in its climate. I have seen South African farmers bury potatoes and oranges, while millions starved, because they (the farmers) could not get the high prices they wanted for their produce. I have seen them withhold their maize for the same reasons, while Africans, whose staple food it is, looked on hungrily. I have seen absentee-ownership of land at work, and whites themselves (let alone blacks) squeezed out of their farms and troop into the towns to become poor whites. My mother, like several other black mothers, died at the age of 45 from sheer hard toil and worry to try to educate her children, without any state help to expect, and the holders of big money didn't care. Four hundred Africans were buried in a coal-mine: what state assistance could they expect? I have seen greed for land and property (thanks to the 'Westernization of Africa') in West Africa. Is it any wonder that several West African states at least *speak* of a Socialist programme for themselves? As for the kind of socialism Africa will create, history will tell.

Often, when I have talked to certain people about the evils of capitalism, sons of white capitalists have said to me: 'What about Hungary?' My answer has been, and still is: Any war of any size anywhere is horrifying. But that's your way of life—you whites of Europe and the Western Hemisphere. You should consider yourselves lucky you still have a conscience in the persons of Bertrand Russell, J. B. Priestley and Michael Scott. Anyhow, Hungary is too far for me to be stunned in the way I know I should be. You see, Jim Crow does it differently in Africa. His is a slow but tight and deadly squeeze. This is the only reality I know. He bestrides this continent from Algiers to Cape Town, and the guns around his belt face east, west, south and north. He wields as many batons. Even although I am in a corner of Africa that is outside his range, I have to live with this bitter thing that he cultivated in me over the thirty-seven years of my life in South Africa. And I see him pull the trigger and let loose his baton every so often just near by. And then I feel the sediment of the bitter thing rise inside me. This is the reality I know: all the others are mere trifles. Even if you blew this globe to bits with your bombs it wouldn't be a tragedy. It would be too cheap and wayward an incident to purify and humble anyone the way tragedy does. Above all this, the humanism of Léopold Sédar Sénghor, President of Senegal, rings sharp, clear and beautiful when he says: '*Man* remains our first consideration: he constitutes our *measure*.'

Mr. Sithole seems to have joined the ranks of the Western world who for a long time been talking about African nationalism as a bulwark against communism. The United States is even now investing money in this mission for Africa. Its leaders have times without number quite unashamedly said their country's foreign aid programme must aim at preventing the entry of communism. Even Buchman's Moral Re-Armament evangelists don't want to be beaten to it: they form a flank of this huge mission.

A second front has been opened in Africa to try to kill Socialist ideas of any kind at the root. It consists of white African liberals, particularly those in Central and Southern Africa. They have set out to give African nationalism a big build-up. Even where, as we have seen in South Africa lately, this nationalist movement has become chauvinist. Some South African liberals sing praises to African chauvinism and are prepared to ride on the back of the tiger: as long as it *declares* it does not hate whites *and* that it believes in non-violence *and* does not like what it imagines to be Communist domination within the African National Congress, but proceeds to stay 'black only' and to place majority and minority groups in their pigeon-holes. The trouble with liberals in South Africa, of course, is that they spend two-thirds of their energy trying to avert a revolution and one-third to verbal protest against repressive legislation. Their attraction for a certain class of the non-white *élite* fits in with their anti-socialist sentiments.

Mr. Duncan said gloatingly in the early stages of the Congo crisis that because of the late Patrice Lumumba's appeal for Russia's help which (in Mr. Duncan's view) automatically made him a Communist, Kasavubu and Mobutu would deal with him as he deserved. One expected that *Contact* and its liberal band would shout: 'We told you so!' after Mr. Lumumba's death. I don't know if they did. But we all know how discredited Kasavubu, Mobutu, Tshombe, the Belgians—the lot—stand in the eyes of the Africans. Suppose Lumumba *were* a Communist, which he wasn't, how could anybody call himself a liberal and still deny the right of any man to choose the ideology he thinks right? It was also plain from the Western press that Britain (almost tacitly) and the United States (noisily) did not mind a cold war in the Congo as long as Lumumba was on their side.

The Americans and white African liberals should take a leaf from Britain's book about her attitude towards communism, liberalism and other divergent 'isms'. She is old, sad, wise and even cynical, as Graham Greene symbolizes so poignantly in *The Quiet American*. The suicidal third force and all that. . . . Granted that Britain's conservatism often renders her so insensible of the colonial people's yawn and irritation which are meant to tell her that she has overstayed her time as a guest and she should leave, she can accommodate conflicting points of view within her borders. What virtue is there in not adopting an ideology because you are not allowed to adopt it and are immunized against it by the help of every conceivable medium of education and witch-hunting?

One is driven to warn the Americans that our poverty should not be presumed upon. Dollars exhaust themselves, ideas give birth to others, on and on. Let Britain tell them so.

Chapter 6

GOING MY WAY?

This is the question we must put to the whites in Africa—those of them who intend to make their home here. It needs an urgent answer. This was brought home to me by an article I saw some time in 1959 in the journal *Encounter*, by Mr. Dan Jacobson, the South African writer now living in Britain.

Mr. Jacobson says the world is seriously expecting or demanding a spurt of literary activity from the new and emergent Africa. To prove that it is idle for people to expect it, he quotes from Hannah Arendt's book, *The Burden of Our Time*:

'Mankind remembers the history of peoples, but has only a legendary knowledge of prehistoric tribes. . . . What made them (the Africans) different from other human beings was not at all the colour of their skin but the fact that they behaved like a part of nature, that they had not created a human world, a human reality, and that therefore nature had remained, in all its majesty, the only overwhelming reality—compared to which they appeared to be phantoms, unreal and ghostlike.'

It is necessary to strip Mr. Jacobson's article of a few sweeping assertions so that we may appreciate the most relevant part—that which treats of the present. We may also be better able to see the peculiar problems of the African writer as part of the larger human predicament. The points we want to get clear in our minds are the belaboured thing about the history of Africa, the 'willed severance from the past', and what Mr. Jacobson's authority calls 'a human reality'.

I don't know about prehistoric tribes and at what point in the line of history a writer's reference ceases to be relevant. But I do know that there is in the oral literature of African nations a considerable body of history which indicates very clearly the moral and social codes that governed the lives of people a very long time ago. I am keenly conscious of where I fall in this long line of continuity among the Bantu-speaking peoples of Africa. It is a history that has been disturbed first by missionaries, then by traders, and then by military conquest.

We should not talk as if someone touched down on some place in Africa and around him communities popped out from under the ground to begin a new life on the surface of our globe. Let me take the extreme case of Africans in South Africa. There are 4,000,000 Africans in the urban areas, 3,000,000 working on white people's farms, and 3,000,000 in the rural reserves. The first two lots consist of people who have lost all tribal affiliations in terms of chieftaincy, and their old moral codes have been battered about. And yet there remains something solidly African in them that has a distinct reference to the past. It has to do with the manner of self-expression through music, dance, song and patterns of behaviour. In all this, there has been a compromise between our past and the present. Listen to the music that has been composed by the post-missionary musicians who have infused European forms with an African idiom and African rhythms. In the simplest forms of self-expression, like jive, there are subtle rhythms which distinguish the European from the African.

If, as Mr. Jacobson says, our use of English and French indicates a 'willed severance from the past', it is simply a position in which we find ourselves as a result of European conquest. And by a twist of irony we can often tell the French and English in their own languages how we dislike their ways! These European languages have been, and still are, a unifying medium for the various tribes that people our continent, and the only way to foster nationalism and to conduct political pamphleteering for the purpose. In fact, there are many more African creative writers using their vernaculars than those who write in foreign languages, even in South Africa. Since 1870, when the first Bantu newspaper was founded by Africans in the Cape Province, the volume of vernacular writings has been increasing. There is a considerable body of verse, drama, and fiction in Sotho, Zulu and Xhosa. And yet, the best thing that could happen to Africa would be to retain English and French as official languages in addition to the common vernaculars. That way we enjoy the best of both worlds. Rather than interpret it negatively as a 'severance', we should realize that its positive value lies in our ability, through the use of these languages, to conquer our present-day external world. We can also make African symbols and images available to the rest of the world, and thus the fusion of cultures takes a more natural course.

Even within the context of apparently deliberate severance, there are cross-currents of political motive and intent. In South Africa, for instance, our past, in its most tattered form, is being used by the white ruling class as a means of entrenching themselves all the more. It is not our traditional culture that is being recaptured for us, but such bits as can be rammed into the local government machinery to give a semblance of self-rule and at the same time arrest the African's mastery of his technological environment and his academic attainment. In countries of British influence, nothing has been pegged, and there is an expedient resort to one or other of two cultures at different times. In French-speaking countries, although the educated African is an assimilated gentleman, he remains an enigma. We have seen how he is now staggering back from the dead-end to which French culture has led him, groping to reach out for his African past as a compensatory response.

I do not know what Hannah Arendt means when she says: '. . . they had not created a human world, a human reality.' What more human reality does one need than that people have socially and politically organized lives? Of course, our civilizations did not float on the back of advanced technology or on stocks and shares. Africans have always been more interested in human relations than in gadgets, even when they realize that they have to operate machines for a living. Africans have always gravitated towards people, not places and things. Why they have not yet, to any significant degree, taken up the idea of a vacation at a holiday resort. People, and not places, give them real pleasure. They want a *social* climate where they can *make* music and fun and not just *listen* to music and *look* at a performance.

For our traditional idea of culture is not a performance for the few who can get into formal dress and afford a ticket to watch it.

Culture is part of the very process of living, of a stream of consciousness, in which a whole community takes part. The Sotho proverb, 'Nothing belongs to you except that which you have eaten', cuts across all the competitive economics of the West. Men and women organized themselves into groups to build one man's house or hoe or harvest his field, and then he joined them to work on somebody else's. The lazy man was outlawed: a man never died of hunger, even when he was too ill or crippled to work.

I am saying, in other words, that this is a human reality that matters more than everything else to the Negro writer in Africa. He is the product of an order that could only generate life and never destroy or corrode it. One is always in the danger of making a *mystique* of national character. I have already indicated that even as I am writing this, the African is changing; which (to risk repetition) makes nonsense of the African personality as a political concept. We can only define the search for it in literary creations as in the foregoing chapters, not the thing itself. But then we are talking about the human reality more or less in retrospect, something we have inherited.

I should be inclined rather to feel sorry for the white writer in Africa, whose problem, as Mr. Jacobson rightly says, is not made bearable by the same consolation and nourishment the blacks derive from their struggle. He is many generations removed from European cultures, and is too scared to come to terms with the indigenous peoples and the human reality they have to offer. His fear has driven him into a civilized posture, in which he fancies that he is the custodian of the very civilization his actions are discrediting. Afrikaans literature, particularly the novel, has not outgrown frontier delusions. The English novel in Africa has been grappling with the immediate problem of race-relations to the exclusion of any reference to a universal context, except in the case of Olive Schreiner's and William Plomer's works. English poetry has just not been able to settle down and reconcile the conflicts that give birth to it. It is essentially still a verse in exile.

The most significant part of Mr. Jacobson's thesis is that which deals with the African writer's present dilemma and the literary material his handicaps and disabilities can afford him. The problem splits itself somewhere. The white writer is at the mercy of the white politician in Africa. His race must simply face up to complete social and economic integration with non-whites in order to create a non-racial society. This way our literature will form part of a common stream of culture in which two or more streams of consciousness influence one another. As long as there are racial barriers our literature will continue to be sectional. In multi-racial communities like South Africa, the Rhodesias, and Kenya, the question of local involvement for both black and white writers hinges on the willingness or otherwise to create mixed societies. The reason why, in the world of fiction, Joseph Conrad, E. M. Forster, and William Faulkner are the greatest interpreters of cultures and character outside their own colour groups is that they had no artificial racial barriers to contend with, such as we find entrenched in the legislatures of Africa.

For the African Negro the problem lies in the struggle to express the larger irony which is the meeting point between acceptance and rejection, once he has felt the impact of Western civilization. This problem is superimposed on the one of local political commitment. And for a long time to come yet, such ironies are going to provide him with literary material. Unlike the whites, Negroes do not resist foreigners as such. They have adopted foreign techniques and, short of being dispossessed and being discriminated against, they are almost always ready to accept whites in their midst. But there are certain things they reject from the West, which have to do with a sense of values in such areas as patterns of behaviour and human relationships. The next move is therefore the white politician's and the white voter's. In a non-racial society, will the white writer go farther than just an appreciation of, or academic interest in, Negro cultures? Will he ever make an attempt to adopt certain Negro ways of life?

Even if he defers decision for the moment, one day we shall all have to answer one way or another D. H. Lawrence's challenge—that the white man may forsake his 'stream of consciousness' for the African's or the Hindu's, or the Polynesian's, or these races may take to the white man's; that one cannot 'express one stream in terms of another, so as to identify the two. . . . The only thing you can do is to have a little Ghost inside you which sees both ways, or even many ways. One man can belong to one great way of consciousness only. He may even change from one way to another. But he cannot go both ways at once. Can't be done. . . .'

T. S. Eliot has said that conflict and diversity between cultures are essential so that allegiances and alliances in other areas may bring about cohesion in larger relationships. One wonders if he would sustain this argument if he were committed to living with Africans and Indians, say, in South Africa, where forced ethnic grouping heightens race conflicts and paralyses literary effort in particular and cultural growth in general. In any case, he abdicates his stand by later advocating a general re-grouping under a Christian banner. Where do non-Christians come in? D. H. Lawrence, I think, could write as he did about the Indians in Mexico because he was not committed to living with them.

In terms of the world into which I am emerging as an African Negro writer, it disturbs me enormously to see how Western culture is continually surrendering intellectual honesty and freedom. Not only have Boris Pasternak and Paul Robeson not been allowed to say things that offend authority in their respective countries, but allied countries have felt obliged to discontinue their patronage of these artists. And there are, of course, several unsung martyrs in Britain and other countries, who suffer because they dare challenge the established order.

If the autonomy of art means anything at all, it is that art should order our experiences and responses and help resolve conflicts inside ourselves as individuals in such a way that we each bring to our groups a personality that could never justify race, colour, and religious discrimination, intellectual dishonesty, poverty, and inequality of privilege.

Just in Passing. . . .

Some white folk think some unwholesome things about black people, and vice versa. A strange man is Lord Malvern, former Prime Minister of Southern Rhodesia and the creator of the Central African Federation. He says: 'Africans, until they are very much advanced, are all liars.' There are whites who say naïvely and patronizingly: 'I like Africans.' Some, especially those who cannot conceive of Africans as anything but servants, will say they hate the educated blacks. 'He's an educated boy, but you wouldn't think it,' some liberals say. 'So humble and respectful.'

When you listen to the following dialogue, then you know you are experiencing an extremely tense situation. A friend of mine I used to teach with, Isaac Matlare, is leaning against a counter in a railway booking office, waiting to be served by a white man. The 'boss' is visibly in a bad mood.

'Listen, this counters is always been standing yere for ten years and it eesn't falling, d'you year?' says white man boss, first thing he comes in.

Isaac gets the hint. The white clerk goes into his cage and glowers at my chum through the expanded metal in front of him.

'Man, your face makes me think of those creeches (creatures) what lives in the zoo—know them?'

Isaac takes off his glasses in his typical fashion, raises one eyebrow and says: 'Oh, I thought they were white!'

White man boss stares wolfishly from his cage and looks impotent. Isaac is, of course, not served; he has to book at another station.

When I worked as a small-town clerk just outside Johannesburg, I was often sent to a European grocery store called Talbots to submit an order for my employer's wife. Every time I entered that shop I felt breathless and some creature seemed to career up and down my spine like the money container that shot up and down a cable between the cashier on some elevated stand and the shop assistants at the counter below. Reason was that there was a white woman who consistently called me *John*. One day, quite beside myself, I said in reply: 'If you've a string of sweethearts called *John*, I'm not one of them!'

A tall white man who heard me made an athlete's leap over the counter to get at me. . . .

Snobbery breeds snobbery. During my visit to Britain in 1959, I attended a conference on race relations at Bangor, North Wales, to which I had been invited. During one of the many intimate discussions, a lady wanted to know from the non-whites in the hall what they thought a non-white's attitude might be towards an invitation to tea by her as a white person. She had experienced difficulty in getting across the conventional barrier and suspected that her failure to do so might have been due to her clumsiness. An Indian member of the audience said he would want to know why *he* had been picked on for tea because past experience with do-gooders had been devastating. I thought the same and added that the lady might consider establishing acquaintance with her prospective invitee before making the 'assault'.

That night in my room I thought about what we had said during the day. Basically, man likes to be treated well by other people; he warms up towards them when they show him compassion. Why, then, I asked myself, do we non-whites often feel triumphant to be able to say *no* and do say *no* to an invitation? I told myself that, having been brought up to look at an invitation as coming from 'the other side', and not just from a human being, and being in a position to say *no*, I should like to feel that I am mentally emancipated; in the sense that I don't have to justify myself to the white man any more, and that my image of him has been cut down to size, stripped of all the glamour and pomp in which he appears in the textbooks we were brought up on.

I sound snobbish. But snobbery breeds snobbery, whether we like it or not. There is a new school of thought in India that is threatening to dethrone E. M. Forster and reinstate Rudyard Kipling as a faithful portrayer of Indians in literature. The latest from this school of thought is that Kipling's bullying tone is more tolerable than Forster's compassion. 'We know where we are with Kipling'—that kind of thing. The Indian intellectual who says this is simply prompted by a feeling of ascendancy. It's mental emancipation run riot; rather like the athlete who goes on a few extra rounds after winning the mile race. But I'm not apologetic for showing this kind of snobbery in other areas. Racial barriers are most brutal and they breed a terrible and grotesque kind of cold war.

Some white folk like Africans in a cheerful and clowning role all the time. As soon as the black man becomes serious and even shows an inclination to ponder about things or about the scheme of things, he ceases to be interesting. It is as if by coming to Africa and 'getting away from it all' (the stuffiness of Europe), they had desperately created an illusion of a 'happy, happy Africa' with a perpetually sunny temperament, a continent that would cure them of some malady, like a Turkish bath.

The South African white, of course, is just outright rude or moronic. The following episode is just one of many.

In 1957, when I was sub-editor and reporter on *Drum* magazine, in South Africa, my editor asked me to go and see the then feature editor of the Johannesburg *Star*, who had spoken to him about the intention of his journal to introduce a regular feature purporting to represent the 'black man's point of view'. I might be interested in offering my services, my editor thought. I soon found myself sitting in front of a tall gaunt white man.

'Would you be interested?' the big man asked.

'Depends on the kind of thing you want.'

'Have you ever written regular features before—for any paper, I mean?'

One has learnt to take South African whites literally, so I replied: 'I'm on *Drum* and I write regularly for *Golden City Post*—er—that's our sister paper, by the way—a Sunday paper. It's published by *Drum*.'

'Is *Golden City Post* published in English?'

'Entirely.'

'Well, you see, what we want need not be in terribly good English. We can always knock it up into shape. I know the Bantu have a peculiar turn of phrase when they write in English. But you shouldn't let it worry you, see what I mean?'

Of course, I saw what he meant—more than he himself was aware of—these poor wretched whites! He meant he had no right to call himself a journalist if he did not know the only Sunday paper in the country published primarily for non-whites—right in Johannesburg. I thanked him for being considerate about my 'peculiar turn of phrase' and was no more interested to hear about the kind of article he would want. Being used to this sort of inanity, I refused to think any more of the incident as I walked up President Street. But once I allowed myself the expensive luxury of saying to myself: 'Who does he think he is, talking to me like that!' Expensive because it generates a wasteful flow of adrenalin. . .

I intend now to explore European literary images of African character. One should really only speak of *human* character. But owing to the racial attitudes that I have gestured at earlier on, which attitudes show that racial barriers are a brutal reality, critics cannot but continue to think in terms of non-white and white characters. The white and non-white authors, writing as they have been in a colonial setting, have made the distinction and it must be treated as such until both sides have willed themselves into alignment somewhere. In Chapter 8 I shall make a brief survey of the non-white's literary image of himself and those of his colour. The grouping of all these images is not absolute: images merge or overlap often. An African often rebels because he is an underdog; a hero is one because he has been a rebel, and so on.

Part Two

LITERARY IMAGES

Chapter 7

THE WHITE MAN'S IMAGE OF THE NON-WHITE IN FICTION

The three outstanding white novelists who portray competently characters belonging to cultural groups outside their own are Josef Conrad, E. M. Forster and William Faulkner. Commenting on a lady critic's statement that writers who sought a setting for their work in far-off countries produced 'decivilized' tales, Conrad writes in a prefatory note to *Almayer's Folly*:

'The critic and the judge seems to think that in those distant lands all joy is a yell and a war dance, all pathos is a howl and a ghastly grin of filed teeth; and that the solution of all problems is found in the barrel of a revolver or on the point of an assegai. And yet it is not so. . . . The picture of life there as here is drawn with the same elaboration of detail, coloured with the same tints. Only in the cruel serenity of the sky, under the merciless brilliance of the sun, the dazzled eye misses the delicate detail, sees only the strong outlines, while the colours, in the steady light, seem crude and without shadow. Nevertheless it is the same picture. And there is a bond between us and that humanity so far away. I am speaking here of men and women—not of the charming and graceful phantoms that move about in our mud and smoke and are softly luminous with the radiance of all our virtues; that are possessed of all refinements, of all sensibilities, of all wisdom—but, being only phantoms, possess no heart. . . . I am content to sympathize with common mortals, no matter where they live. . . . Their hearts—like ours—must endure the load of the gifts from Heaven, the curse of facts and the blessing of illusions, the bitterness of our wisdom and the deceptive consolation of our folly.'

Conrad's greatness as an artist lies in his disinclination to recognize boundaries in human character when he writes about Malays and Arabs. Mrs. Almayer (*Almayer's Folly*) is superstitious and depraved, but that has nothing to do with her half-caste blood; any more than this has anything to do with Nina's disillusionment in Christian teachings. Nina is an individual, her mixed ancestry is incidental.

Nina (Mrs. Almayer's daughter) is enchanted by the recital of 'savage glories, those barbarous fights and savage feasting' typical of her people's past. She 'saw with vague surprise the narrow mantle of civilized morality, in which good-meaning people had wrapped her young soul, fall away—and leave her shivering and hopeless as if on the edge of some deep and unknown abyss. . . . Her teachers did not understand her nature, and the education ended in a scene of humiliation, in an outburst of contempt from white people for her mixed blood.' Nina's going back to barbarism is not necessarily a process of degeneracy or depravity; her failure in the end is at least tragic and credible, because she has turned to the 'uncompromising sincerity of purpose shown by her Malay kinsmen' as an escape from 'the slick hypocrisy, the polite disguises, the virtuous pretences of such white people as she had had the misfortune to come into contact with'. No such conflicts exist for most of the characters in African writing where they appear either as mere creatures of fate or victims of political cruelty. Almayer does not understand why Nina has given herself to Dain whom he regards as a savage. 'I am not of your race,' Nina replies. 'Between your people and me there is also a barrier that nothing can remove. . . . You wanted me to dream your dreams, to see your own visions—the visions of life amongst the white faces of those who cast me from their midst in angry contempt.'

Conrad's *An Outcast of the Islands* carries the theme of *Almayer's Folly* further. Babalatchi and Lakamba lead the Malays and Arabs against the white traders in the Macassar area. The revolution is successful. Captain Lingard warns Babalatchi that the whites will yet prove his (Babalatchi's) undoing.

'This is a white man's talk' (Babalatchi says). 'I know you. That is how you all talk while you load your guns and sharpen your swords, and when you are ready, then to those who are weak you say: "Obey me and be happy, or die!" . . . You think it is only your wisdom and your virtue and your happiness that are true. You are stronger than the wild beasts, but not so wise. A black tiger knows when he is not hungry—you do not. He knows the difference between himself and those who can speak; you do not understand the difference between yourselves and us—who are men. You are wise and great—and you shall always be fools.'

Babalatchi uses Aïssa, the Arab woman, to entice Willems the white man with the intention of conducting a make-believe love affair. Almayer will then lose Willems' allegiance and Lingard will be broken. But the love affair becomes extremely serious. Lingard admits to Aïssa that she is capable of dominating a man with her love. 'How can you know?' Aïssa says to Lingard. 'How can you know? I live with him all the days. All the nights. I look at him; I see his every breath, every glance of his eye, every movement of his lips. I see nothing else! What else is there? And even I do not understand. I do not understand him!—Him!—My life.'

Still with intense feeling, when she realizes she has Willems in her spell and he cannot fight, Aïssa says:

'And I knew then he would not fight you! Before—many days ago—I went away twice to make him obey my desire; to make him strike at his own people so that he could be mine—mine! O calamity! His hand was false as your white hearts. It struck that strong hand, and—O shame! It killed nobody! . . . Round me all was lies. His strength was a lie. His strength was a lie. . . . And to meet you—you, the great!—he had no one but me! But me—with my rage, my pain, my weakness. Only me! . . .'

Willems, a white man who from the start feels proud of his European descent, marries a Malay woman. He misuses her, but she drives him away from home. He later meets Aïssa. 'She, a woman, was the victim of her heart, of her woman's belief that there is nothing in the world but love—the everlasting thing.' Rather than allow Willems to return to his Malay wife, Aïssa kills him. She does it out of a sense of defeat: she has fought like a cat to keep him but has failed.

This is characterization that follows no prescriptions usually determined by the 'race problem'. The fate that hangs over Conrad's characters is a subtle and inscrutable one.

William Faulkner's Joe Christmas, a Negro in the novel *Light in August*, develops a twisted personality under the guardianship of the McEacherns. He is driven by McEachern's brutality and ascetic principles to anti-social habits. He kills his guardian and runs away. Whether with white or Negro women, his sex life is violent. The knowledge that he has Negro blood haunts him and gives him passionate delight in seducing white women. Then there are the orgies with Miss Burden, a white woman who comes of Yankee parents. To get out of this woman's possessive love, Joe Christmas kills her. But he is tracked down and lynched.

This is not just a 'race relations story', even within the narrow boundaries of Deep South life with its very parochial and stock attitudes which constitute a passing political phase. Joe is not just a Negro whose problems are externalized in terms of racial discrimination: the big problem is inside himself more than with the bare situation of colour conflict.

Faulkner's sense of irony shows us an interesting aspect of Joe Christmas's character in the Negro's response to Mrs. McEachern's benevolence towards himself: 'It was not the hard work which he hated, nor the punishment and injustice. He was used to that before he ever saw either of them. He expected no less, and so was neither outraged nor surprised. It was the woman: that soft kindness which he believed himself doomed to be for ever victim of and which he hated worse than he did the hard and ruthless justice of men. "She is trying to make me cry," he thought, lying cold and rigid in his bed, his hands beneath his head. . . . "She was trying to make me cry. Then she thinks that they would have had me." '

It is a long distance to travel between Kipling's view of India and E. M. Forster's. Kipling, with his fanatic sense of authority, sees the British club in India as an exclusive institution that must rightfully protect the British way of life against the alien influence of the Indian people and perhaps the almost corrosive fierceness of the Indian sun. What interests Forster here is the pathetic manner in which the Anglo-Indian maintains a pipe-smoking complacency that pretends to transcend the isolation of club life, to which Indians are not admitted. Forster is out to depict the various shades of attitude, the slights, the hurts (big and small), the interchange of pride and humiliation, the violent hates and the comforting sense of companionship, when Indians and Europeans are thrown together—especially Indian intellectuals. There are sharp contrasts in this picture. The Indians have their own caste prejudices. But these are never given prominence over race prejudices between the British and the Indians. This is the motif of Forster's *Passage to India*.

Dr. Aziz is a mixture of East and West at their best; of the mystic Moslem, the poetic sentimentalist and the cynical materialist. He admires and respects Fielding, Mrs. Moore and her children, Ralph and Stella: he can show them hospitality as if it were all that mattered at the moment. He is deeply touched by their show of friendship, and goes out of his way to conduct Mrs. Moore and Miss Quested to the Malabar Caves. For those who despise him, like the Calendars, Ronny, the Turtons and so on, Aziz has an equal measure of contempt.

Here is a picture of Dr. Aziz: 'Like most Orientals, Aziz overrated hospitality, mistaking it for intimacy, and not seeing that it is tainted with the sense of possession. It was only when Mrs. Moore or Fielding was near him that he saw further, and knew that it is more blessed to receive than to give. These two had strange and beautiful effects on him—they were his friends, his for ever, and he theirs for ever; he loved them so much that giving and receiving became one. He loved them even better than the Hamidullas, because he had surmounted obstacles to meet them, and this stimulates a generous mind. Their images remained somewhere in his soul up to his dying day, permanent additions. . . .'

Aziz turns extremely anti-British after the farcical trial at which Miss Quested accused him of indecent advances and later withdrew the charge. 'It disgraces me to have been mentioned in connection with such a hag,' he says, determined to claim damages from Miss Quested, and gloating.

When Fielding visits him, Aziz anticipates him: 'I know what you are going to say next: Let, oh let, Miss Quested off paying, so that the English may say, "Here is a native who has actually behaved like a gentleman; if it was not for his black face we would almost allow him to join our club." The approval of your compatriots no longer interests me, I have become anti-British, and ought to have done so sooner. . . .'

There is that final parting between Fielding and Aziz. The English must clear out of India, says Aziz: it's too late now for the Indian to try to know the English, a thing they wanted to do ten years before. Only political reasons can bring them to the same committees. Aziz prophesies that the English will yet quit India one day.

What message there is in *Passage to India* is subtly conveyed: it never, as in Paton's *Cry, the Beloved Country* and so much of our other fiction, supersedes character. Forster is content to tell his story, explore character and depict it in the round, like Conrad and Faulkner, untrammelled by labels and provincialism, leaving us to our emotional catharsis.

Aziz, Joe Christmas, Conrad's Nina, and Aïssa are memorable literary creations because they cannot be hewn and carved to fit into the frame of local politics; because they are endowed with the human characteristics which have permanence and which suffer and endure historical change. They are greater creations than those in African fiction because they have much greater freedom of movement than their African counterparts. They are not tethered to any sort of didactic standard. They are not there to justify themselves, to vindicate themselves and their race. As a result they can be carried through several emotional states and react to different situations in various ways that indicate a development.

Nowhere else in the world today do we find so many ghettoes as we have in Africa: social, intellectual, and political ghettoes. In South Africa, I knew the white man either on an intellectual plane or as a worker in his employ. Between these two points there are millions on either side of the colour line who have no way of contact. How, then, can I faithfully portray the whites in my writing, and how is a white writer expected to project himself sufficiently to keep us in proper focus? He belongs to a privileged class and he stands in greater danger of falling into snobbish ways than I.

It is the writer who, if he can live down his innate prejudices, is in the unique position to unveil the sham and stupidity with which the politicians of his race (who hold the destiny of the race in their own hands) are perpetuating the yawning gulf between us. I take my cue from Lionel Trilling's *The Liberal Imagination*:

'The characteristic work of the novel is to record the illusion that snobbery generates and to try to penetrate to the truth which, as the novel assumes, lies hidden beneath all the false appearances. Money, snobbery, the ideal of status, these become in themselves the objects of fantasy. The greatness of *Great Expectations* begins in its title: modern society bases itself on great expectations which, if ever they are realized, are found to exist by reason of a sordid hidden reality. The real thing is not the gentility of Pip's life but the hulks and the murder and the rats and decay in the cellarage of the novel. . . . The novel, then, is a perpetual quest for reality, the field of its research being always the social world, the material of its analysis being always manners as the indication of the direction of man's soul. . . . Its classic intention . . . is the investigation of the problem of reality beginning in the social field.'

A word in passing about Afrikaans literature. One cannot say much more because Afrikaans literature is restricted to two million whites, if not less, in South Africa, and it is part of a defensive mechanism. The Afrikaners have put up barricades around themselves and the writer has to screw up his face and squint in order to see the outside landscape. They have been justifying themselves ever since S. J. du Toit and other leaders launched the Afrikaans Movement in the nineteenth century in order to establish the language as a literary and official medium.

The pioneer poets Leipoldt, Celliers and Totius were preoccupied with either the struggle of their people to free themselves from British rule or with a lyrical expression of eternal verities or natural phenomena. So much of their poetry is in turns fighting, moaning and sniffling talk against concentration camps, banishment, African 'savagery', and extols Boer bravery. Totius ostensibly built up in his poetry an image of his people as a persecuted race who, like the Israelites, traversed miles and miles of desert to look for a Canaan and, in the process, to bring salvation to barbarians (Africans). Alas, that persecution complex has released a great number of excesses in Afrikaner domination.

Like South African English fiction of the nineteenth century, this was a gloating literature. More recently, a few novelists began to concern themselves with contemporary 'problems', but still with a defensive and wounded manner about them: the 'colour problem'; the 'Jewish problem', the 'poor-white problem'. Mikro the novelist, like Sarah Gertrude Millin, depicts grovelling, degenerate Coloured labour squatters (Uncle Toms among them), and like Mrs. Millin, he dislikes mixed blood. Jochem van Bruggen is a sort of one-eyed Dickens: he sees only the poor whites and not the complete setting. With C. M. van den Heever, the African is part of wild nature, and the writer himself, until his death a few years ago, was still bogged down in his Voortrekker boots. The Hobson brothers think of Bushmen as sub-human, and write about them in the same context as baboons. There is Frans Venter's novel, translated into English under the title *Dark Pilgrim*, in 1959, soon after its appearance in Afrikaans. In him, the Afrikaans have only just caught on about the black man come to the city—thirty years after Plomer's famous short story, *Ula Masondo*. But Mr. Venter sees this black man as nothing more than a stranger in town.

What Professor G. H. Durrant of the University of Natal says in a review of Professor Guy Butler's *A Book of South African Verse* is most relevant to the predicament of South African English writing: 'What I complain of is an exaggerated concern for oneself as a member of a particular group—as a Christian amongst heathens, a white man among blacks or Coloureds, an Englishman among Afrikaners, a European in Africa, or a South African in Europe.' This is the weakness, he means, of the poetry represented in the anthology. In the same way, English fiction in South Africa is obsessed with race relations. The *plot* is the thing, and as race conflicts provide innumerable facile plots, we are in for a gold rush; and so character counts for little or nothing. In fact, I rather suspect that we, both black and white, unconsciously want to maintain the *status quo* so as to delay as long as we can the coming of the day when we as writers shall be faced with the greater responsibility of inventing plot and reconstructing character in broader human perspective. In actual dealing with whites we non-whites have, rather good-humouredly, often exploited our position as underdogs: so much as to say, 'You're my friend and you're privileged, so . . . get me out of this mess, or else . . .' Oppression and the protest it excites tend to falsify human behaviour, and are a passing phase, at any rate, as between white and black. Deep under these layers of emotive interpretation and colour distinctions you will realize that human beings are basically the same. This is a platitude, but I must risk raising a yawn in order to drive this point home: that as long as the white man's politics continue to impose on us a ghetto existence, so long shall the culture and therefore literature of South Africa continue to shrivel up, to sink lower and lower; and for so long shall we in our writing continue to reflect only a minute fraction of life.

Against this rather gloomy background, it is most refreshing to turn to two writers whose names do not excite much clamour at all. These are Uys Krige and Ethelreda Lewis. Uys Krige, the most emancipated of the Afrikaans writers, brings to English prose a distilled quakerism that sounds at once aloof and native to the soil. His short stories, *The Dream and the Desert* (written in English), have no full-blooded race conflict and yet the Africans in the stories are real. The black man emerges as cosmopolitan and universal man. He is primarily a soldier and only a black man incidentally. In the story *Two Daumiers* a Mosotho, who is in the army in North Africa, has been feeling bitter because he has come all the way from his country, Basutoland, only to do petty jobs instead of being armed with a rifle to fight. (Non-whites in South Africa are not allowed in the regular army and during a war they cannot enlist as combatants.) The African tells a war correspondent when they meet again: 'No' (the Basuto laughed again), 'today I do not use my slit trench. Today I fight. Did I not tell the Morena (you, sir) yesterday I did not come here only to be a drawer of water that in these parts one finds nowhere? This morning the big Morena (boss) gave us rifles for which I thank the good Modimo (God). For we are the men of Moshesh and we must fight like the men of Moshesh . . . for our mountains, our people. And the sooner we fight the sooner we shall be back amongst our people. Yes, war is fighting, Morena, not lingering in the desert. Now, at last, we fight. That is good. . . .'

Ethelreda Lewis's brilliant and moving short story, *Blind Justice*,[1] came out in 1926. She was perhaps best known in the late twenties and early thirties as the editor of the Alfred Aloysius Horn tales, but she later picked up the threads of original fiction again, this time under the pen-name of R. Herneken Baptist. In

[1] From *Stories of Africa* (ed. E. C. Parnwell, 1930).

Blind Justice the blind African, Sandasa, is 'colourless'; he is not a justification, an instrument of protest in the narrow sense, not a romantic medium. He is just a human being.

Sandasa, a sculptor, has had his eyes dug out with a knife by a man who, caught in the act of killing Sandasa's cousin, decided to blot out all visual memory of himself. For twenty years Sandasa makes a great number of clay heads representing the one-eared criminal, with one hand holding a knife: he must never forget that face. 'When the voice in the night comes to wake me no more,' he says to a visiting white sculptor, 'then will my task be done. I shall know when he is dead, white brother.'

There is the spellbinding moment when Sandasa waits in a passage at the police station while a group of labourers file past, with the suspect among them. He senses the presence of the murderer: 'Sandasa had risen to his knees. His hands mowed the air with a scythe-like movement. On his knees he moved forward, mowing, mowing. . . . The first touch and grip of those mowing hands round his (the murderer's) knees brought an indescribable shuddering roar from his wide-open mouth—the noise man makes when nightmare gently touches him. . . .'

The man is led away. Sandasa weeps. 'For Sandasa, his work filched from him by the unnatural processes of legal justice, turned his face to the wall and ceased to live. Who but Death may wipe away the chill tears of the artist bereft of impulse?'

The difference between the writer who exploits plot as presented by race conflicts and the one who is interested mainly in human character whatever the circumstances, is clearly symbolized by the difference between Plomer the poet and Plomer the fiction writer using the South African setting. Although he had a sensitivity to the nuances of racial injustice, Roy Campbell, his one-time co-editor of a South African journal, could never have had, he did not have the latter's pretensions to a native poetry. That most insolent of South African poets, Campbell, could say: 'My task demands a virgin muse to string/A lyre of savage thunder as I sing.'

Plomer the fictionist, on the other hand, was a very angry man, and although he was clearly the best of a kind, he wrote best when not emotionally involved in race prejudice, when he was not protesting outright. For instance, his Japanese tales, *Paper Houses*, are most beautiful and moving. Here he makes his characters *live* the clash between East and West, without letting them explain it by word of mouth. Few of the minor wolfish white characters in *Turbott Wolfe*, a novel about South Africa, also live the conflict convincingly. What makes *Ula Masondo* succeed is that its protest is merely implied.

And now for the grouping of our images.

Savages, brutal and noble

For several years in the history of South Africa the white man gets to know the non-white merely as an enemy on the battlefield or as a slave—whether it be as a labourer on a farm or carrier on an expedition. Often he knows the non-white as a convert of a mission station. The emotional circumstances of a contact between fighters on the battlefield or between master and servant allow for little more than a tendency on the part of the white man to see the non-white as one of a group rather than as an individual. The missionary tries to deal with the individual personality. If he fails to use this advantage profitably, it is because he believes he is dealing with a 'ward' who represents an inferior culture, which must be completely destroyed as an antithesis of Christian culture.

The early literature produced by the 1820 British settlers is a pioneering literature written in the heat of brutal historical circumstances. The writer of this period hardly touches the fringe of the problem that lies in the so-called clash of cultures; still less that of the irony that lies in the conflict of cultures that need not always clash but are supplementary. The irony of the 'clash' should be rich material enough to interest a novelist and a poet; to say nothing of the real clash as it exists in economic and religious systems.

Thomas Pringle came to South Africa with the British settlers and later became secretary to the Society for the Abolition of Slavery. Pringle writes about the non-white with humanitarian feeling. Apparently the non-white does not present an enigma to him. In his *African Sketches*, Pringle tells of an African woman who is being given over to a colonist to work for him as punishment for crossing the frontier without permission. While she pleads her case with finger raised to the sky, Pringle observes what he calls the beautiful flow of the Xhosa language—the music of it—and her natural, graceful manners. He remarks that he could not help feeling that whites are greater barbarians than savage blacks. Of the conduct of a congregation in a religious service, Pringle says that they cannot be called 'savage', despite their lack of 'accessories of civilisation'. 'There was, even amongst the rudest of the people, an aspect of civility and the decent respect, of quietude and sober-mindedness, habitually under the control of far other principles than those which regulate the movements of mere savage men', he observes. All these experiences surprise Pringle, as when he finds that there is respectable peasantry intellectually advanced.

He writes sympathetically about bands of Africans who have been forced into hiding by colonists and later raid the latter's settlements to recapture their cattle; about Hottentots who are under contract of service, and about their mellow singing: 'sweet, solemn, and pathetic harmony'.

Thomas Pringle's humanitarianism is sincere, but the non-white in his *Sketches* emerges as a passive creature of history. He seemed, in his remarks about the admirable qualities of the Hottentots, to be trying to explode the myth about 'darkest Africa'. There is a large volume of verse by him that is sheer romantic glorification of the non-white and his way of life. One of the poems in *African Sketches*—one of the many rather maudlin ones in the collection—is *Bechuana Boy*, about Marossi, an orphan, who first came under the poet's protection in 1825. The boy had been carried off by the Bergenaars, a Hottentot clan, during a raid, who later sold him to a Boer for a jacket. The Bechuana Boy accompanied the writer's wife to England. He later died, but left a good impression on them.

'By Christians we were bought and sold
. . . And roughly from each other torn,' says the boy.

And

'Englishmen will never know
The injured bondmen's bitter woe.'

Pringle hears in a Xhosa song, *Afar in the Desert*, the longing to go out into the desert with 'the silent Bush-boy alone by my side'. The Xhosa man wants to live away from 'scenes of oppression, corruption and strife', which are the bane of his life.

The humanitarian uses much of his verse to vindicate the aborigine, to crusade for the freedom of African tribes scattered by the white man's superior war machine, and of the 'enslaved Madagass', the 'dejected Malay' and the 'degenerate Belgian'.

Professor Guy Butler of Rhodes University, Grahamstown, is perhaps right in saying that the British settlers brought to the frontier the concept of the 'noble savage', with them a romantic rebellion against the 'too self-conscious eighteenth century, in favour of primitive, wild, unsophisticated man who lives close to "mystic nature" '. The nakedness of the aborigine, he says, suggested innocence, a clear morality. Pringle poetry expresses this romanticism eloquently. To this he brought his personal values, his sympathy, although he pays so much attention to group behaviour rather than character.

The Zulu wars towards the end of Pringle's century released a large body of verse, much of it quite savage and gloating. African armies are said to be coming on like a 'herd of black game' with the 'speed of flame', but so efficient is the white man's warfare that the morning finds 'the devils silently gone'.

A good deal of the fiction of this period is crude. It concerns itself with externals and glib insulting descriptions of the black man.

J. Percy Fitzpatrick, whose volume of South African tales, *The Outspan*, appeared in 1898, thought African life had a mystical power to destroy the white man. In the title story we are told of a white man who goes native and disintegrates when he is back among his own people. 'It seems like—like a sort of judgement . . . civilization, scorned, and flouted, being the instrument of its own revenge.' The white chief in the story dies suddenly. One character says: 'Even in the urchins of the race (Africans) there is the instinct of evasion which enables them to baffle the closest inquiries.'

We shall never know what this mystical power is that causes the white man's ruin. In fact, when dawn comes, we realize that we have been listening to a hunter's or transport-rider's yarn, with so much plot that it swamps character.

For the first time in the fiction of the late nineteenth century we see African life at close quarters in William Charles Scully's *Kaffir Stories*. The distant, shadowy figures are gone, together with thundering epic events that trampled them down. Scully comes to grips with the enigma that emerges from the impact of the Christian outlook on the non-Christian.

The story, *The Fundamental Axiom*, is about Samuel Gozani, at one time a pupil evangelist at a mission station, and Martha Kawa, a woman of mixed parentage, with a very fair complexion. She had an English father and an African mother. 'When five years previously she was sent to the mission, she was in a condition of absolute savagery,' says the writer. 'In the mission school her Aryan blood told; she kept easily ahead of the girls and took all the best prizes.'

Martha loves Gozani, but he takes no notice of her, because he loves Miss Blake, a new white woman on the staff. The standard of his work drops very low because he broods too much over the barrier that lies between him and Miss Blake. He feels lonely. He tells her that a black man becomes a stranger to his own people when he takes to the white man's ways. 'Even you only tolerate me because you think it pleasing to God that you should do so; but you would never be my friend or let me be yours.' She, on the other hand, protests that she likes Gozani as much as if he were white. She doesn't mean it, really.

A Rev. Robley Wilson comes on the scene and falls in love with Miss Blake. In a fit of jealousy, Gozani kills Wilson. The only other witness to the murder is Martha. She loves Gozani and so she will protect him. The two flee the mission and go to live elsewhere as man and wife. Decay sets in, for no reason we can fathom. Gozani, now insane, kills his wife and takes his own life.

Scully makes wild assertions in an attempt to understand the characters of this African couple: 'It was for Miss Blake that he (Gozani) was striving to qualify as a minister; it was of her that he thought all day and dreamt all night. Into his wild and elemental nature, in which hereditary savagery was simply covered by a thin veneer of civilization, this strong love for a woman of an alien race had struck its roots deep down. But instead of the savage element being transmuted into gentleness, his love absorbed into itself the savage and thus became savage in its character. This resultant was a highly explosive psychic compound.'

Later, 'In Martha, the Aryan element manifested itself mainly in force of character, and ability; for in her tastes and desires, as in her physiognomy, she followed her mother's race. Whilst Samuel was secretive by nature, she was rendered so by force of circumstances.'

We are never sure what Scully means by 'savage' or 'savagery' and we do not know whom Gozani inherited his savagery from. The writer gives us the impression at one time that this 'savagery' is merely a *state* and can form some compound with love. The only time it appears as an overt thing is when Gozani kills Wilson. And we don't see what is so hereditary about jealousy. Again, we have no proof in the story of how Martha's tastes and desires are taken over from her African mother. After Hitler, we need not go into all that business about people's ability being inherently Aryan.

Scully's creative ability—there is no doubt about this—is bedevilled by his preconceived ideas about 'Aryan superiority' and 'African savagery'. Neither Martha's 'Aryan ability' nor Gozani's education saves the couple. She and her child die a dog's death.

The 'fundamental axiom', says Scully, is that the 'average barbarian' is fully the 'equal of the average civilized man'. We do not know the terms of reference in the phrases, 'average barbarian' and 'equal of the average civilized man'. And so the 'axiom' falls to pieces.

Sir H. Rider Haggard ends this period that began with Pringle and the 1820 settlers. He arrived in South Africa at the age of 17 and moved a lot among the Zulu people, learning much about their history, customs and heroes. Haggard's *Nada the Lily* appeared in 1892. As in his other books, the African is romanticized in this novel. And like James Fenimore Cooper's tales about Red Indians, Haggard's world—the fake-legendary—interests juveniles.

The Degenerate

When Sarah Gertrude Millin's *God's Stepchildren* became a best-seller in the United States in 1925, the catharsis of it must have rubbed the white Americans the right way. Here's the tragedy of mixed blood, and we're in it too, brotherman, they must have thought. A shattering guilt complex set in: not over the white man's rotten treatment of the Negro, but over his 'sinfulness' that produced the Negro. Mrs. Millin was trying to show that miscegenation between black and white is an evil thing, evil, she thought, because it produces a degenerate race in social and political conditions that outlaw mixed marriages.

The missionary, the Rev. Andrew Flood, marries a Hottentot woman in order to prove something: that he regards blacks and whites as equal in the eyes of God. He hopes his non-white converts will better understand Christ's Gospel when he has married one of them. The members of his congregation often ask him awkward questions about the Gospel, but there are some who haven't the slightest intention of taking the missionary's word seriously or being converted. There is no indication that any of these Hottentots are capable of any deep thinking about religion and the meaning of existence.

Naïvely, the missionary abandons his European standards of cleanliness, again in order to prove that God doesn't make any distinction between black and white.

Mrs. Millin tells us that the community in which Flood has come to work are a very indolent, *dagga*-smoking crowd who thrive in dirt. They are also addicted to witchcraft. In fact, they regard Flood as a fool rather than as a brother. He degenerates. 'He was himself in many ways a savage,' and he dies a miserable person.

No doubt, the author means to tell us, Andrew Flood has by marrying a Hottentot decided the fate of future Coloured generations. One by one these characters crumble; external conditions have no influence on character any more, and Sarah Gertrude Millin cannot save her characters. Deborah, Flood's daughter, cannot go straight, although she grew up under another missionary at some other station—Mr. Burtwell, who lived normally. To satisfy her animal instincts, we are told, she falls in love, first with a Hottentot, and then with another man. We are treated to such generalizations as: 'She (Deborah) had, *as most half-caste children have*, a capacity for imitation' (my italics). Deborah's learning ability reaches a limit, because 'inevitably the point would be reached where a solid barrier of unreceptivity would hinder all further mental progress'. Another label. Again, 'native children arrived at their full capacity very early—at fourteen or fifteen they would begin to falter, to lag behind, to remain stationary while their white competitors went ahead'. Adam Kok, half-caste leader of the Griquas and Hottentots, with whom Deborah and her son, Kleinhans, subsequently go to live, is described as a 'leader of shamefully born savages and fugitives and outlaws and emancipated slaves'.

'In that community where work was universally despised' Kleinhans is said to be by nature a husbandman. 'Heaven knows what germ in his distant white ancestry had quaintly chosen to establish itself in Kleinhans's character.' He hates the 'meek, dark bearers of shame'.

Kleinhans is not accepted by whites in spite of his conscious efforts to live down his Coloured blood by engaging in money-making projects. A group of whites beat him up. Those qualities which his white ancestry is supposed to have brought with it collapse in him. No, they never go beyond the ordinary level, these half-castes, the writer suggests. No firmness of character at all! Kleinhans ends up as a farm manager and marries a Coloured.

Elmira is born of this marriage. She is sent to a European school to 'try for white'. For himself Kleinhans admits defeat: he cannot cross over; but his children must not go to an African school. Elmira is thus offered as a pathetic sacrifice, and we see her walking on a very tight rope in that school for whites. It snaps by accident, and her personality crumbles. It is her illness which brings her parents to the school to see her. Her real identity is unveiled. She never puts up a fight during her stay in the school. Shame has done it again; she is ashamed of her parents. But more than that, the accident of colour, which forms the motif of the whole novel, has brought about the inevitable collapse of Kleinhans and his wife, Lena.

'What does it matter when she is going to die that we are brown and she is white?' Lena asks. 'But we are unlucky people. We are unlucky to be born, and still more unlucky was Elmira to be born.'

Lindsell, who has been responsible for Elmira's schooling, undertakes to marry her. She must do it, not because she loves this old man, but because she is a creature of circumstance, and, like all the rest, a slave to a hereditary fate. 'She (Lena) shudders to think of her pretty child married to this hateful-looking old man (Lindsell). But, on the other hand, there flowed in her the blood of submissive slaves and acquiescent Eastern wives. There were women in her ancestry who had come young to the harems of old men, there were some who had been concubines casually taken up and casually cast off.'

For the first time in the story, someone in the Flood line—the last in the line—starts thinking about colour and mixed blood in a manner no other fictional character before him has done. This is Barry, Elmira's son by Lindsell. In Cape Town, Barry looks around him and thinks how unambitious and unenterprising Coloured folk are. A black man, he observed, can scale up as far as an English or Scottish university even without the political and social privileges enjoyed by the Coloured man. And still the Coloured man remains behind.

Why? Hottentot blood, that's the trouble, according to the author. 'Imitative and monkey-like . . .' Barry's blood has something of this. Mrs. Millin admits that there are South Africans who have coloured blood in them in spite of their very fair complexion, but who are by no means hopeless.

Someone tells Barry that an ancestor of his once blundered into a marriage with a Hottentot. Because of this, a line of Coloured children had been born, each one of them continuing the 'evil'. Barry must see that he does not repeat the blunder. He tries to fight back, but he fears his blood and is harassed by a sense of inferiority. He succumbs to the suggestion, and decides to be a minister of religion. 'It would be some recompense for what his ancestors had done.' This is the millstone to which his character is tied.

Barry's experiences at Oxford and later as a soldier in the first World War have a wonderful effect on him: they seem to broaden his vision and the colour issue is no longer an obsession with him, just as it isn't in Europe. He marries an English woman and returns home. When she is expecting a child, he is nagged by the same person as before into telling his wife the truth about his coloured blood. His nightmare is not softened when he goes back to his folk to see his dying mother, Elmira. The sight of her, his great-grandmother and all other Coloured folk living in poverty and misery decides Barry to start missionary work for their uplift. He gives up his English wife.

We are made to understand that Elmira's slavish acquiescence to Lindsell's demands is the same as that of her grandparents, of her parents, of her tribe—that 'unluckily born', grovelling, defeated breed of 'God's stepchildren', 'who must always suffer'.

Sixteen years after *God's Stepchildren*, Sarah Gertrude Millin continues the story of Barry Lindsell in the *The Herr Witchdoctor*. Barry is still atoning for his forefathers' miscegenation. He fails, and is aware of his failure as a missionary. But being born for failure, he does not get our sympathy. He has the grand opportunity of returning to his family—his wife and child—but he rejects it. 'Had he ever in his life stopped crying: "Don't let the brown people take me."'

John Nsingasi asks a number of questions about the black man's position in the polity. He wants to uplift his people. But he breaks down under the weight of the intellectual arguments the author introduces. John eventually joins the German missionary church. He knows that by so doing he is 'throwing himself from stony earth into uncharted, immeasurable space. But in that space still lay his dream. . . . Whomever he betrayed, whatever he risked, he had to pursue it.' John only threatens to grow into something big as a character.

Aaron, the leader of the Levite sect in Mrs. Millin's *The Coming of the Lord* is another fate-driven creature. He is a religious fanatic and no one can reason with him. 'God will fight on our side,' is his stock reply to all who beg, persuade, order, urge him to leave the Heights where he has established his town against Government regulations. For the rest, the Levite masses are described as people who love an idle life, the implication being that they mean to enjoy themselves on the Heights while they wait for the coming of the Lord—the Revelation.

The Levites are forced out by the authorities. Once again, character tumbles down to an inevitable end.

Again and again in Sarah Gertrude Millin's novels we see non-whites driven or goaded by a fate. Her works reveal in turn Mrs.

Millin's strong will and an uncompromising tenacity to her ideas and ideals. She succeeds best when she does not impose her own will on her characters, e.g. in her volume of short stories, *Two Bucks Without Hair and Other Stories*. These are intimate portraits of Africans in one predicament and another. Particularly striking are those of her servants, chief of whom is Alita, the domestic.

Alita is always fighting other people's battles, trying to stretch her meagre wage a long way to provide for a number of dependants. Her grown-up son and daughter are always creating responsibilities which she is ever ready to shoulder. And in the typical African fashion, she claims her daughter's illegitimate child as hers and does not feel ashamed of her daughter or grandchild, no matter how wayward the daughter is.

Although she takes a deep interest in Alita and her children, such as only few South African whites are capable of, Mrs. Millin records objectively the emotional twists and turns that she observes in her workers and her own failures and successes in handling Africans. Her beliefs do not stand in the way of character development at all.

There is that delightful story about Thomas the gardener. He doesn't see why Mrs. Millin should fuss about holes being dug deep for roses just when (Thomas thinks) *he* is working for her. He reckons that if he has been working for her for only six years, and she had lived on the property for twenty-seven years, she might have got her former gardeners over the first twenty-one years to dig deep holes for the roses. At this point she admits she is stumped.

Sarah Gertrude Millin is a historian as well as a novelist. Hers has been a prolific writing career in both fields. One cannot help but feel that the ever-present element of fate that weighs so heavily on her fictional creations comes of her strong sense of history, a desire to place things within the spectrum of cause and effect. And who knows, there has probably been a tug inside her between a love of history and an ability to write fiction. And then there is that other and overriding factor which must always confront the serious South African writer as long as politics maintain their present drift: the need for a writer to come to terms with himself in relation to his position as either one of an underdog majority or as one of a privileged minority. Within this context the urges to preach, protest, hand out propaganda, to escape, sentimentalize, romanticize, to make a startling discovery in the field of race relations, to write thrillers, and other urges, all jostle for predominance in the writer. A practising critic is just as apt to be angry and impatient in a set-up like this as the writer is, particularly when, as I am compelled to do, the critic identifies himself with the underdog characters of his colour. Because of this, I may appear to be unduly hard on Mrs. Millin.

Children of the Wasteland

Non-Europeans do not loom large in Olive Schreiner's classic, *The Story of an African Farm.* The non-white character appears as a butt for the wrath of Tant' Sannie, the Dutch woman of the farm, and for the treacherous Bonaparte's intrigue; or as a servant. These non-whites are really seen as an organic part of the African setting: violate the black man, you violate the setting; respect the one, you respect the other.

Part of this setting are the Bushman rock paintings. They make the contemplators, Waldo and Lyndall, feel the presence of the artist '. . . and it seems that the stones are really speaking—speaking of the old things, of the time when the strange fishes and animals lived that are turned into stone now, and the lakes were here; and of the time when the little Bushmen lived here, so small and so ugly, and used to sleep in the wild dog holes, and in the "sloots", and ate snakes, and shot the bucks with their poisoned arrows. It was one of them, one of these old wild Bushmen, that painted those'—one who was different from the rest. He did not know why, but he wanted to make something, so he made these. . . . Now the Boers have shot them all, so that we never see a yellow face peeping out among the stones.'

Bonaparte comes to the Dutch woman's farm to ask for shelter. When the German overseer warns him not to stare at the woman so much—the probable reason for her hostile attitude—Bonaparte 'turned his nose full upon a small Kaffir of two years old. That small, naked son of Ham, became instantly so terrified that he fled to his mother's blanket for protection, howling terribly.' That is how Tant' Sannie regarded blacks and we are also warned what attitude to expect from Bonaparte from now on. He is going to be just as spiteful, contemptuous and brutal towards the servants as Tant' Sannie.

'Because Tant' Sannie held they were descended from the apes, and needed no salvation' the African servants are prohibited from the Sunday services on the farm. The Coloureds (those of mixed blood) receive a somewhat preferential treatment.

There is a beautiful picture of simple trust in the German overseer's attitude towards the servants. For instance, he just cannot disbelieve the herd who denies stealing twenty sheep. 'How can I think he lies?' says the German, like a child. 'I know his heart. It was under my words that he first felt his need of a Saviour.' (He conducts prayer services for the African servants.) Of Tant' Sannie's coloured maid, he says:

'I have confidence in her. There is that in her which is pure, that which is noble. The rich and high that walk this earth with lofty eyelids might exchange with her.' We are under no illusion that the overseer is Olive Schreiner's spokesman as the champion of the underdog surrounded by a pack of wolves. 'He had more sins than all the Kaffirs in Kaffirland,' Tant' Sannie tells Waldo after his father, the overseer, is dead. He dared to give the herd's wife and child sanctuary when they were expelled from the farm.

There is mute suffering among the servants on this farm; like a piece of earth that erodes noiselessly under the relentless flow of running water or under the lashing of a South African storm. Only in one spot does mirth erupt and bubble on this landscape. This is when Tant' Sannie's maid laughs—often at the victims of the Boer woman's lashing tongue or punishment.

Like Charles Dickens's underdog, Olive Schreiner's non-white characters enjoy the little that individual philanthropy can give. In her *Trooper Peter Halket*—which is a moving sermon—the African is part of a setting that is being ravaged by war. The story takes place in Mashonaland, Southern Rhodesia. The Mashona and Mandebele are being forced out of their land to give way to a gold-prospecting company. Again, the African is a mute sufferer when he is tied up by the British, ready to be shot for spying. Peter Halket releases him and dies for it himself.

Often, because there is mute response to suffering, the African and Hottentot servants on Tant' Sannie's farm move about like shadows. Often, again, their very reticence is laced with agony. And Olive Schreiner's warmth and compassion never escapes us. 'When the drunken Kaffir lies by the road in the sun we draw his blanket over his head, and put green branches of milk-bush on it,' she writes. 'His (God's) Kaffir; why should the sun hurt him? . . . There is no justice. . . . The black man is shot like a dog, and it goes well with the shooter. . . .'

The same warmth and compassion comes out in Olive Schreiner's short story, *Dream Life and Real Life.* Here, Jannita, a Coloured girl, is shot dead by a Bushman, Hottentot, and an English navvy just before she can tell her former master that they are plotting to steal one of his sheep. Jannita, who looked after the flock ran away from her cruel white master. Somewhere in the caves she overhears the plot, but the three, on hearing a rustling noise near by, go after her and intercept her in the farmyard.

These three men, however, are not mute sufferers: they have a live intellect, and there is a mixture of wanton and vindictive attitudes at the back of their mischief.

In William Plomer's fiction, as in Olive Schreiner's, we are dealing with African characters who, deliberately or unwittingly, are made to appear as a personification of the natural setting. William Plomer writes in his autobiography, *Double Lives*:

'To speak of it (*Turbott Wolfe*) as a novel is perhaps a misnomer: it was a *violent ejaculation, a protest*, a *nightmare*, a phantasmagoria —which the dictionary defines as "a shifting scene of real or imagined figures"—judged as a novel it is very deficient. By realistic standards, the story or plot is exiguous and somewhat absurd, and it was not even well constructed. The main characters are neither well drawn nor convincing, the development is episodic, and the whole proceeding is crude and immature, and disfigured by an unpleasant superficial smartness or vulgar cleverness. Nevertheless, the book is not wholly without merit. If it was crude, *it had vitality*; some of the minor characters are noted with skill and true feeling, and there are scenes, passages and phrases which are at least not banal. In my opinion its justification was that of an original sketch-book, an outburst of poetic frenzy on the part of a solitary and emotional youth who had not reduced his thoughts to order but had reacted convulsively to his surroundings; and also (in the words of, surprisingly, a South African critic writing fifteen years after its appearance) as a picture of a world "dominated by race fear and race hatred" and "a revelation of savagery in a vaunted civilization".' (The italics are mine.)

Indeed, he tells us he wrote *Turbott Wolfe* between the ages of 19 and 21. Even so, after reading much of the South African fiction of the last thirty years, it is refreshing to go back to 1925 and read Plomer's *Turbott Wolfe.* Its intellectual interest is more intense than ever before in South African English fiction writing.

The characters in this novel feel they have something to contribute to the polity. There is a third dimension to them, as it were, unlike the two-dimensional characters in *God's Stepchildren,* who are but creatures of fate. . . . Turbott Wolfe is a bit of a romanticist himself, but we never lose focus, any more than we confuse Flaubert's Madame Bovary's romantic impulses with the realistic setting and events surrounding her life.

Nordalsgaard, the Norwegian missionary, is a gentleman 'looking to his work to reward him only with affection of the half-awaking consciousness of the simian, mystical childlike, man-like and the woman-like obscure attractive soul of the African'. The idea of the African being something of an anthropoid ape coming out of a prehistoric fog is a romantic one. Like Wolfe's intention to train his eye 'to admire to excess the over-developed marvellous animal grace of each Lembu individual', and his ecstasy 'over the bright-eyed ingenuousness of every child, over the patriarchal grace of each old man, over the youthful grace of every young one. . . .'

It is in 'violent ejaculation' and protest that Plomer says of the African girl, Nhlizinyombi, with whom Wolfe has fallen in love: 'She was a fine rare savage, of a type you will find nowhere now: it has been killed by the missions, the poor whites and the towns. The missionaries brought them the sacrament, but . . . syphilis too. They took away everything from the natives—all those vague mysterious savage ways of mind on which their lives are conducted, often very honourably and even nobly.' And he goes on to say how the African soul became the battleground for white denominationalism.

It is true that white denominations have been warring among themselves over the African's soul. True, also, much of the beauty of Africa has been replaced by wasteland on which towns and missions now sprawl.

We get a close-up of Nhliziyombi when she and Wolfe meet. She receives a present of a gold pin from him. She is overjoyed and exclaims: 'O, white men!' She runs off. Again, for a brief spell, we see the two in a banana-grove. He tells her how much he loves her; she takes the white man's hand and looks at it, evidently full of pity and gratitude, knowing that her place can only be among her community.

Wolfe's servant, Caleb Msomi, is an educated and trustworthy man. Wolfe skips the conventional master-servant relationship in his dealings with Caleb. Caleb plays an important role in the society of Young Africa and he exerts a subtle influence on his employer. Otherwise, he is one of those characters Plomer would be the first to recognize as vaguely drawn. The Africans live in the midst of white neurotics like Friston, who begins talking about the world's becoming quickly and inevitably a 'coloured world'; amidst a pack of white wolves like Flesher, who degenerates into a grotesque hater of 'nigger-lovers'—maybe he even hates them more than he hates Africans; Soper who is forever spitting vitriol to hide his remorse over a ghastly murder he committed when he castrated an African. Soper tells his friends that he nearly married a Coloured man's daughter and yet he thinks Africans are nothing more than animals. Another time, he orders an African to destroy the sheep belonging to Romaine, his accomplice in the murder. Frank D'Elvedere warns Friston: 'Never suppose that you can elevate the black man to your own level. You can't. . . . But it is very easy for a white man to lower himself to the level of the native. . . .' And perhaps to prove this, he says he cannot claim that no black woman has ever shared his bed. . . .

The presence of the black man exerts an uncanny influence on relationships between white and white. This is constantly happening to these white characters. The Schwerts take to terrible acts of witchcraft; Bloodfield's hatred of the blacks and anger with the likes of Wolfe never let up. Roumaine's servant, conquers, in a drunken state, the farmer's white governess. She loves him.

Clearly, these whites are up against a violent setting. Plomer shows a poetic sense of irony in his vision of the frustrated Norwegian missionary and of the other side of the story relating to missionary endeavour and Christian civilization: its defeat.

It is easy to see how the vitality with which the white characters are drawn and the vicious light in which he shows up their 'vaunted civilization' and inflated sense of self-importance should have infuriated the South African white public—thirty years ago or today.

The Migrant

In 1926, young Plomer, after giving literate white South Africa a rude jolt with his first novel, wrote a long story, *Ula Masondo*. This started off a school of writing which was to exploit the migrant labour system of South Africa as literary material. Laurens van der Post, then his friend, followed with his first novel, *In a Province*; and then *I am Black*, by Grenfell Williams. Among others were Peter Abrahams, Alan Paton and, most recently, Frans Venter, whose Afrikaans novel, *Dark Pilgrim*, has been translated into English.

The African who comes to the city from the rural reserves to work on the mines on contract, presents an interesting range of personalities for a creative writer to explore. When the theme has been beaten out, the hero of the piece, in the hands of various writers, goes through a number of experiences, some very harrowing, gets sick of it all and limps back to the reserves. We have grown weary of this wretched creature, but Ula Masondo has survived them.

Ula gets himself entangled with a spiv-like character, Vilakazi, and his comrades in Johannesburg. Vilakazi is also a mine-worker. Ula has to surrender first a portion of his wages and then all the money to Vilakazi as his 'protector'. Vilakazi in turn is associated with a rogue, Stefan. House-breaking, drinking, women, are now regular items of entertainment for Ula.

Right from the start Johannesburg gets a grip of him:

'As though he had lived through it all before, as though he would live through it all again, he suffered and never forgot the routine of work and rest at the Simeon and Steck Amalgamated, the sight of shivering groups standing in a darkening or a brightening air and waiting to descend at the skips, the voice of the shift-boss, the dampness and darkness below, the sensation in one's ears at the deeper levels, the dimness, and the moving lights, the hum of work in subterranean stillness, the stale fumes of gelignite and acetylene, and in the narrow stopes the loud staccato stutterings of the compressed-air drills, which men held in their hands like powerful animals that wanted to get away. . . .'

Ula Masondo is fascinated by Emma, the only girl in the gang, no less than Vilakazi himself is. The other character who has considerable influence on Ula is Smile, the Christian dandy who works as a domestic: 'On Sunday mornings Smile wore a black coat, and carried in his pocket a Lembu Bible, for he belonged to one of those innumerable native sects that make of Christianity an exciting cult, and quote the Scriptures to their own purposes. In the afternoons he still had the Bible with him, and used also to carry a little cane, which he would wave like a wand, saying of somebody he disliked, in a tone of the utmost contempt: "*Hau?* He's just a heathen!" or, describing something he liked: "Truly, this tobacco is Christian!" ' Masondo even buys a cane like Smile's.

Ula and Emma escape arrest by the breadth of a hair when detectives pounce on Vilakazi. The two start off for home in the reserves. At the station, Ula refuses to recognize his mother who has come to meet him. Two of his brothers are treated to the same snobbish indifference, and he takes Emma to her home, where he tells them he is going to stay. This experience drives Masondo's mother literally mad. She hangs herself.

A white storekeeper who once sold Ula a blanket is telling his wife all this: he thinks he knows what the city has done to Ula: 'Hanged herself! Mind you, it's only the second time I've ever heard of a native committing suicide. By Jove, there's an example for you, of a boy going away quite all right, and coming back with all this Christian dandy business that I can't stand at any price. Give me the raw nigger any day, is what I have always maintained.'

It is fascinating to see how Plomer's image of Ula Masondo grows. For instance, when the black migrant is trapped in a mine by a fall of rock. Before the rescue party comes he dreams of Bushmen paintings back in his home district. He has heard of the extinct Bushmen and this idea fuses now with that of his own possible extinction:

> What are you doing,
> Ula Masondo?
> Do you follow the Bushmen?
> Are you lost in the hollow
> Root of the city?

Laurens Van der Post came of Dutch parents and in 1926 became William Plomer's friend and co-editor of the literary journal, *Voorslag*, together with the late Roy Campbell, in South Africa. I still consider Van der Post's *In a Province* the best fiction he ever wrote. He has become a mystic. Apart from a portion of his volume of lectures, *The Dark Eye in Africa*, he is quite unintelligible to me.

In a Province rings an echo of *Turbott Wolfe*: Johan van Bredepoel is another version of Turbott Wolfe. Like Wolfe, Van Bredepoel is assailed by doubts about Western Civilization. Has it not suffered in its self-imposed mission of transforming Africa? Both men are haunted by a sense of failure, and they are the only characters in their South African fictional world who are sensible of this failure. The others of their colour, with a few exceptions, are just stupid brutes.

Van Bredepoel takes an interest in Kenon, an African lad who comes to the city to work. The white man is also a stranger to city life. Kenon is an artless, gullible child of nature when his friend meets him. But soon the lad finds he has to adjust himself to the tempo of town life. He buys a cheap gramophone from a white hawker. Van Bredepoel acts in time to save Kenon from the tangle of an unwritten hire-purchase agreement that a white vendor wants to foist on the lad.

'He (Kenon) had also a genuine and deep desire to improve himself which exposed him to all sorts of dangers of which he was not aware, and made him particularly vulnerable to the disdain of his more sophisticated companions. . . . It did not take him long to realize that, in the strange and complex life in which he found himself, the traditions of his people were no longer certain guides. . . .' First, a brothel. During a raid by police Kenon is arrested and tried on a trumped-up charge. His remorse gets the better of him and he is disinclined to plead for himself. It's prison for him—six months. He chooses to go it alone, refusing to disclose the names of his friends.

Life can never be the same again for Kenon when he comes out of prison. A corrosive bitterness builds up in him. Van Bredepoel is, in the meantime, battling with his own thoughts about Kenon. He has no ready-made arguments. He finds the dialectics about changing the whole system useless, even in the face of a riot, when Kenon tells him that he knows him (the white man) but that his assagai does not.

The magistrate of Paulstad has something to tell us, something relating to ritual murder and other acts of witchcraft among Africans: 'We don't allow the black people to enter into the system of living for which our justice was obviously devised. By refusing to do so, we imply that they are psychologically and racially in a different class. Yet we proceed very logically to inflict our system of justice on them as if they were like ourselves. . . . We forbid them the sort of life their law demands, and give them our law without the sort of life that our law demands.'

Van der Post is much more sensible about this than other writers and politicians who reduce the problem to simple terms like 'clash of cultures'.

Kenon sways about like a door on one hinge: he roves about, smokes a narcotic weed, develops a lust for violence; he seems beyond rehabilitation. What is the significance of Van Bredepoel's idealism and philanthropy against a vicious machine that reduces people of Kenon's colour to all this? Van Bredepoel feels his own inadequacy poignantly. But he is still prepared to lay a bet on 'individual responsibility' which he thinks we are bound to lose if all attention is given to an overhauling of the whole system—a mere 'approximation', as he regards it. 'It seems to me fatal. The starting- and finishing-point is in the heart of each man. At one time the responsibility for action was placed on the individual, and I think the world was relatively a good deal happier.'

Of course, collectivism and communal responsibility have overtaken the world in several fields of economic activity since the 1920's when Van der Post wrote. The place of the individual in all this continues to exercise the novelist's mind: how are private and social interests to be reconciled?

Frans Venter's novel, *Dark Pilgrim*, presents its hero as a Jim-comes-to-Jo'burg type of caricature: Jim stands for the stock clumsy bumpkin who comes to the gold mines. Venter's character joins a crime syndicate which has the incredible function of politicizing its members: steal from the white man because he oppresses you, and hate him. Venter, writing from his cosy couch in a privileged, perhaps even posh, residential area, wouldn't know that people steal primarily because they are hungry or else they are psychopathic cases. After it all, the author sends his hero limping back home, shattered by his experiences in the city. This vindicates the determined attempt of the white ruling class in South Africa to drum into the black man's head that his real home is in the rural reserves, not in the 'white man's town'.

Someone will have to tell the whites one day—writers, politicians, the lot—in a language they can understand, that a meaningful literature that uses the South African setting will have to draw its power from the ironic sense of permanence with which the black man sticks it out in a city where he is not accepted by whites except as a servant: not from the theatrical antics of Jim and his facile exit. To this latter kind of stuff I should even prefer to read the dream-like story in *I am Black*, by Grenfell Williams and Henry John May. Here, the man goes to the city to seek a fortune, is battered about, and returns to his home to succeed his father as chief—like the valiant prince of fairy tales: that is, if we were short of alternatives. Ula Masondo is still very much alive. His exit is not just that of a black man, but of any human being who is hounded out of a place and seeks refuge in the last stronghold of a man's personality: the belief that he is, at any rate, superior to those he is going back to. He doesn't have the money they will be expecting from him as one who comes from the golden city, but he has a walking stick and they are heathens!

Man with a Halo

The story means everything to Alan Paton and character is of secondary importance in his *Cry, the Beloved Country*, the first work in the history of South African fiction in which the black man looms so large. E. M. Forster says in his *Aspects of the Novel* that when a novelist wants to strike with direct force, it is convenient for him to use 'flat' characters; characters who can easily be labelled and therefore managed. Paton's characters are nearly all flat. We can almost hear them groan under the load of the author's monumental sermon, a sermon packed with a very deep sincerity, the text of which is 'Comfort in Desolation'.

The Rev. Stephen Kumalo can be summed up by 'so in my suffering I can believe'. Msimangu, Paton's commentator, remains untouched by the events in the story. He can be summed up by: 'It is the law, Mother. We must uphold the law.' Kumalo also remains the same suffering, Christlike, childlike character from beginning to end. He is always trembling with humility. He accepts the scheme of things: 'No, nothing, only more fear and more pain. There is nothing in the world but fear and pain!' He is always bewildered. Even after his bitter experiences in the city, he can still address the white boy from Jarvis's farm as 'inkosana' —little master. He can still say to the boy, 'When you go, something bright will go out of Ndotsheni.' The priest can still end his letter of condolence to Jarvis, 'Your faithful servant'. Kumalo represents the Africans of the older generation who behave ordinarily in the presence of their fellow-Africans, but with self-effacement in the presence of white people; the long-suffering type that gets all the kicks and wishes to give none; the type that gives a stock response to violent situations; bear and suffer. It absolves them from the responsibility of reacting humanly. But it also makes for a tough hide that can absorb the cruder processes of life while they move about on the spiritual plane.

Paton has thought fit to use this type for Kumalo's role, for highly sentimental reasons. In the midst of so much pain, fear and dishonesty, he seems to say: 'Here is a man who does not hate, who harbours no bitterness. And he is a black man, too, one of a race that is often despised. Have you no reverence for such dignity? . . .' and so on; a variation upon the theme of 'comfort in desolation'.

We are in Sophiatown that was. A township of night screams, violence, of streets peopled with sluts and men in dishevelled as well as sleek dress, a township of backyards that harbour a debauched, dissipated existence. But Mrs. Lithebe remains untouched by all this. She fits into the sermon and mustn't get out of hand.

Gertrude, the hardened shebeen queen, really adds nothing to the desolation and is soon removed from the story.

The priest's brother, John Kumalo, pretends to a roundness and one is tantalized into hoping that the interplay of opposite personalities such as his and the priest's is going to grow into something memorable. John Kumalo is a political speech-maker; he always seems to be addressing a crowd even when he speaks to one person; he does not like Christian convention; he is sensible of the insecurity around him. He will do anything to avoid more pain than is already being inflicted upon him and his people. For this reason he must get a lawyer to defend his son and talk him out of the crime in which John's son and the priest's are involved—of shooting the younger Jarvis, a negrophilist.

But John Kumalo falls back into line and even becomes a political caricature.

Paton makes the most of his setting. Without it he would not have a story. Beneath the illusion of progress and prosperity Johannesburg is a sordid city, a city of disgraceful slums . . . a city of bus boycotts and political strikes; a city where the crime machine spits a bullet here and a knife there to take human life; but all these features of city life do not develop in a vacuum. They can only mean something to us in the context of the larger social setting of South Africa. Paton might have attempted to study the characters of people in a process of change in such a setting. As it is, we get ready-made characters, because he wants with a swift stroke to convey a message. We merely hear about the deterioration of Absalom's morals (Kumalo's son) from those he has been in contact with. But those who tell us are not a very informative lot. Even the reformatory official is not very helpful. Absalom's lover is a dumb, bashful girl who has been so ravished by slum conditions that she has developed a disposition to allow things to happen to her, as if she were held down by something too big for her to understand. We do not actually see Absalom's demoralization in process. We do not even know what he thinks about himself and the social order he finds himself in. When we come face to face with him, he is just a fear-stricken creature being sacrificed.

One may remark: 'But Bigger Thomas in Richard Wright's *Native Son* is also a fear-stricken creature.' Yes. But Wright gives us an almost minute-by-minute account of how that fear started and grew into something far larger than Bigger, and how he lived the fear. Bigger Thomas is not a mere vehicle of a message such as Alan Paton puts across: that juvenile delinquency demands sympathy rather than vengeance; even although Paton's novel is an echo of *Native Son*, and Bigger Thomas is the American Negro counterpart of Absalom. Because the message keeps imposing itself on us in *Cry, the Beloved Country*, we cannot but feel how thickly laid on the writer's liberalism is: let the boys be kept busy by means of club activities and they will be less inclined to delinquency; work for a change of heart in the white ruling class (Jarvis's final philanthropic gesture and his son's practical interest in club activities together with his plea to South Africa indicate this). Human nature is falsified because there are bad characters as against good ones—in two distinct groups.

Paton's 'vision of humanity' makes his flat characters 'vibrate a little', like Dickens's; but hardly any of the chief characters are as significant as Dickens's. Paton is much more progressive than Sarah Gertrude Millin and there is a warmth in him which the latter doesn't have. But both of them present flat characters who are a mechanical instrument for the execution of plot and the communication of a clearly defined message. Olive Schreiner and William Plomer, on the other hand, regard non-Europeans as an organic part of the setting.

The Menacing Servants

This is a continent of servants—servants of all kinds. There are as many conceivable kinds of relationship between master and servant as the writer cares to explore; especially in the case of white master and black servant, the usual pattern in Africa.

Nadine Gordimer's method is not to portray an obvious interplay of personalities or cross-impacts between master and servant. The reticent, ant-like, non-committal manner in which the domestic servants move about in the house releases a mysterious but real force that upsets relations between the white members of the same family. And the servants themselves stay unperturbed, in a sense, like catalytic agents.

Let us review first her volume of short stories, *Six Feet of the Country*. In the title story, when Lerice's husband brings Petrus word that his brother's corpse cannot be retrieved, Petrus first looks at him 'out of his knowledge that white men have everything, can do anything; if they don't, it is because they won't.'

Miss Gordimer's characters do not talk or think about their race relations. They simply feel the little world around them narrowing and crowding in on them as a result of their class prejudices, fears and doubts. The characters look helpless. Petrus, Lerice's domestic, never told her or her husband that he had a sick brother sleeping in his room (on their premises). They get to know about this only when he is dead. Says Lerice: 'You would think they would have felt they could tell *us*, once the man was ill.' Lerice may be thinking that there is a tacit conspiracy among domestic workers not to confide in their employers. The trouble is she may think a number of things, but because there is a barrier between master and servant, she is not in a position to know what is at the back of a black man's mind: all so exasperating!

Madam will never know what the servant's attitude is towards the work he or she is given. She can only guess. It plagues the McClearys (*Horn of Plenty*) not to know what the non-committal Rebecca thinks about the work they pile on her. 'Rebecca always waited to be spoken to; it was as if she had decided that hers would never be the responsibility for opening verbal negotiations of any kind. She did not fidget while she waited; she was, it often appeared to Pat (the mistress), without nerves.' Rebecca cannot get used to calling Mrs. McCleary by her name, and although her mistress insists, she doesn't think it is important. 'She didn't even say it was a nice dress,' says Mrs. McCleary of her maid. Perhaps

Mrs. McCleary is too thick-headed to sense that nineteen years' domestic work under whites has conditioned Rebecca to these conventional relations between master and servant.

Lena hardly ever says anything either (*Happy Event*). Ella, her mistress, doesn't know her. Thomas, the house servant, has contempt for her, but Lena continues to be the defenceless, passive woman. The point Miss Gordimer wants to make is that not many employers *want* to know anything about their servants except when something goes wrong in the household duties. A servant's personal problems are apt to upset employers unduly. 'She is not a *motherly* figure,' Ella thinks. 'One cannot imagine her mother to anything.' The enigma seems to loom larger when Lena looks at her, 'suddenly, directly, without a flicker of evasion, without dissimulation or appeal, not as a woman looks to another women or even a human being to another human being.'

Non-white characters interest Miss Gordimer only as far as they throw light on the subtleties of group attitudes and pig-headedness among whites. 'You never know with *them*. . . . You can send them to a doctor to make sure you aren't harbouring someone who's diseased, but you've no way of finding out what sort of person a servant is. . . . "Ah, Thomas," someone would murmur, "now he's a good old thing." '

One's attention is always drawn to the white man's reaction to the presence of the black man in Miss Gordimer's stories which portray non-white characters. The white detective who comes to investigate Lena's killing of her baby adopts a manner that 'has changed to the impatient one customarily used for Africans by all white persons in authority—a manner that arose perhaps quite legitimately in defence against the circumlocution of the rather poetic Bantu languages, with their delicate formality, and now has hardened into indiscriminate use.'

Again, in the title story, our eyes have been focused on Lerice and her husband in their reaction to the difficulty of finding the corpse of Petrus's brother, until we get to the climax when the coffin is opened and it is discovered that indeed Petrus has got the wrong body. Our eyes shift to Lerice's husband when, with devastating ruthlessness, Miss Gordimer shows the man with golf stick in hand on the day of the burial. We are almost embarrassed for him when he awkwardly joins the procession.

In another volume of short stories, Miss Gordimer uses the same technique—*The Soft Voice of the Serpent*. With the same sensitive touch, she probes and reveals the indignation, the anger, the laugh, the indifference, the desire to patronize, the desire for some entertainment and other shades of emotional reaction when whites are in the presence of a non-white.

Ah, Woe is Me is a moving story about a domestic, Sarah, and her struggle against ill health which is always threatening to prevent her from maintaining and educating her three children. Her white employer tries desperately hard to understand her, but the barrier is a formidable one. Sarah's mistress is anxious to help her, now bedridden, but it's a futile effort, really. The children come to see the white woman. She can only elicit information from them by means of questions. She says: 'I always had the curious feeling that they were embarrassed, not *by* me, but *for* me; as if their faces knew that I could not help asking these same questions, because the real state of their lives was unknown and unimagined by me, and therefore beyond my questioning.'

Throughout the story the spotlight is focussed on the white woman and her response to the presence of Sarah and her children. Perhaps it is in a gesture of despair that she says of Janet (one of the children): 'Then she lifted her head and looked at me, without interest, without guile, as if she looked into the face of the sun, blinded.' Despair over her utter inability to reach out to the black girl.

If you want someone who is more of the white archetype of the strong menacing black servant than a human being, you will find him in Doris Lessing's *The Grass is Singing*.

I read this novel in 1950 (the year of its publication), one of the bitterest periods of my life in South Africa. I was then churning out protest short stories by the dozen. There was a liberal leak in the barrel of gall inside me. Everything I thought and did was a loud protest against whites. *The Grass is Singing* seemed to fulfil my innermost dark strivings. Although I am still angry, I can, at this distance in time, make a reassessment. Besides, I feel cloyed and weary after a decade or so of protest creative writing.

Being the daughter of a white settler in South Rhodesia has affected and determined Mrs. Lessing's image of the African. She revolts against the social conditions into which she was born, against the white settler's inhumanity towards the black man. Moses, the African servant in her novel, must have fulfilled that revulsion and protest. I happen to know that today, because she is preoccupied with that larger and universal protest, she would create a different character from Moses. Already in her short stories and short novels, written later, her servants are only subtly and ironically menacing. In the same way as Nadine Gordimer's are, except that there is full-blooded interplay of personalities between black and white in Miss Lessing's characterization and only a one-way impact in Miss Gordimer's. Their servants release a poison—silently and unknowingly—that sets their masters against each other and precipitates a neurosis in those who boss them.

Mary Turner in *The Grass is Singing* is a South African. She marries a farmer about twenty years her senior, chiefly as a result of scandalous talk she overhears among other white women about her old-maid existence. They come to farm in Southern Rhodesia. From the beginning they know their marriage was a frightful mistake. Mary hates farming and the loneliness that goes with it; she is indifferent to sex; she loathes Africans, the heat, the bush around her house, and the poverty into which she has married. Until now the 'servant problem' has been to her like mere middle-class gossip. She hates the smell of Africans, she tells herself, and their being Africans.

Mary fails to keep her black domestic workers. She flies into a temper with each one that Dick provides from the farm gang, and one after another leaves her on his own initiative. Dick himself is a dismal failure as a farmer and he can ill afford to lose so many workers. Progressively he loses all patience with her, and relations between them worsen even as bed companions.

During Dick's illness, she reluctantly goes to see about the farms. She is armed with a sjambok. In a temper, she strikes one man on the cheek. Later, when she is in need of a domestic worker, Dick drafts this same man, Moses, on to housework. Mary lives in perpetual fear of him, and tries to cover this by barking at him and making him do unnecessary work. By one of those strange processes of disintegration in human character in its relation to the thing it hates, Mary lets Moses undress and dress her. By this time she has already once begged him to stay when he wanted to go as a result of her temper.

On the advice of a neighbour, who wants to buy out Dick and save him from final ruin, the Turners employ a manager who is to hold things together while they are on leave. One day this new hand sees Moses dressing Mary. He drives the African out of the house. Moses, believing that Mary is leaving the farm because she has found new love, kills her on the eve of her departure. But since the new hand drove Moses away and he failed to turn up for work the next day, Mary has been expecting and waiting for her death. She has reproached herself for disloyalty towards Moses.

Mrs. Lessing's African characters talk and respond visibly to the white man's dealings with them. Like Miss Gordimer, she is keenly sensible of the shattering effect of the non-committal, ant-like way in which blacks serve whites.

'He (Dick) sat heavy and silent through the meal, a nervous tension between his eyes. The planter had broken down, a water-cart had lost a wheel, the waggon had been driven up a hill with the brakes on in sheer lighthearted carelessness. He was black in it, over his head in it, with the familiar irritation and the usual sense of helplessness against cheerful incompetence (of his workers).'

Another 'boy' (Europeans *and* middle-class Africans alike speak of their servants as 'boys' or 'girls' or 'houseboys', no matter how adult or juvenile) is sent to work for Mary. 'He had had years of experience working for white women who treated him as if he were a machine; and he had learned to present a blank, neutral surface, and to answer in a soft neutral voice. He replied gently, to everything she said: "Yes, missus; yes, missus," not looking at her. It made her angry that he would never meet her eyes.'

Again, at the farm (during Dick's illness): 'She (Mary) hated it *when they spoke to each other* in their half-naked, thick-muscled black bodies stooping in the mindless rhythm of their work. She hated their sullenness, their averted eyes when they spoke to her, their veiled insolence; and she hated more than anything, with a violent physical repulsion, the heavy smell that came from them, a hot, sour animal smell.'

Until Moses enters into the fatal relationship in the last weeks of Mary's life, she dreads him in spite of his reticence and obedience. One morning, she stumbles upon Moses washing his body, as he usually does. He senses her presence: 'A white person may look at a native, who is no better than a dog. Therefore she was annoyed when he stopped and stood upright; waiting for her to go, his body expressing his resentment of her presence there. She was furious that perhaps he believed she was there on purpose; this thought, of course, was not conscious; it would be too much presumption, such unspeakable cheek for him to imagine such a thing, that she would not allow it to enter her mind. . . . She felt the same impulse that had once made her bring down the lash across his face.'

A little later in the kitchen, Mary reflects: 'Remembering that thick black neck with the lather frothing whitely on it, the powerful back stooping over the bucket, was like a goad to her. And she was beyond reflecting that her anger, her hysteria, was over nothing, nothing that she could explain. What had happened was that the formal pattern of black-and-white, mistress-and-servant, had been broken by the personal relation; and when a white man in Africa by accident looks into the eyes of a native and sees the human being (which it is his chief pre-occupation to avoid), his sense of guilt, which he denies, fumes up in resentment and he brings down the whip.'

So she orders him to scrub the floor, which he tells her he has done earlier. She confirms the order, and 'for a moment they stared at each other exposing their hatred'. Here, for once, and only for these brief moments, Mrs. Lessing shifts from the general to the particular, groping to reach out to the workings of the black servant's mind. During one of Mary's ravings, Moses replies: 'Madame asked me to stay. I stay to help Madame. If Madame cross, I go.' More than she is aware, she feels he possesses a 'dark attraction' for her. 'She was being forced into contact, and she never ceased to be aware of him. She realized, daily, that there was something in it that was dangerous but what it was she was unable to define.'

In her short stories, collected under the title, *This was the Old Chief's Country*, most of them set in Southern Rhodesia, Mrs.

Lessing, now on surer ground, ventures farther into that world of black servants, sensing always their inscrutable capacity to be misunderstood by whites. She has begun to take notice of and to record cross-impacts between black and white. Gideon in the story *No Witchcraft for Sale* is a devoted domestic of the Farquars'. His son and Teddy, the Farquars' son, are playmates. 'Ah, missus,' says Gideon, 'these are both children, and one will grow up to be a Baas, and one will be a servant. . . . It is God's will.' When Teddy frightens Gideon's 'piccanin' (an objectionable term used by Teddy and whites in real life who think themselves superior), because 'he's only a black boy', Gideon merely lets his face fall.

One day a snake spits into Teddy's eyes and there is no doubt that he is going to be blind. Gideon takes the situation in hand and rushes into the bush. He plucks a few leaves, chews them and spits the juice into the boy's eyes. He is saved and the parents never cease to thank Gideon. A white man, hearing the oft-repeated story, comes to ask Gideon where he can find the herb so as to produce quantities of the cure. Gideon becomes difficult, and when his employers press him to show them the herb, he leads them a long way through the bush. Six miles from home, he finally picks a handful of blue flowers from among the grass. They all know this can't be the thing they want. They know from his accusing manner that he is deliberately keeping something back.

That enigmatic silence is there, but the servant visibly reacts to the white man's attitude to him: 'I'll serve you and you pay me,' Gideon seems to say, 'there our relationship ends. And you keep out of my private life.'

This non-committal attitude of the silent servant is his most effective weapon against the white master, who has all the instruments of power on his side. Both of them know this.

There is the same 'black menace' in the story, *The Second Hut*. It exasperates the farmer, Major Carruthers, not to know who of his labourers burned down the hut they have built for his hateful Afrikaner foreman. The African worker will accept orders from above and refuse responsibility.

Little Tembi, in the story of the same name, is an enigma to his white employers, the McClusters. They have brought him up, but as a youth he grows away from them. He steals, drifts away to the cities and comes back to steal from them. Finally, when he is arrested, McCluster remarks: 'They don't think anything of prison. It isn't a disgrace as it is for us.' He means, perhaps more than he intends, that white rule in African rests on a tangle of controls and restrictions which Africans are continually being jailed for violating. 'What did he *want*, Willie?' Mrs. McCluster asks in desperation. 'What is it he was *wanting*, all this time?'

Mrs. Lessing moves among farm labourers and, the dramatist that she is, observes closely the whole irony with which master-servant relationships are ridden. Nadine Gordimer shows the same sense of irony, but where she is interested in the one-way impact (from black on whites), Mrs. Lessing shows the labourer responding to, as well as influencing, the whites. A worker, however justly dismissed, can spitefully make a mark on a tree near the farm where passing Africans will see clearly: 'This is a bad farm with a bad master.' An employer may never know why his servants leave or why he has a bad name.

'Leopard' George in the story of that name has an elderly black worker, Smoke, who once worked for his father. The white man has the habit of sleeping with old Smoke's daughter. She comes to him one day, in a coquettish manner, while he is in the company of several other whites. He never expected that a physical relationship would lead to this kind of presumptuousness. In spite of Smoke's appeals, George sends the girl off to a mission school at his own expense. Another girl presents herself. This time he has rubbed Smoke the wrong way. Why does he not marry, Smoke wants to know, and observes that his daughter, being used to George's money and physical love, is not likely to stay long in school. But this second girl came of her own accord, George argues. It dawns on him later, when he remembers Smoke's accusations, that the girl is his labourer's wife. 'And now this one, this one! You, Little Baas, should take this woman.'

When she comes again, he drives her away. It is too late in the night for her to go back to her home over the hill. He locks her out. Next morning he sends for old Smoke, who comes, supported by two young men. A dramatic scene is enacted:

'He said at once: "Smoke, I am very sorry. I did not know she was your wife." Still they did not look at him. Already irritation was growing inside him, because they did not accept his contrition. He repeated sternly: "How was I to know? How could I?"

'Instead of answering directly, Smoke said in the feeble and querulous tones of a very old man: "Where is she?"

'This George had not foreseen. Irritation surged through him with surprising violence. "I sent her home," he said angrily. It was the strength of his own anger that quieted him. He did not know himself what was happening within him.

'The group in front of him remained silent. The two young men, each supporting Smoke with an arm under his shoulders, kept their eyes down. Smoke was looking vaguely beyond the trees and over the slopes of grass to the valley; he was looking for something, but looking without hope. He was defeated.

'With a conscious effort at controlling his voice, George said: "Till last night I did not know she was your wife." He paused, swallowed, and continued, dealing with the point which he understood now was where he stood accused: "She came to me last night, and I told her to go home. She came late. Has she not returned to you?"

'Smoke did not answer: his eyes were ranging over the kopjes tumbled all about them. "She did not come home," said one of the young men at last. . . .

'After a delay, the old man looked straight at George for the first time, but it was as if George were an object, a thing, which had nothing to do with him. Then he moved himself against the arms of the young man in an effort towards independence; and, seeing what he wanted, his escort turned gently round with him, and the three moved slowly off again to the compound.

'George was quite lost; he did not know what to do. He stood on the steps, smoking, looking vaguely about him at the scenery, the familiar wild scenery, and down to the valley. But it was necessary to do something, Finally he again raised his voice for the servant. When he came, orders were given that the garden boy should be questioned. The houseboy returned with a reflection of the garden boy's insolent grin on his face, and said: "The garden boy says he does not know what happened, baas. He went to bed, leaving the girl outside—just as the baas did himself."

This final phrase showed itself as a direct repetition of the insolent accusation the garden boy had made. . . .'

George goes out the next day armed with a rifle, knowing full well that Smoke's wife has been killed and eaten by a leopard. Smoke leaves the farm.

The Long One is a strange character in *The Nuisance.* The writer's father says of him: 'He knows how to handle oxen, but he can't handle his women.' And the writer remarks with absolute candour, in a way that sums the results of black-white cleavages: 'We gave our natives labels such as that since it was impossible ever to know them as their fellows knew them, in the round. That phrase summarized for us what the Long One offered in entertainment, during the years with us.'

Two of Doris Lessing's short novels in her volume, *Five,* are particularly interesting in their portrayal of cross-impacts between white master and black servant: *A Home for the Highland Cattle* and *The Antheap.* The former is about an idealist and romantic, Marina Giles, who comes from Britain to settle in Southern Rhodesia. Her husband is a scientist in Government service. To the consternation and horror of her white neighbours, Marina treats her domestic, Charlie, as a human being. He is a cheerful soul. She is keeping the house and its servant while the owner, Mrs. Skinner, is away on leave. She is shocked to see the bare room in which Charlie is 'expected to fit his life, the dirty sanitary lane bordered with stinking rubbish cans and also his unreasonable cheerfulness.' Marina is in constant conflict with her neighbours over the 'servant question'. She gives Charlie 25s. a month instead of the 20s. he received from Mrs. Skinner.

Theresa, a domestic who works for another European, and a friend of Charlie's, is pregnant. Charlie is responsible. What is he going to do about it, Marina wants to know. Theresa is going to have a baby, is Charlie's reply. His apparent indifference infuriates the white woman, and she says: 'Everybody has a good time. You and Theresa enjoy yourselves, all these females have a lovely time, gossiping, and the only thing no one ever thinks about is the baby.' Charlie doesn't appreciate this whole emphasis on the baby—a baby who is going to be born in quite an ordinary way.

What does she suggest? he wants Marina to tell him. Can't

Theresa go and stay with her father? No, the old man is no good, and Theresa must work to maintain him. Charlie realizes the situation is a little problematic, so he waits for Marina to help him get out of it. His attitude said: 'I have unbounded trust and confidence in you!'

True to European type, Marina suggests that Charlie marry Theresa. She is pursuing a moral code which is almost completely irrelevant in an urban African community whose sense of values has been shattered by the migrant labour system which breaks up family life. She wouldn't know, of course, that illegitimacy is not a shameful thing among Africans, Christians included. A woman is always very happy to look after a daughter's or son's child born out of wedlock, with all the loving care she is capable of. In fact a man or woman will do everything to stake a claim to get a son's illegitimate child even if the son cannot be persuaded to marry the child's mother.

Mrs. Lessing is sharply conscious of the helplessness in which a well-intentioned and justice-loving person usually finds herself in Southern Africa, because the little good she may do is rendered virtually useless by the corrupt but powerful system in which she lives, a system in which it becomes a crime for a white person to be decent towards the underdog and vice versa.

The Antheap tells of Mr. Macintosh, a gold miner. He employs a large labour force because he insists on making the workers dig with picks and shovels, in order to save himself expenditure on mining machinery. Mr. Clarke, an engineer, works for him. He has a son, Tommy, who is in the habit of playing in the African compound. Mrs. Clarke continually tells him not to play there. 'You get sick from the natives,' she says. Or 'You're too big now to play with a lot of dirty Kaffirs.'

Mrs. Lessing records in minute and interesting detail the cross-play of minds and emotions between Tommy and his playmate, Dirk, who is Macintosh's child by an African woman living in the reservation. Tommy repudiates the miner's patronage, wondering all the time why he neglects his own son Dirk. Throughout their childhood these boys learn to adjust their respective social positions and to become real friends. But not without mental and emotional upheavals that cause them pain.

In one of those dramatic scenes between black and white in which Doris Lessing excels, Macintosh is talking to Dirk who is refusing to go and work in the pit.

' "You can't make me," said Dirk.

' "Who's boss on this mine?" shouted Mr. Macintosh.

' "There's no law to make children work;" . . .

' "Why do you want to loaf around the compound, why not work and earn money?" (asks Macintosh, trying to be reasonable).

'Dirk said: "I can read and write, and I know my figures better than Tommy—Baas Tommy." '

After Macintosh has set fire to Dirk's hut, where Tommy used to teach him privately during vacations and where Dirk kept his library (bought for him by Tommy with money given by the miner), Dirk bursts out:

' "When I grow up I'll clear you all out, all of you, there won't be one white man left in Africa, not one."

'Tommy's face had a small, half-scared smile on it. The hatred Dirk was directing against him was so strong he nearly went away. . . . "I'll try and get you more books."

' "And then he'll burn them again."

' "But you've already got what was in them inside your head," said Tommy, consolingly. Dirk said nothing, but sat like a clenched fist, and so they remained on that tree trunk to return to their different worlds, it was with a deep sadness, knowing that their childhood was finished, and their playing, and something new was ahead.'

Tommy wins in the end. If Macintosh must sponsor his education, he must also do his duty by Dirk—send him to school. He must also make good the loss of Dirk's library.

Both Nadine Gordimer and Doris Lessing, in their image of the African—the servant in particular—bring out clearly this one fact: that the whites in Africa live in fat feudal comfort which the servant class affords them. And even although they do not pay the workers well, the whites lose heavily: their humanness. A kind of moral corrosion has set in in this privileged society. And what is more, they are never sure, by virtue of this master-servant relationship, what goes on in the mind of this seeming black automaton. But it is a menacing automaton. There is a Sotho saying that goes:

'Take me, protect me, together with the lice on my blanket.' This is another way of saying: Take me for what I am. So, have your servant, white man boss, and thus sign on to live with a perpetual enigma.

The Rebel

Africans loom larger in Nadine Gordimer's second novel, *A World of Strangers*, than ever before in her short stories.

'Trouble with me, I don't want to feel miserable, I don't want any glory out of it. Sam and Peter and all those others, yap-yap all the time, chewing over the same old thing, this they've taken from us, that they've denied our children, pass laws, injustice—agh, I'm sick of it. Sick of feeling half a man. I don't want to be bothered with black men's troubles. You know that, Toby? . . .' This is Steven Sitole speaking—the cynical, unstable, uncommitted, a-moral, a-political rebel. Anna, a white woman who has deep sympathies with the African's political aspirations, considers Sitole's whole outlook irresponsible *vis-à-vis* the political struggles of the bulk of the black people: 'The only defiance he's interested in is not paying his bills, or buying drink. He's got this picture of himself as the embittered, devil-may-care African, and, believe me, he's making a career of it. He doesn't care a damn about his people; he's only concerned with his own misfortune in being born one of them.'

Toby Hood, a young English publishers' representative who has just arrived in Johannesburg to take over an office, has become, in his unobtrusive manner—prompted by no desire to 'prove' anything—Steven's friend. It has slowly come home to him what different worlds he moves between. The easy, apparently carefree and well-provided little world of the Alexanders, Cecil Row, the Baxters, the Pattersons, on the one hand, and the slums that are the home of the Sitoles, the Sams and millions of other blacks, on the other. Besides Anna Louw, he is the only other white person in the story who can talk at length about Africans. This is how he defends his friend (or does he excuse him?):

'The public life people have always responded to pressure from within—their own conscience, sense of responsibility towards others, ambition, and so on; but the private livers, in whom these things are latent, weak, or differently directed, could go on simply going their own way, unless the pressure from outside became too strong. Well, now it's just bloody irresistible. It isn't enough that a chap like Steven has all the bother of being a black man in this country, on top of it he's expected to give up to political action whatever small part of his life he can call his own. . . . He's a rebel against rebellion. On the side, he's got a private revolution of his own; it's waged for himself, but quite a lot of other people may benefit. I think that about Steven. He won't troop along with your Congresses, or get himself arrested in the public library, but, in spite of everything the white man does to knock the spirit out of him, he remains very much alive—getting drunk, getting in debt, running his insurance racket. Learning all the shady tricks, so that, in the end, he can beat dear old white civilization at its own games. . . . While Congress chaps are pounding fiercely on the front door, he's slipped in through a back window. But, most important of all, he's alive, isn't he? He's alive, in defiance of everything that would attempt to make him half-alive. . . .'

Sam, the grave black man, on the contrary, was 'full of dogged hope, a person whose life was pinned to a future. Just as Steven was hopeless. A person committed entirely to the present.'

The black rebels in this story are detribalized, urbanized: Steven, Sam and their like. No individual white character influences any of them perceptibly. But without any conscious overt conduct on their part, they make an impact on Toby in a way the Alexanders and their minions do not. He feels drawn to them without displaying the missionary ecstasy so many whites might do in similar circumstances. He is even afraid he may be so committed to the African side of his world that it might not be easy to bear the pain of living away from it when he is back in England. Steven lives much the same way he did before Toby became his friend; and yet the news of his violent death touches the Englishman deeply. He thinks: 'What had I known of Steven, a stranger, living and dying a life I could at best only observe; my brother. A meaningless life, without hope, without dignity, the life of the spiritual eunuch, fixed by the white man, a life of which he had made, with a flick of the wrist, the only possible thing—a gesture.

A gesture. . . . He was in the bond of his skin, and I was free; the world was open to me and closed to him; how could I recognize my situation in his? . . .'

Toby senses in African jazz the vitality, the rhythm, the passion which he missed among the jazz-crazy youths and girls at home in England. 'I had seen them (the English) writhing, the identity drained out of their vacant faces, like chopped off bits of some obscene animal that, dismembered and scattered, continue to jig on out of nervous impulse. . . . And it was true that that very night I was struck by the strange innocence of their (Africans') dancing. In all its wild and orgiastic shake and shamble, there was never a suggestion that it was a parody of or a substitute for sex. There was none of the dreamy concupiscence that hangs, the aura of a lean, wolfish sex-hunger, about the scarcely moving couples in a white night-club. For these people, the music and the dancing were not a dream and an escape, but an assertion. . . .'

And here we have a rebel among rebels.

As long as Miss Gordimer moves among those she knows very well—those of her colour, naturally—her portrayal of people is full-blooded and capable. She has utter contempt for the smug, moneyed suburban white folk who engage in petty meaningless diversions like hunting, horse-racing and dinners, for their silly talk, and for the ghetto they have created for themselves. They do not care to know how three-quarters of their country live. And yet the non-whites they meet, servants or rebels, articulate or not, exercise a palpable influence on them. Miss Gordimer herself has no means of knowing the African better than she knows Steven, who is articulate and can speak her language, because of racial and social barriers. But she knows the catalyst can remain where she wants it to be. She can watch its action on her side of the colour line, and with the tail of her sharp eye, she can observe a number of things on the periphery of the field of action. Within these limits she is efficient and does not lack precision.

The edgy rhythm and texture of Mrs. Elspeth Huxley's prose suggest the brutality that characterizes the setting of her novels—Kikuyu country in Kenya. She is familiar with every twist and turn, promontory and valley of that part of Africa, as she is with the ways of Kikuyu and Masai. On Mrs. Huxley's own admission in her first Kikuyu novel, *Red Strangers*, 'no person of one race and culture can truly interpret events from the angle of individuals belonging to a totally different race and culture'.

Red Strangers tells of the crashing of the white man (the stranger) into relatively serene country in the 1890's, and the indigenous people's response to his high-handed ways. Four persons in a family line each react differently to the red strangers' methods, more often crude and bullying than humane. There are Muthengi; his brother, Matu; Karanja, the latter's son; and Kaleo, Karanja's brother. Muthengi is corrupted by European influence after an abortive attempt to rebel; Matu shows at first a non-committal admiration for whites and later finds himself a squatter on white man's land; Karanja, on his own initiative, learns how to write. He and his father eventually resist a rabble-rouser's incitement to kill the white man on whose farm they live. Karanja displays a moonstruck pursuit of things European, and it seems he cannot help himself. Like a character out of a fairy tale, he goes away to seek knowledge in Nairobi, and, like his father, Matu, he takes to European cultivation on his *shamba* (cultivated piece of land). Of the four characters, Kaleo is the most captivated by European ways: schooling, dress and so on, and he learns to despise the customs and cultural activities of his people.

Mrs. Huxley has documented Kikuyu customs and beliefs in great detail and has captured much of the African's symbolic manner of talk. They move freely from one patch of ground to another; they raid and are raided by Masai for cattle and goats; the elders dispense justice as a council; everyone goes through recognized initiation ceremonies, like circumcision; there is a strong sense of communal responsibility, belonging and ownership of property.

Come the 'red strangers'. They bully the people off their land, force them into labour gangs, sometimes shanghai them and beat them up when they have run away; levy taxes on the people; separate others from their families and communities. The missionaries discourage circumcision of girls; whole communities of Africans are moved forcibly from one place to another. Where formerly a murderer paid blood-money to the bereaved and a thief was fined goats, now all criminal and civil offences are handled by some big white man in Nairobi or his agents; often the whites seem to favour the offender. Then British justice simply does not see any use for the African judicial system. Cattle raids come to an end and the youth idle and drink because the traditional challenge has been removed. Their religious beliefs are also being battered about, by white missionaries and administrators. Says Imuru, the witch-doctor, of the whites: 'At first I thought that these strangers would go, but now I know that they intend to stay, and that because of their magic we cannot drive them away. It is the will of God. Now the power of the elders is broken like the bones of a goat beaten before the Council. Men steal and evade punishment, for thieves need no longer pay compensation. Instead, they are taken to Tetu to work for the strangers. What sort of justice is this, where the judge receives something and the injured one nothing? Is it not in itself a kind of theft? The country is like a swarm of bees when the queen is dead. Soon I shall die, for I have seen enough.'

Once again we see the African setting in revolt. The African characters are an organic part of this setting. They rebel at first, but one after another they buckle up in the face of European intrusion on their land and upon their way of life. Somewhere along the line we feel we are not looking at people but rather at a piece of earth being tamed by the white man, resisting and responding in turn, rising and breaking under plough and harrow but continually changing. Muthengi, after an initial abortive attempt to drive away a white man, who replies to the attack with gunfire, allows himself to be made headman and to supply cheap labour at the bidding of his white superiors. He grows wealthy and is arrogant towards his people and expropriates any piece of land for his purpose. His musings about the strange and awkward ways of white folk do not go deep enough to prompt him to assert his traditional system of life. Perhaps because he is just an adventurer at heart and not a thinker. Irumu the witch-doctor always threatens to be a thinker, but remains ordinary. There is a note of rebellion in his acquiescence: 'My kinsmen, you have seen a more powerful magic than mine come into the land. Your feet are set on strange paths; they travel away from the knowledge that has been handed down to us from our ancestors . . . towards wild cold places of which we can know nothing at all. Against this new magic the wisdom of our ancestors is as dust blown against a rock, or as a twig carried down by a river in flood. . . . Why they (the strangers) have come I know not, but they come in peace, and perhaps one day God will send them sense, so that they will be able to understand our customs and our law.'

Matu, Muthengi's brother, and his son, Katanja, evince a kind of innocent and even naïve curiosity in the white man. They can leave their families quite easily and work for a white man, not for the cash wages offered but for the experience of it. The reasons for which Karanja wants to be a Christian are pretty vague, too.

The rebels, Benson Makuna and Jehoshaphat, are not convincing at all. They are fraudulent oafs, and some of the things they use for recruiting a following for their organization are puerile. The missions, they point out, are breaking down their custom of circumcising girls, and taxes go to buy motor-cars for District Commissioners.

A Thing to Love takes up the story of the Kikuyu from where *Red Strangers* left off. It is a pity that a writer of Elspeth Huxley's esteem could not employ her wealth of anthropological material about the Kikuyu to create memorable characters in her earlier novel. The characters in *Red Strangers* are very much like prehistoric man to whom so many things happened without stirring in him a will that he could impose on the scheme of things and deflect its course. In *A Thing to Love*, on the contrary, there is a clear focus on character. The story is about the beginning of Mau Mau activity. It begins with an academic conflict between Gitau, a Kikuyu teacher, and leader of a secret movement, and Sam Gibson, once a wealthy Englishman and now a farmer.

One is a stock nationalist type and the other a stock English settler type whose judgment is bedevilled by a sense of superiority and an exaggerated sense of indispensability, and who thinks missionaries are wasting their time and energy trying to educate the blacks. Colonel Foxley is also the typical settler-farmer. His daughter, Pat, is a school teacher in a mission school, something which her parents are not happy about.

Gitau and his colleagues, Banduki, George Rutinu, Jonah Kimani (son of a highly-respected chief who is later murdered by nationalists) and the Spokesman (leader), are ruthless in their methods of organization. People are compelled to 'eat the oath' to break which is supposed to bring death on the eater; they pay as much as a thousand shillings each (like Foxley's worker, Raphaelo) to the movement on the feeble but sparkling promise that certain of the farms will belong to them after the white people have been wiped or driven out; individual collectors seldom surrender all the money realized at any one time; unwilling persons are killed; Gitau murders a youth in order to make an escape. And then, of course, there are the wholesale Mau Mau atrocities.

But there is the stock appeal, again, to the lowest motives among their people: Europeans must be servants and Africans the masters; the people must not allow the whites to break down their custom of circumcising girls. And none of these leaders is anything but a savage at heart. Gitau has his mental conflicts. We are told that he once believed in Aggrey's parable about the harmony that is made by both the black and the white keys of a piano. But he was dismissed from a school for seducing a girl—a trivial misdemeanor to him; he was once humiliated by a white post office clerk and he is now bent on revenge. Is it right to hate, to teach boys to read and write and the next moment teach them to carry gun and panga? What has happened to him, Gitau? Accuse the responsible ones—the whites, who have lied and cheated to procure Kikuyu land. Christianity says God loves all men equally. But are he and the white man treated equally? It is not right to kill, and Africans condemn killing, as much as Europeans do, and the lad whose life he ended was not white. But he broke the oath by hesitating to help me escape. . . .

And so Gitau debates the ethics of his actions. But the conflict is short-lived. He does not flinch. Eventually he is killed by Sam Gibson's bullet during a man-hunt. And there you have the stereotyped fire-eating rebel.

Matthew, a Christian son of Chief Kimani, is an interesting character, to start with. Like his father, he is against all these atrocities. He lives in terror of death much of the time. His wife turns unfaithful, carries on a clandestine affair—on a purely physical plane—with Gitau, who is in the same town, working on a murder plot to destroy Matthew and his father. We do not know why the woman suddenly turns against her husband and helps Gitau. Matthew is thus tortured, but not before he has seen Zachariah, a martyred evangelist whose eyes have been taken out by the rebels; and not before panic has churned his bowels, making him waver between taking the required oath and remaining a Christian. He has before now been the battleground as it were of the Christian God versus the Kikuyu God whose seat is Kerinyagga Mountain. His faith triumphs. An accident saves him from death.

An even more fascinating character is Raphaelo, the Foxleys' foreman. He is the very picture of pathos as he sends word demanding the Foxleys' farm for which he has paid a thousand shillings to the movement. An official of the movement tells him the white man hasn't died or gone away yet. Raphaelo should in fact intensify his recruiting effort. He wants no part in the killing of the Foxleys—the man and his wife. He hopes they will run away so as to make murder unnecessary. But he is caught up in the tide of inevitability, and plays a leading role in the murder of the couple. He leaves the farm, a broken man, with Foxley's coat on and a paper with which to claim the farm. The local official of the movement laughs at him for his *naïveté*, and sends him back to the farm.

Raphaelo does not go back to Foxley's farm. He goes towards Nairobi. Despair overwhelms him. Where could he have gone wrong? He couldn't track down the mistake. He had eaten the oath, paid the two thousand shillings to the organization for Foxley's farm, enrolled a large number of devotees and so on. He had been told the time would come when the whites would run out and the Kikuyu way of life be restored; taxation would go. But it must have been all lies: the Europeans had not gone, more were coming every week.

Raphaelo has immense possibilities as a character. But I think Mrs. Huxley concentrates too much attention on plot and stereotypes to build him up and allow him to develop. It seems she has also a magnificent opportunity to explore the interaction of feeling and thought between Pat Foxley, who develops admirably, and Raphaelo: she as an educationist and he as a trusted worker in a brutal setting. But this aspect remains unexplored.

Pat does a good deal of thinking about her place and that of the Europeans in general in this set-up. Even after the death of her parents, she can still say that arrest and revengeful punishment do not go down to the root of the trouble. So she must continue to teach. She rejects Sam Gibson's offer of marriage because she realizes their lives are incompatible, and reaffirms, within herself, her dedication: 'Now she was too committed, there was too much she couldn't leave undone, and those she had once presumed to teach had set too stringent an example. If they, without question, staked their lives, could she withhold the small counter of her own contentment? Only with a mind whole and single could she stand with those fighting the battle that never ended on the side that must not lose, and meet the destiny to which it seemed she had been assigned.'

Mrs. Huxley's rebels are full-blooded, fierce rebels—as fierce as the African setting makes them. But one wishes there was much less of the conventional rebel in them, except for Raphaelo who is the best-drawn of them all. There is a kind of inevitability in Gitau's make-up, and Matthew is the conventional, ready-packed article, destined for martyrdom by virtue of the fact that he is a Christian.

The most brilliant portrayal of the African rebel is to be found in *The Day of the Monkey*, a novel by the American, David Karp. I make no apologies for including American fiction in a survey of European literary reflections of Africa. I am aware of only two other American novels on Africa—Robert Ruark's *Something of Value*, a book about Kenya, and Saul Below's *Henderson and the Rain King* the former is trashy—just the kind of thing Hollywood would jump at.

Dr. Luba, leader of a nationalist movement in a British protectorate, is witty, cunning and has a profound sense of history. At first he uses the sex act between a European army officer and an African priest's concubine on a temple altar as a symbol of the white man's arrogance, a symbol round which to rally his people for a rising on the day of the religious feast of Rama. An artist's drawing of what he imagines took place at the altar is pasted all over town to incense the people.

Governor Lysander Pellman, an intimate friend of Dr.

Luba's, tries to plead with the nationalist not to make an issue of such a 'trivial' affair which he can easily persuade the priest to disavow.

' "But my dear Lysander, its truth never has been of any importance. Did it actually happen?"

' "Yes. As I understand it, almost the way it was drawn by the artist."

'Dr. Luba smiled. "Remarkable. For once a popular issue has some basis in fact. A charming change."

' "You know, however, how little real importance it has whether it occurred or not."

' "Of course, my dear Lysander. A thinking man in possession of the facts would look down his nose at this whole affair."

' "Then why aggravate it into something of importance?"

' "Because that is my political function, Lysander. We've talked of this before. You should not act so surprised."

' "Jackson will be back in a moment so I can't possibly argue this with you properly. But may I say one thing?" Dr. Luba nodded agreeably. "That this is irresponsible behaviour."

'Dr. Luba put his black, wrinkled hand on Lysander's sleeve affectionately. "But Lysander, as a nationalist I am obligated to be irresponsible. It is not my government. It is yours. It is not my law and order. It is yours. Until the function of law and order is in my hands I must disrupt it. If you are not made uncomfortable as our masters, why should you then leave us alone?

' "The trend of the world is to break up empires, to give colonial peoples the rights to self-determination," Lysander reminded the little doctor.

' "Only in those places where the imperial power has been chivvied and exasperated and matters brought to a head. . . ." '

When an American doctor invites both him and the Governor for a drink at a club, Dr. Luba declines on 'principle': 'Until I can offer the European the hospitality of a club from which he is barred unless invited, I shall decline his hospitality to a club where I am barred unless invited.'

The Governor again tries to plead with Luba to call off the demonstration planned for the Feast of Rama and save the young army officer an embarrassment. The African argues that blood and violence must attend the birth of a nation as they do the birth of everything else.

' "Does this mean that I will have to be killed before you're satisfied?" [asks the Governor]. "No, my good friend, I'm not interested in the blood of Europeans. They, after all, are not the ones who must give birth. It is the blood of my own people. . . . I have every confidence in your guns, your tanks, and your soldiers to see to it that they are badly beaten in their attempt [to cut the throats of the whites]. And that is what I want—an uprising, noisily and bloodily, if you please, quelled. It begins the history of my nation. The more you kill and maim, the happier I shall be. Notice the handful of people involved in the American Boston massacre. It is an historic landmark for them. What had they to complain about before then? Taxation? Is that a cry to raise a man's blood or his spirits? Taxation without representation. It is a pathetic bleat in the roll of historic clarion calls. My people are landless, propertyless. Will they respond to commercial slogans? Blood, Lysander, blood. It has always had a mystical significance to man. Let me see blood and I will show you patriots. . . . I am the leader of a ridiculous group of men, embarking on an almost petty and ridiculous adventure. I cannot help these things. But I shall not hold myself up to myself as an object of laughter—a man who withdrew a revolution to save some silly young soldier social and official embarrassment. You ask too much, Lysander. You presume too much on our friendship." '

Such friendship between a Governor and an indigenous revolutionary is unusual anywhere. It could hardly exist. But it is made credible. The Governor's character is no less brilliantly drawn. Both fall as a result of the abundant faith they have in each other. Governor Pellman firmly believes that by releasing Dr. Luba from prison in an unorthodox manner and promising him the independence of the Protectorate, the African, through his sense of responsibility, will stop the uprising. Dr. Luba has before this promise told his colleagues that the temple incident is no more a suitable rallying point. They must use the black man's sheer hatred of the white skin. When the Governor puts to him the offer of independence from the Colonial Office, Luba says that once the British have left the chieftains in the mountains will come down and pillage the towns. Only if the people have fought for their freedom and bled and died for it will they be able to resist the marauding chieftains. 'They'll come down into the town and the small villages and they will stop the clock of our history as surely as a bullet in its guts would. No, if we are to hold this state we must fight for it. We must put the wrath of desire, the iron of victory, into our people. Then we can arm our people, train them into modern military units, equip them with all the machines we will need, and we won't wait for the warrior chieftains, we shall go up into the mountains for them. Those who are against us, we'll hang, those for us, will be placed in charge. . . . These aren't the Dark Ages. We needn't invent and build our own machine tools. We can buy them with the gold we'll find in our mountains. We'll train our people with teachers we'll bring in. . . . We must fight on the Feast of Rama. We must fight and bleed and win.'

Luba, after debating with himself, decides to put a halt to preparations for the Rama demonstrations. A white Communist, supposed to be an *agent provocateur*, together with an African leader whom the white man has influenced against the 'dangerous intellectual', kill Luba: they are bent on the revolt. Governor has relied too much on Luba's ability to stop the rebellion, and also has foolishly not reckoned with Luba's personal enemies. To the end he has refused to call in troops from Britain for fear of 'playing up' the revolt and therefore fanning it. There is shooting on the feast day, resulting in a loss of life and damage to property. Pellman is retired.

David Karp brings out very ably the gullibility of the Colonial Office with its traditional fanatic faith in its Governors. Let a Governor minimize or exaggerate the seriousness of a local situation, the Colonial Office rushes to his assistance. Either way, he pays for it with his prestige. What detracts from *The Day of the Monkey* is Mr. Karp's introduction of the stale, boring and now well-known American image of Communists—just as if Africans were incapable of an uprising without Russia's intervention or as if there *must* be a Communist about wherever there is an African uprising. It may flatter the Americans' vanity, in real life, to feel that they have a keen nose for Communist agents in Africa or anywhere else, but such material is irrelevant to a novel like Mr.

Karp's and it tends to falsify his characterization. Another thing: it is enough that the incident of the army officer with an African girl at a temple altar is used to incite violent feelings among the Protectorate folk; but for an artist to depict the incident and for the drawing to be pasted all over in public places is sensationalism gone to the wildest limits. Not even Luba's intelligence is revolted. Mr. Karp's tone here lets him down.

One of Joyce Cary's rebels is Aissa. The setting is a province in Northern Nigeria which he knows so well. Of conflicting religious beliefs, which are the theme of *Aissa Saved*, Cary says in a preface to his *The African Witch*: 'The attraction of Africa is that it shows these wars of belief, and the powerful often subconscious motives which underlie them, in the greatest variety and also in very simple forms. Basic obsessions, which in Europe hide themselves under all sorts of decorous scientific or theological or political uniforms, are there seen naked in bold and dramatic action.'

Aissa is a Christian living with other African converts in a Mission run by a white man and his wife. Across a piece of water there are non-Christian communities. The leader of this enthusiastic band of converts, Ojo, takes them on a trip across the water to the other side with a view to bringing the gospel to the heathens just when there is a pagan feast on. The missionary pair are troubled by the risk, but Ojo defies anyone once the spirit 'talks' to him. The whites decide to accompany them. Aissa, taking the lead in hymn singing, sees her sweetheart and ex-convict Gajere among the crowd. Her long-lost baby is also there. She goes to him, and her old drinking friends she left behind when she was converted are elated at the reunion. They are lost in the crowd, and a riotous orgy follows at the drinking place, Aissa and Gajere being the centre of the scene. Abba, their baby, is with her.

Soon more non-Christians arrive, and someone incites an attack on the Christians. Aissa defies them, defending her faith and cursing their god and priestess. She is badly hurt and is cut off from her mission people who have fled. She loses her foot in jail because it is infected. A travelling Christian performed the surgery, because the Bible says: 'If your leg troubles you, cut it off; if your eye, take it out.' She escapes being killed by the non-Christians, and finally reaches the mission, a human wreck.

When she is well again, Ojo organizes a holy war on the heathens. Unknown to the white missionaries, the converts are guided by a scriptural text which they draw from a box to the accompaniment of black magic. This is what they do whenever they find it difficult to agree. The text justifies their project.

A spate of ruthless killings ensues. Aissa allows Gajere to be killed to show that she loves Jesus. Her baby is likewise sacrificed by the Christians near a wooden cross and the non-Christians offer up a mother and her child: all this is intended to make rain fall. Violence on both sides turns inwards and the Christians slit their noses in a frenzy. The native authority is completely confused and incapable of restoring order. Aissa and Ojo are killed; as she dies, she fancies she sees God 'in a white riga and a new indigo turban', and her baby sitting on a goat near God.

In the preface cited above, Joyce Cary says also: 'The African setting is dramatic, (it) demands a certain kind of story, a certain violence and coarseness of detail, almost a fabulous treatment, to keep it in its place.' Until we get the great novel on Africa, we must suspend judgment on a statement like this. In the meantime, as the author explains in a prefatory note to *Aissa Saved*, we are always confronted by converts who accept the letter of the articles of their faith, because they have come in at a much later point in the evolutionary line of Christianity than old believers; these now only accept Biblical texts as metaphors and symbols.

Mr. Johnson and Staffnurse

The heroes of Joyce Cary's *Mister Johnson* and Sylvester Stein's *Second Class Taxi* do not easily fall into categories. Each of them is a crossbreed between a servant and a rebel. Mr. Johnson, a government clerk, is a rebel in his own noisy, funny, boisterous and boastful way. He is not consciously pitting himself against convention and asceticism both in white officialdom and in the society of which he comes. No, otherwise Cary's characterization would not be the splendid success it has turned out to be. He is just a living repudiation of 'stuffy' decency. As a clerk in a Northern Nigerian administrative office, Mr. Johnson has delusions of grandeur, but never in a neurotic way. He regards himself as a servant of the King of

England, to whom he often sings praises. He regards his wife, Bamu, as a government lady, although she knows nothing about such things. When he is drunk and happy—which he often is—something tells him 'he doanno how to be so happy, he got no practice in dem great big happiness. . . .'

Sylvester Stein, who is a great admirer of *Mister Johnson*, was inspired to create Staffnurse in his *Second Class Taxi*, published in 1958. Both Staffnurse and Mr. Johnson are a living condemnation of their white superiors and some aspect or other of the machinery the two of them are required to work. No white official is ever disposed to take Johnson in hand and treat him as something more than just a lever in the administrative machinery of British 'indirect rule'. If and when the lever jams, Blore, Rudbeck and Tring—the officious lot of them—knock it out of joint and that's that: the lad stands condemned.

Staffnurse, in a greatcoat emerging from a concrete drain pipe where he sleeps, tells us a story of oppression. Neither he nor Johnson *speaks* rebellion: they simply act it. Staffnurse in the Hampshire household becomes an uncomprehending butt for Professor and Mrs. Hampshire's domestic liberalism—a liberalism that is the shadow of that other kind which glories in the short-circuit operation of pious amendments and objections from a safe parliamentary back-bench; all which does not touch Staffnurse's 'greatcoat existence'.

Staffnurse and Johnson are inarticulate and yet articulate. A servant, by virtue of the very relationship in which he stands to his employer, is always in a position to do the latter down; he is often disposed to get his own back at an employer, especially where a non-white person works for a white one. And yet we mustn't overstretch similarities. These two characters are as diverse as the environments that make them. Mister Johnson's colonial existence is not harassed right and left by 'white supremacy'; Staffnurse, being in a multi-racial society, is. Johnson derives a good deal of moral strength from the communal life the administrative set-up makes it possible for him to live. He can tell his folk every good or bad story about himself, imaginary or real, and be sure they will feast or sympathize with him. This makes for a solid sense of social security. Staffnurse is not only detribalized; he is rendered insecure by oppression. The community that gives him moral support is an amalgam of ethnic groups brought together by common suffering. But he meets whites every day and they order his life for him in every direction. A black intellectual's response to this situation is a political one—academically and overtly. A black man of Staffnurse's educational level may follow the political lead of the intellectual. But because he lacks the equipment that helps his fellowman to speak out and to find other outlets, in intellectual and cultural pursuits (alas, even here the difficulties are savage), the Staffnurse type has to try to fit into the pattern of master-servant relations. He cushions himself against insult and injury by lying to his master, cheating him when there is no chance of being found out. He gets little or no material gain out of this but it gives him a sense of triumph.

There is no such straitjacket for Mr. Johnson: he lies and cheats alike to black and white. Although he is in a homogeneous community, he lives above his fellowmen. There is a 'Johnsonian world' he moves in where 'Johnsonian standards' operate. And he applies them to the only reality he knows. If this does not accommodate his vitality, it is not his fault. He will go to the gallows just as if it were everybody else's destiny. Mister Johnson is a universal character. Outside his greatcoat, Staffnurse would be one; but then he wouldn't be Staffnurse: the South African underdog with a dim identity and origin in a country that requires other bits of identity than that a black man is a South African.

All in all, if society must have masters and servants in conditions of vast disparity between groups and classes, it must accept Staffnurse and Mr. Johnson. Accept Mr. Johnson? He is in bad odour among West Africans generally. They regard him as a buffoon and suspect that Joyce Cary is laughing at some foible which he may have detected in the African who has to adjust his thinking to European ways—or who need not. I flung away *Mister Johnson* with exasperation when I tried to read it for the first time, in South Africa. I had seen too many journalistic caricatures of black people and 'bongo-bongo cartoons' showing Africans with filed teeth and bones stuck in their hair—too many for me to find amusement in Johnson's behaviour, always on the verge of farce. There is not much to laugh at in South Africa. When there is laughter, it is often tight-jawed in a self-assertive way. When I took up *Mister Johnson* again—in West Africa—I found it most entertaining.

The Aspiring Zulu

It is always annoying to read of 'Zulus' or 'Basuto' or 'Xhosas' in South African fiction, because both culturally and politically these ethnic groupings are unreal. One doesn't know when Jack Cope wants his novel, *The Golden Oriole*, to be judged as regional fiction and when as purely a South African novel. But as we are confronted by Zulu characters, Zulu they must remain.

In this context, Glanvill Peake, the hero, is an interesting fellow as a departure from the conventional school of writing that spotlights the black man's emergence from a rural life and his arrival in the city. He is not a migrant labourer, and his return to the Reserves has nothing to do with disillusionment in town life, or frustration. Like Plomer's Ula Masondo, he is hounded out of town: in his case, by the immediate fact of the bullet wounds inflicted on him by whites, among them the profligate, Tommy Seddon.

Glanvill is aspiring to be a writer. He does write a poem that attracts the attention of a white member of the Inter-Race organization, Mrs. Foxon. At the 'literary evening', to which he has been invited by Mrs. Foxon to read some of his verse, he gets a humiliating reception from most of the whites, and is assaulted by a drunken Tommy Seddon.

For some inexplicable reason, Glanvill goes to an Inter-Race again, this time to receive a bronze medal for his famous poem that has appeared in a Belgian journal. Perhaps the purpose is to have the last laugh. Indeed he gives a few thrusts at some whites, and is rude to Mrs. Foxon by virtually declining her invitation to tea at her house. But he does all this after a few drinks too many.

Peake often tells himself that he doesn't like the patronizing friendship of such people as Mrs. Seddon (who is soon to divorce her useless husband), and the missionary sponsorship of people like Mrs. Foxon. 'He hoped she was not the sort of white woman who forced herself to have stiff mission tea-parties with black parsons and their ladies, sat on charitable committees and philanthropic societies.' He is also cynical about Paul Devenham's literary interest in his writings. But he accepts the help of these whites when they offer it—from whatever motive. We never really see Glanvill at grips with the problem of bitterness or with the question whether he should or should not accept white patronage—in the light of his past unpleasant experiences. He likes to be thought highly of by the whites.

The reader must feel cheated here, especially if he does not know what the 1930's were like for black-white relations—on which the story is based. When one thinks of this, Glanvill, Zulu or no Zulu, can be seen as the veritable product of the times in which he lived. In the 1930's enlightened Africans were still a pretty isolated minority. They loved the patronage of white liberals who of course were regarded by government authorities as 'experts on natives' and were applied to for 'confidential' reports about Africans who wanted jobs, mainly in the teaching and clerical fields, the latter in the then Native Affairs Department. There were always liberals at the gates of voluntary welfare agencies who decided which black man had an 'unimpeachable' or 'irreproachable' character. This meant most times that you did not go about insulting whites who 'had the welfare of natives at heart' and therefore 'alienated their sympathy'.

Not that Glanvill wanted a job under liberals. But such contact with whites as multi-racial bodies like Inter-Race afforded had a prestige or status value. The Glanvills have increased in proportion to the leap in the literacy percentage among non-whites over the last quarter of a century, but they do not enjoy the popular confidence our hero himself enjoyed among the masses. The Glanvills today are despised and their motives suspect.

The Foxons and Jubbers who made the Inter-Race in the 1930's have changed little. Today a black employer still does not go to another African (however well placed) for a testimonial: no white employer would be impressed by it unless the sponsor were himself cited by a liberal, whether clerical or lay, who must still act as referee. The Foxons of today appear in new robes and even come out unashamedly to tell the African what methods he should adopt to liberate himself: whatever he does, he mustn't break the law;

he must respect the constitution of the country; he must be a passive resister, and all the other claptrap.

Because Glanvill is an artist at heart, he does not keep aloof from the illiterate masses. He mixes with them and listens attentively, keeping his finger on the pulse. For this reason it seems only natural for him, after working at a non-political job and another on the fringe of politics, to climb the platform when asked by the workers to speak for them. Even then, his heart is not really on the thing. His literary urge gives him no peace, and he must raise money to send his sister abroad for treatment of her failing eyesight.

The Zulu remains an individualist. The manner in which he is shot by a group of white racialists might easily have been irrelevant, but Mr. Cope has contrived it so that it arouses the conscience of people to the point of donating money for his sister's passage and treatment: his social position, when publicized, evokes sympathy from the people.

What keeps nagging one throughout the story is the improbability of Glanvill's social pull as a writer. It would have been credible for a teacher or trade unionist to be known widely, to be talked about in Durban and outside, to be known by a reckless slum teenager, as Glanvill was; not a writer. But it is not an artistic fault to create non-types. The important thing is that the hero is not a freak.

Another aspect of the 'aspiring Zulu' is Dr. Luke Njilo in Jack Cope's ironic and comic short story, *The Tame Ox*. On the afternoon when he is to be awarded an honorary Ph.D. degree at his college, Dr. Njilo helps himself liberally to home-brewed beer brought by well-wishers who come from the surrounding villages. He walks about in his gown, making himself pleasant to all the simple guests, who, however, do not appreciate the significance of the occasion. Dr. Njilo is often referred to as a 'tame ox', the kind of 'good boy' who must always justify himself to the white man.

Miss Poynton, a wealthy patron, arrives. She is sure she understands 'the Zulu mind'. She is shocked to see Dr. Njilo take off his boots to feel freer and more comfortable.

When the Chancellor sees Dr. Njilo come barefoot to conduct

him to the platform, the white man charitably thinks how simple and unaffected the man is.

Before all the distinguished guests on the platform, Dr. Njilo lets go of himself. He jumps down and, to the accompaniment of hand-clapping from the audience, does the Zulu war dance, shouting at intervals. Of course, Mrs. Poynton feels let down and looks 'like a guinea-fowl shot on the wing. . . . Her ideal of progress seemed in ruins, the feet of the idol crumbling away'. The Chancellor is 'amazed but full of admiration'; the Police Commandant thinks: 'How right I am about these black devils.'

'They say he is a tame ox,' chants some old warrior. 'There he is, hau! hau! a black-maned lion among the herds!'

When Dr. Njilo has seated himself, sweating profusely, he says simply to the Chancellor, 'I think they would expect it,' and 'I am afraid, Sir, the trappings of civilization were somewhat in the way' (meaning the gown).

Here is an aspiring man who is not sophisticated at all in certain directions. But then he comes of a race that indeed is not easily sophisticated, one that does not easily lose its identity, and that is wrapped up in itself, always living in the memory of its military history—thanks to British indirect rule administered by men like Shepstone.

Although *The Tame Ox* is a really funny story and efficient, and there is poignant realism in *The Golden Oriole*, Jack Cope is at his best when he applies a microscopic lens to human suffering among non-whites. He singles out a character who is in some predicament and shows us agony at work. No lofty aspirations come into the picture: we are face to face with simple people. He does this in his other short stories that appear under the title *The Tame Ox*.

Chapter 8

THE BLACK MAN'S LITERARY IMAGE OF HIMSELF

In the 1870's the South African Negro in the Cape Province was already writing creatively, to say nothing of the journalistic writings he was producing. While the whites were writing gloatingly about their victories over the blacks and over each other (English and Afrikaans) and Afrikaans writers were spitting vitriol, the Negro was protesting; but at the same time he was trying to reconcile the white man's violence with the Christianity he (the white man) was preaching. Although he was as bitter against the whites as the Afrikaner was bitter against the *rooinek* (English), the Negro simply couldn't release as much vitriol in his literature as the Afrikaner. His image of the white man was charged with prejudice and hate, in the same way the white man's image of him was. But because of the other preoccupation (with the impact of a new religion) the Negro was inclined to be introspective. The white man seemed too huge a reality to fit into his spectrum. And then the nineteenth-century black writer was not a member of a coherent nationalist-minded group. The Afrikaner was. Everything the latter did was in the interests of the *volk* and of a cultural and political body.

What is the African's literary image of himself? We are dealing here with the African who emerges as a writer because of the presence of the white man (sometimes in spite of it) who brought formal classroom education with him. In Southern and East Africa, where the white man is a settler and therefore influences the black man who in turn influences him, the African writer appears in a number of roles.

First, there were the writers who wrote religious stories or verse with a strong moral bent. These men were the products of missionary teaching, and they wrote in the Bantu vernaculars. Such writers appeared in Basutoland, where the Paris Evengelical and Roman Catholic missions printed plenty of religious matter. In the Cape Province where the Presbyterian Church was strongest and the North-Eastern Transvaal, where the Lutheran Mission operated, religious writing was encouraged among their communities. And then there were the American Board of Missions in Natal and later the Anglicans and Methodist churches there and elsewhere.

Second, since the first group of independent Africans broke with the missionaries and founded the newspaper *Imvo Zabantsundu* (now 80 years old) in the last quarter of the nineteenth century, writers have fanned out into various modes of expression. Furious pamphleteering followed after Union in 1909 in response to the notorious Act of Union itself, then the Land Act of 1913 which compelled Africans to be labour tenants on white people's farms, and several other laws.

Political thinking was taking shape among the oppressed as Britain abdicated her position, leaving the non-whites at the mercy of the white settlers. These ganged up and by the Act of Union dedicated themselves—Boer and Englishman—to the cause of white supremacy which was to rest on the pillars of black serfdom.

The response of the creative writer swayed between romantic-escapist at the one end and protest literature at the other. Always the religious tone reinforced this writing, but never in the mawkish self-pitying manner that characterized early American Negro verse. A Cape Province author signing himself 'Hadi Waseluhlangeni' (Harp of the Nation) wrote this in 1884, which appeared in a vernacular journal, *Isigidimi*:[1]

> Some thoughts till now ne'er spoken
> Make shreds of my innermost being;
> And the cares and fortunes of my kin
> Still journey with me to the grave.

[1] Translation by Dr. A. C. Jordan in *Africa South.*

I turn my back on the many shams
That I see from day to day;
It seems we march to our very grave
Encircled by a smiling Gospel.

For what is this Gospel?
And what salvation?
The shade of a fabulous *hili*[1]
That we try to embrace in vain.

In 1925, Mqhayi composed a mock-praise in honour of the Prince of Wales (now Duke of Windsor) when the latter visited South Africa:

Ah, Britain! Great Britain![2]
Great Britain of the endless sunshine!
She hath conquered the oceans and laid them low;
She hath drained the little rivers and lapped them dry;
She hath swept the little nations and wiped them away;
And now she is making for the open skies.
She sent us the preacher: she sent us the bottle,
She sent us the Bible, and barrels of brandy;
She sent us the breechloader, she sent us cannon;
O, Roaring Britain! Which must we embrace?
You sent us the truth, denied us the truth;
You sent us the life, deprived us of life;
You sent us the light, we sit in the dark,
Shivering, benighted in the bright noonday sun.

Later, we hear B. W. Vilakazi, the Natal poet and scholar (who died recently) romanticizing in Bantu the idyllic setting of his early life and also protesting against the white man's policies. His *In the Gold Mines*[3] is a protest against the white man who unfeelingly sends the black man to his death at the bottom of the mine against the whole system of migrant labour that breaks up family life. The machines do not care, they 'heed not'

[1] Another name for a *thikoloshe* (a spirit).
[2] Translation by Dr. A. C. Jordan in *Africa South* (Cape Town).
[3] op. cit.

The groans of the black labourers
Writhing with the pains of their bodily wounds
The air close and suffocating.
With the dire and sweat of their bodies
As they drain their hips till nothing is left.'

In despair the mine worker says:

Thunder away, machines of the mines,
My hands are throbbing with pain
My swollen feet are aching
But I cannot relieve the pain,
For the white man's cures call for money.
Thunder away, but wake me not,
Great things I have done for the white man chiefs,
And now my soul weighs heavy on me.

He wants to go on sleeping:

Sleep and wake up far away
Far away in the land of spirits and dreaming,
Sleep and never wake again,
But rest in the arms of my father's fathers
Down in the fresh-green pastures of heaven.

In later years we saw the emergence of poets like Jolobe, Moses Mphahlele, H. I. E. Dhlomo. Mqhayi wrote in the Xhosa vernacular, Mphahlele and Dhlomo wrote in English, producing some of the most vigorous protest writing of the 1920's and 30's. Outside protest and romantic escapism, there are vernacular writers in South Africa who had in a sense come to terms with the position assigned to them by the white ruling class and are responsible for most of the anaemic writing that is meant for juveniles.

The Romantic Hero

The Tshaka-figure has always excited the most heroic instincts in the African: this, in spite of the array of white historians who have always represented Tshaka, the Zulu King, as nothing more than a barbarian; a sadistic savage without a drop of mercy.

Thomas Mofolo, a Mosotho of Basutoland, wrote a beautiful historical romance, *Chaka*, in Sotho, translated into English by F. H. Dutton in 1931. Mofolo was born in 1875 in Basutoland. He was educated in a school started by a Mosotho pastor of the Paris Evangelical Mission. He later went to Morija, the oldest teacher-training school in Basutoland, also a P. E. M. institution. After qualifying in 1899, Mofolo studied theology and then taught in Maseru and later became proof reader for Morija Press. He is said to have read Rider Haggard and Marie Corelli.

Mofolo's first novel, *Moeti oa Bochabela* (The Pilgrim of the East) gives an account of African life in ancient days. It is about a boy who wanders away from his home in search of 'the unknown Creator'. He believes that the Creator does not like the brute behaviour of his people, disgust in whose drunkenness, hatred and other moral lapses has caused him to leave home.

His next novel, *Pitseng*, also in Sotho, is set in a village that is built in a hollow (*Pitseng*—at the pot). It is a love story telling of the education and courtship of a modern African. It is a classic in its language and idiom.

In his introduction to *Chaka*, Sir Henry Newbolt says Mofolo's first novel is something like a mixture of *Pilgrim's Progress* and Olive Schreiner's *Story of an African Farm*. Although it is not likely that Mofolo was acquainted with Christopher Marlowe, *Chaka* is an interesting mixture of Tamburlaine and Dr. Faustus. The Tamburlaine in Chaka can be expressed in Professor Wilson Knight's words in his *The Sovereign Flower*:[1] 'Throughout he (the Scythian king) feels irresistible, backed by destiny.' Professor Knight says Marlowe's drama is a 'tyrannic progress shown with all its superficial glamour, but none of those inward depths of psychic conflict shadowed by Shakespeare even in *Richard III*'.

Chaka is in a sense a religious king. He might not feel that he is the scourge of the ancestors, but he believes that his witch-doctor, Isanusi, is an efficient intercessor between his people, epitomized by himself, and his ancestors; inasmuch as the witch-doctor in traditional African society is not a mere dealer in charms and potions, but is the moral conscience of his people. It is to him that the people appeal when they want to know what to do so that

[1] Macmillan, New York, 1958.

they do not offend the community and thereby the spirits of the ancestors.

Mofolo's king commits tyrannical acts in alarming succession. But he has his moments of 'psychic conflict'. His career began as a compensatory response to people's despise of him which arose from the fact that he was a chief's illegitimate child. It was also a response to his brother's lust for his own blood, and to his father's ill-treatment of his mother (she was expelled from the royal house). After the last attempt by his brothers to take his life, 'he resolved that from that time on he would do as he liked: whether a man was guilty or not he would kill him if he wished, for that was the law of man. Chaka was always a man of fixed purpose. . . . But until now his purposes had been good. Henceforth he had only one purpose—to do as he liked, even if it was wrong, and to take the most complete vengeance that he alone would imagine'. We can almost hear Edmund in *King Lear* or Richard III speaking.

This is where the Faustian element comes in. Chaka meets Isanusi, the witch-doctor, who is to 'work on him', so that he conquer the chieftainship which he believes rightly belongs to him. Isanusi tempts him further and confronts him with the 'moral problem of choice'. Chaka can procure another kind of medicine which will make him king of a much bigger empire than he ever dreamed of. 'It is very evil, but of great power,' says the witch-doctor. 'Choose.' He asks Chaka to give this serious thought first, because he will have to murder and shed much blood in the process of becoming the desired monarch. Isanusi provides Chaka with two attendants: Ndlebe (ear) with long ears that could catch the faintest whisper from miles away and report back to the king; Malunga, whose work was to doctor the regiments so that they are brave and obedient.

Chaka succeeds to the stool. He has been to the river and seen a serpent which came out of the water, coiled itself round him, licked his body, and receded, staring at him. This is the messenger of the ancestors, which is to assure Chaka that his career deserves their watchfulness and assistance.

Isanusi comes up again with that suggestion of a potent medicine. The king must give the blood of one he loves most, to be mixed with the medicine.

'I Chaka had no need of deep thought. I have decided upon the chieftainship of which thou hast spoken. But I have no children and I do not know if the blood of my mother or my brothers would be sufficient. But if it is, I will give it you that ye may compound your medicines of it.'

'But among those whom thou hast promised there is not included the one thou dost love with the love of which I spoke. *Her* thou hast passed over. Think of *her* and tell us thy decision.'

'Apart from these, the one I love is Noliwe.'

'So be it. Think well which thou dost desire. The chieftainship without Noliwe. . . . But thou wilt not win it unless thou kill Noliwe, thou thyself, with thy own hand. [Isanusi smiles and continues.] Today, Chaka, we are teaching thee the highest kind of witchcraft when men kill their children or their parents so that the spirits may receive them and prosper them.'

Isanusi is a symbol of Chaka's other self. Whenever he is in a tricky situation he need only shout, 'Isanusi', and the witch-doctor will be there to assist. The decision is confirmed, and Noliwe, who has already delivered Chaka's child (unknown to him) is killed by his own hand in a scene that is full of pathos.

Chaka makes several reforms and gathers a number of small tribes under him and they become part of the Zulu nation, protected against the plundering expeditions of men like Zwide and Matiwane. Chaka's military genius creates the most formidable army in Africa at the time.

At the peak of his power and manhood, Chaka begins to be plagued by nightmares. He leaves his homestead in order to be 'alone' outside the city. Even then he continues in lust for blood and sends one division of his army to destroy another. Bodies continue to feed a very large pit just outside the city. But he feels the approach of death. Here is one of his dreams:

'He saw himself at his hut . . . and the gorge seemed to be spread out below him. He felt a strong wind blowing, a hurricane, which was followed by a great din of people crying out, and at that moment he saw the gorge. The people he had killed were there raging with anger, but some merely looked at him in pity without saying a word. He saw the screech owl circling round in anger and crying, "Chaka, Chaka, Chaka". It was clacking its beak. And Chaka saw, too, all the evil spirits gathered there, and his friend, the Lord of the Deep Waters, as well. And all were looking towards Chaka. And as Chaka watched them thus in his dream Isanusi came with his companions . . . silent as if they were rejoicing over Chaka with an inhuman joy, like the joy of one who has overcome his enemy when he was prepared to kill. It was the joy of those who perceive their day has come. And Isanusi said: "Chaka, today I have come to seek my reward. I told thee that when I should pass here again thou wast to await me with all preparations made; there was to be no delay; thou wast to give me what is mine with no disputation. For I have worked well for thee, and thou hast won the chieftainship and power and honour and riches and great fame." '

Chaka knows death is near and he cannot flee. In his other dream he sees Noliwe, the woman he loved; Dingiswayo, now dead, who was against unnecessary bloodshed and forgave those he conquered; the trusted soldier of whose popularity he was so jealous that he sent him to distant lands to fetch a stone from which metal is made so that he perish, and who dragged his living corpse back to his king.

Isanusi does come to claim his price in cattle. Chaka's attendants, Ndlebe and Malunga, simply disappear without a word of explanation. Chaka must pay the supreme price. His brothers murder him. The hyenas do not touch him; they merely circle round his body.

Indeed Chaka's life story stripped of all the romance still reads like a romance, as can be seen in E. A. Ritter's magnicent biographical epic, *Shaka Zulu*, which was published in 1955. Mafolo tells his story as a Christian, who is concerned with the battle between Evil and Good in Chaka. The manner of telling it is in the tradition of African oral literature—interspersed with songs and snatches of moralizing. When Chaka's father, Senzangakona, has disowned him and his mother at the instigation of his wives, Dingiswayo, to whom Chaka's father is subordinate, fines Senzangakona for employing warriors to commit the cowardly crime of trying to kill Chaka. Mofolo says at this stage: 'In this chapter we have seen that the fruit of sin is wondrous bitter, for we know that

Chaka had not been to blame for what happened, but none the less, his father had ordered him to be killed.'

Although he was Tswana-speaking[1] Sol. T. Plaatje[2] wrote in English as well as in his native language. He translated *Julius Caesar, Comedy of Errors, Merchant of Venice, Othello,* and *Much Ado About Nothing* into Tswana, and his political work, *Native Life in South Africa*, published in 1916, ran into five editions. Plaatje wrote other political works in English and also African folk-tales and poems in Tswana.

Sol. Plaatje's novel, *Mhudi*, could have been published before 1920, but for some reason the author does not indicate, it did not come out till 1930. Before he wrote *Mhudi* he had to raise money to finance a trip to U.S.A. and tour nineteen states. This he did by writing a booklet, 18,000 copies of which were sold. 'It was a disquisition on a delicate social problem,' he writes of this booklet, 'known to Europeans in South Africa as the *Black Peril* and to the Bantu as the *White Peril*. I called it *The Mote and the Beam*.'

Mhudi itself is a love story set in the Orange Free State and Southern Transvaal, just around the Vaal River. Mzilikazi, the historical hero who broke away from Chaka, fought his way over the Drakensberg Mountains. His enlarged army and collection of tribes spilled over into the Free State and conquered the Barolong (a section of the Batswana) and all the other neighbouring tribes. The story opens with the destruction of Kunana, the Barolong city, by Mzilikazi's son, as reprisals for the killing of two of the Zulu king's tax collectors at the instigation of the Barolong chief Tauana.[3] Gubuza, Mzilikazi's astute general, condemns publicly the attack on Kunana as cowardly—resulting in a cheap victory over defenceless people.

Ra-Thaga and Mhudi, refugees from Kunana who met far away from their home and became man and wife, encounter Boers for the first time in Moroka's country. Moroka is a peace-loving man, and has kindly received Sarel Cilliers' party after most of it has been exterminated by Mzilikazi's warriors.

Moroka makes a pact with Sarel Cilliers to join forces and

[1] *Tswana*—the language that originated in Bechuanaland.
[2] Pronounced Pláh-iki.
[3] Pronounced *Tawana*.

march against the Zulu king. Mzilikazi is routed finally, and he just manages to trek northwards with a severely depleted army, with his faithful Gubuza covering his flight. Ra-Thaga has also been caught up in this strife.

Plaatje's women are more impressive than his men. Next to Mhudi is the stately Nandi, Mzilikazi's best-loved and chief wife. For a number of years she chooses the path of an exile in order to escape the wrath of her husband who has been influenced by a jealous junior wife to kill Nandi, on the strength of some false story about the queen's unfaithfulness. When her husband has been reduced to the status of a monarch without an empire, she follows him in order to console him, knowing that he must need her. Just as the Chaka-figure excites images of heroism and fighting grit in the South African Negro, the Nandi-figure, whether in Chaka's mother or Mzilikazi's wife, is a symbol of beauty, long-suffering motherhood, gentleness and dignity.

Mhudi has been travelling with Nandi, and now they have to part because Nandi has to follow her husband, Mhudi has found Ra-Thaga whom she followed to the war.

' "Good-bye, my sister," (Mhudi) said. "I am returning to Thaba Ncho for I have found my husband: mayest thou be as fortunate in the search for thine own."

' "Umnandi salutes thee also and thanks thee for the brief but happy time we have spent together. Thou hast a welcome destination in Thaba Ncho while I (supposing I meet my husband) know not what the future may have in store for me."

' "Nay, not so, my Matebele sister, for the gods who protected thee from the wrath of Mzilikazi will surely accompany thee in the search; seek him and when thou hast recovered the lost favour of thy royal lord, urge him to give up wars and adopt a more happy form of manly sport. In that he could surely do much more than my husband who is no king."

' "Nay," retorted Umnandi ruefully. "Thine is a royal husband, the king of the morrow, with a home and a country to go to. What is my lord without his throne, for what is a defeated king with his city burnt? It is no bright destiny I look forward to, but a blank gloom. . . . But now I regard it my duty to seek him and share his doom if he will but permit me." '

Plaatje writes as a politician and historian; not, like Mofolo, as a moralist. Also, he is less of a romanticist than Mofolo. He writes as one of a people whose land was ravaged by both Zulu and Boer; yet he is never bitter. He had cause to be bitter. The Land Act of 1913 forced large-scale migration of Africans from European farms because they resented being compelled to become labour tenants and the law abolished the squatter system by which they could have a share of the crops they produced on the white man's farm. On behalf of the African National Congress Plaatje visited a number of those farms to find out the extent of suffering caused by the new law. He describes that period in bitter terms in his political work, *Native Life in South Africa.*

Perhaps Plaatje was too much of a historian, journalist and politician to visualize character independently of the historical events in which people were involved. But he had compassion, and this balanced the historian's detachment in him; his love for human beings was profound, and for this reason Mhudi comes alive even in the midst of epoch-making clashes, even if we consider her dialogue stilted. Somehow he sees his pathetic villain's (Mzilikazi's) fate as poetic justice, but he never gloats over it. This kind of poetic justice, the dream-like quality of the narrative, the use of the pathetic fallacy, and the weaving in of songs, are in the tradition of Bantu oral literature. Sometimes Plaatje, in his enthusiasm, comes into the narrative, as when he says of Umnandi: 'She was a daughter of Umzinyati (the Bison-city) the offspring of a lineage of brave warriors with many deeds of valour to their credit. *Such was the description of her given to the writer by a hoary octogenarian that it reminded him of a remarkable passage in the Song of Songs.*' (My italics.)

Ra-Thaga is expressing Plaatje when he says to Mhudi on the first meeting: 'The Barolong, noted for their agility and dexterity with the sword—a clean sword that never stained itself with the blood of a woman, are wiped out. . . . In our wars men killed other warriors, and captured the unarmed and non-resisting. They took the women and children home. But the Matebele, oh, the Matebele!'

The Pathetic Hero

Peter Abrahams, now living in Jamaica, was the first South African Negro to write an English novel after Sol. Plaatje's *Mhudi* came out in 1930. Political pamphleteering was given a violent spurt by the pass laws of 1932 and the equally notorious Hertzog Bills of 1935 which reasserted white supremacy in land ownership and political representation. Abrahams's first short stories, *Dark Testament*, and his first novel, *Song of the City*, came out in the early stages of the war. They are in the Richard Wright and Countee Cullen tradition. *Mine Boy* follows the line of Plomer, portraying a country lad who comes to the mines.

At St. Peter's Secondary School, Johannesburg, which we both attended in 1935, Abrahams was a dreamy boy who wrote a good deal of verse inspired by Marcus Garvey's call to the American Negro to come back to Africa, and most probably by Langston Hughes' verse written in the idiom of

I am a Negro:
  Black as the night is black,
  Black like the depths of my Africa.

I've been a slave:
  Caesar told me to keep his doorsteps clean,
  I brushed the boots of Washington.

He left South Africa just before the outbreak of World War II and has since then revisited his people about twice for very short periods. Although his fictional work owes everything to his life in South Africa, Abrahams's writing has been done in Britain.

He takes up Plaatje's story twenty years later and blows it up so that Mzilikazi and Gubuza attain life-size proportions. In the best-written of his novels, *Wild Conquest*, Mzilikazi's first serious reverses at the hands of the Boers make him look a most pathetic hero as he limps northward, as it were. New characters are added, like the cosmopolitan witch-doctor, Mkomozi, and Dabula the sentimentalist. The non-white character in this novel appears as a slave, as a citizen of an ever-widening empire, and as a victim of the deadly Boer war machine.

The first part of the novel is an episode of the Great Trek. Slaves have been freed, and feelings between Boer and master and slave are running high. Before one Boer family leaves its farm in the Cape Province, it sets all the houses and barns on fire so that the free Africans should not use them.

In the second part, the Boer trekkers clash with Mzilikazi.

Peter Abrahams has introduced 'a new will into past time', thus bending history to a point in order to tell more of the truth than the historian. This 'unhistorical will' operates within a short space of time in history, so that the characters produced short-lived unhistorical effects. For a time, we forget we are travelling a time-distance in history. Mzilikazi and his people are not the unfeeling savages who revel in beer, war and women, such as we are used to reading about.

Dabula and Gubuza, Mzilikazi's generals, defy custom. Far away from his home, Dabula is treated to one of the wives of a chief as a sign of hospitality (a most unlikely thing to happen). Contrary to custom, he has one wife, and is stricken with remorse for seducing the chief's wife. He broods over it with tedious sentimentalism, and tells his wife about it. He knows the sting of fear, before a sex experience as well as before a battle.

There is that bold speech of Gubuza's after the sack of Kunana: 'Wise men of different tribes and nationalities are agreed that cheap successes are nearly always followed by the shadow of tragedy. Wise men are agreed that nations should in their strength tread carefully.' Mzilikazi also says the 'unhistorical' thing: 'Without you (the people), I cannot be king. Without me, you cannot be a nation.'

It is Gubuza the idealist who says to his wife: 'Perhaps, my head is turned by power. How does a man know? All I know is, if I seek power, it is for what I can do with it, not merely that I should be powerful. But how does a man know the secret motives of his heart?' Somewhat theatrical, as Gubuza is often inclined to be. After a witch-hunt during which forty-one innocent people have been killed, he is worried. 'Why is it so with our people?' he asks Mzilikazi and Mkomozi the witch-doctor in conversation. 'We are cursed by a bloodlust,' answers Mzilikazi. 'I'm afraid of the darkness of our people,' Gubuza says.

But when the Boers have arrived, Gubuza acts with decision.

Dabula is a soldier through and through. His king sends him to go and fetch his queen, Mnandi, who fled to Basutoland to seek Moshesh's protection. He learns much from the Basotho king and comes back a changed man.

'Now life is real for you, my son,' Mkomozi says to Dabula. 'It will never again be just a spear and a battle cry.'

'The world is so big,' Dabula replies.

The much-travelled and knowledgeable witch-doctor, Mkomozi, seems to know all the answers:

' "Why do you mourn for forty-one, my friends?' he asks after the witch-hunt. "I will tell you. It is because the darkness that you cry of in these others, is in you too. . . . These matters are the scheme of things. If you must mourn, mourn for our world that is in darkness. . . . Perhaps in the distant ages that are to be, there will be, among our descendants, those who can answer your questions, and when they can do that, perhaps the darkness will be lifted from the minds of people, and there will be only good medicine men. . . ." '

Here Mr. Abrahams fails to control the character of his witch-doctor because he tries to make him bigger than he really is. This is what Mkomozi is saying in effect: when people know why there is evil in the world, perhaps they will not be ignorant any more, and then perhaps evil will disappear. Which does not make sense. Mkomozi is credible when, instead of taking the cosmic view of life, he contemplates things within the limits of his community's experience; as when he says of Gubuza: 'He made instruments of people. And always, that is wrong.' Our image of Mkomozi is also distorted by his psycho-analyst's explanation of the wicked Ntongolwane's spell over Ntombi, who cannot move from where she is standing. 'Ntombi!' says the witch-doctor in an attempt to break the spell. 'Listen, child, listen! There is no spell on you. The spell is in your mind only. It is because you believe it that it is so. Do not believe it. It is not real. It is in your mind only. In your mind only.'

Evidently the writer is trying to break away from the Rider

Haggard tradition of bloodthirsty witch-doctors (Ntongolwane in *Wild Conquest* is like Gagool the witch-doctor in *King Solomon's Mines*). A commendable effort. As in the rest of the novel the author gives the 'unhistorical will' free play. I think that Peter Abrahams should have been content to make Mkomozi announce, as he later does to the spectators after he has triumphed over Ntongolwane's charms that there are good and bad doctors. 'For the bad doctor gets drunk with power. He does not think of the comfort of the people but only how to have power over them.'

The Underdog

'No, my friend, not mad. He's a human being now. The love that is between him and that girl has made him human. The inhibitions caused by the oppressor have left him. If it were possible he would become a complex person in a very short time, but anything might happen between now and then. The tragedy is not in Swartz and this girl. The tragedy is in this land and in our time. You must be first a native or a half-caste or a Jew or an Arab or an Englishman or a Chinaman or a Greek, that is the tragedy. You cannot be a human being first. That is the crime of our time, my friend. For that reason Swartz and this girl who have now become human beings will suffer. This love of theirs is a symbol of man's attempt to move forward beyond the chains that bind him.'

This is Mako speaking—an African to a Jew friend—in Peter Abrahams's *The Path of Thunder*. He is referring to a Coloured friend of theirs, Swartz, who is in love with an Afrikaner girl, Sarie. Although Mako has warned Swartz before that he is playing a dangerous game—in a society the European section of which forbids mixed marriages or discourages them—he turns his wrath on this society. It is an underdog speaking about the underdog. But it is just this kind of protest which limits the emotional and intellectual range of characterization.

We are in a country where it is considered a crime for two people to love each other if one is white and the other black. The characters in such a setting must not exceed the boundaries of ready-made group attitudes and response. This pattern of response: Lanny Swartz, a Coloured, and Sarie Villiers, white, fall in love. They know the possible consequences. The communities from which they come still cling to their traditional racial prejudices. We anticipate disaster, if the action of the story must be played out in South Africa: it could not be otherwise. There is an excessive play of fate in the lives of the characters and their experience is such a minute fraction of life.

Much more interesting in this novel are Fieta, the Coloured woman who has emerged from a dissipated life and is now being steadied by her love for the crippled Mad Sam, whose own life is perpetual pain. The image of Fieta is not limited by any impending disaster from outside herself or Mad Sam: the image is capable of development. Yes, they are underdogs, and this makes them vulnerable, but there is a wide area of response open to them.

Wild Conquest and *The Path of Thunder* clearly show the British influence plus Mr. Abrahams's own impetuosity. His *Tell Freedom* is autobiographical. It echoes the earlier influences again. He is now completely anglicized and seems to be fighting to recapture his roots. His is a childhood of millions of other non-whites in South Africa. During the period he talks about, covering about twenty years from 1919 (the year of his birth), the Coloured people (in the South African sense, i.e. those of mixed blood) believed, as a result of brutal historical processes, that they were superior to blacks. They enjoyed privileges that blacks did not have. The blacks, on the other hand, believed that, because they did not have evident mixed parentage, they were superior to Coloureds.

Since the last war, however, both the Smuts and Malan governments have narrowed the material difference between blacks and Coloureds down to a hair-line. And in spite of what the South African herrenvolk think, the concept of race purity in that country is just so much eyewash. Such a high percentage of South African whites have coloured blood anyhow.

But even among the Coloured underdogs themselves there are subtle class distinctions. Peter Abrahams describes a poignant scene in a 'high-class' Coloured area. The community here feel ashamed of their slummy origins in Vrededorp, then a predominantly Indian and Coloured suburb of Johannesburg.

'A new family was moving into a house in the little alleyway that connected our dead-end street to the next. These loudly spoken remarks were for the benefit of that family. I watched the new family and the pile of junk they stacked on the pavement from the dray-cart.

'The women were right. This was a slice of the slummiest, filthiest, Vrededorp and Malay Camp moving into our "select" area. The beds were of the wooden variety we had called "bugs' heaven" in Vrededorp. They had cracks and nooks in which armies of bugs lived. . . .

'And the people were slumland's children: the old woman, hard and ageless, whose rasping voice carried to us as she interspersed her instructions with curses; the tough, brutal-looking young man who carried all the heavier things; the two fat, squat, ribald younger women who spoke at the top of their voices; the litter of dirty children of all shapes and sizes; all this was slumland suddenly catapulted into aspiring City and Suburban.

'And we, the aspiring, were ashamed to see ourselves as we had once been. We resented being reminded of our origins. Having escaped the slums, we dreaded slipping back, and we resented savagely the turning of our new homes into a new slum area. All this resentment was slung at the new arrivals. Had they left their junk, dressed in their best and moved in with even one suite of new furniture bought on the instalment plan, the women would have turned out with cups of tea. . . .'

It may be of interest to the reader here to make brief mention of what African verse there is in South Africa which sounds the cry of the underdog. Of the large body of protest verse that has come from the South African Negro whose image of himself is that of the underdog, much has been written in the three main Bantu languages. Of course there was such maudlin English verse as the late Moses Mphahlele's which appeared in 1920. Depicting a pass raid by mounted police he wrote:

> Horses to right of them,
> Horses to left of them,
> Horses behind them!
> Prancing and trampling,

On woman, man, and child,
While horse, now mild and rider wild,
Are ranged in full parade!
On them the proud Brigade!

This was his hope:

As sure as dewdrops can remove
A boulder which strong winds defies,
So sure can tears make God reprove
The tyrants who our cries despise.

He was in Britain during the first World War, and later wrote laudatory verse about the African volunteers who went down with the *Mendi* ship. He shows in much of his verse a soft spot for King George V and the Union Jack.

Then there was H. I. E. Dhlomo's long English poem (about 1,000 lines), *The Valley of a Thousand Hills*, published in 1941. Up to his death in 1957, Dhlomo was editor of an African weekly in Durban. He also published fourteen plays in English on African historical heroes: *Shaka, Moshoeshoe, Cetewayo, Dingane* and others, and on themes of a more general nature. Some of the plays have been staged in South Africa.

The Valley of a Thousand Hills in Natal Province is the most beautiful scenery in the Union of South Africa. Throughout the poem runs the wailing of black people who were once proud and majestic but now lie in the dust, but whose conscience is still alive. The poem is Dhlomo's struggle to understand himself, an underdog, the meaning of pain, the problem of power and greed, and also a struggle to invoke his ancestral spirits whose presence he feels in the Valley. Dhlomo sees the plight of the South African non-white as part of universal suffering. His protest imagery is drawn from Byron and Shelley, and his nostalgic melancholy from Keats.

In contrast to the Valley—this 'heaven-sculptured land',

Our human arts in chains of fungus soil
Of crippling laws and forms have now become
Commercial pantomime, a reaping field
For swollen pundits . . . crude and dumb before
This artless Art, this form-defying Form!

There is a romantic Keatsian image in Dhlomo's bird that sings in the Valley a song that was never heard before by man:

> From whence you come, pain, beauty, love and joy
> Have mingled out into a bloom of song!
> But here on earth man's soul remains the toy
> Of inharmonious processes which long
> Have raged; here where our youth and joys are mocked
> By want and tears, where, like the dead, foul dust
> Shuts tight our door; where age, deemed wise, is rocked
> By scourge of fear and hate!

At a certain stage on this soul-searching journey, the poet falls into a mood of dejection; he feels despised and sick in body and in mind. He wants to die, but a little voice inside him tells him to look at the beauty of the Valley of a Thousand Hills and live. And then there is peace inside him. He discovers the importance of the Self.

> Our world, our thoughts, our all is in the Self.
> God is as great as the individual soul!
> Our bigness makes life big; our smallness, cringed
> Not God or man or Devil or the world,
> But Self chastises or enthrones the soul.
> Our God or Devil is the feeling Self,
> Catastrophe or life the self-same Self.
> Thus I am God! and God is I . . . this Self!
> So purity and peace reigned everywhere
> Deep in the Valley of a Thousand Hills
> For purity and peace in me then reigned.

Hope and light have come to help him fight despair and weariness and evil ways. Nostalgic memories crowd in on him of the 'Tribal Village State' that existed in these hills, the true republic:

> A land of homes and only homes!
> Commercial hells here burn no soul!
> No social institutions dark
> To right men's wrongs (wrongs just men, wronged,
> Find wrongs just done!)

Where today the girls show drooping breasts—'drooping low with shame and use'—in their primitive purity breasts stood 'haughty, full, defiant bulbs'. Those days, men were

> like rock hewn strong
> Not bent nor burdened with small things
> Of avarice, but bred and taught
> To wrestle with immensities.

And then the bitter protest:

> The song and pace now widen out into
> A flooded stream all dark and fierce with Wrong!
> No longer mine but tortured visions of
> The race I see; a groaning symphony
> Of grim discordant notes of race and creed,
> Of writhing snakes of ideologies
> And twanging tunes of clashing colour themes,
> Where Wealth and Power and Blood reign worshipped gods
> And Merit, Truth and Beauty serve as slaves!
> But on these heights of Time, Event, I gaze
> Into a future tragic with Greed's ways.
> With din and pain fraught is the sight!
> For hills find we mountains of strife;
> For rills deep streams of blood and sweat;
> For trees the swelling song of woe;
> For herds the broken people of the land;
> For heights and depths the depths and heights of woe,
> Where joys of life drip hot with pain;
> Where but to live is sacrifice. . . .
> A fog of tribulation spreads,
> Engulfs and robes the Wrong-torn land. . . .

And again:

> This beauty's not my own! My home is not
> My home! I am an outcast in my land!
> They call me happy while I lie and rot
> Beneath a foreign yoke in my dear strand.
> Midst these sweet hills and dales, under these stars,
> To live and to be free, my fathers fought.
> Must I still fight and bear anew the scars? . . .

The Valley remains at once a symbol of despair and hope for the underdog.

Only a romanticist, such as Dhlomo is, can pray for a world without pain, where life is not a sacrifice—in a scheme of things where life is always pain. Even in his protest, Dhlomo remains a thorough-going romanticist, like Mofolo and Plaatje, although the writer of *Mhudi* does not show it in his political writings. This romanticism and a spontaneous inclination to dramatics, pervade African character. To this, and to the African's fatalism which enables him to face and carry the tragic moment, add Christianity, and you get a personality that is at once submissive and violent, accommodating and uncompromising, full of laughter and tears—no, we can't define it: we can only search for the African personality. Nor shall we gape in surprise if we find the flags and landmarks we had planted in our wake blown away by winds of change.

During the last twenty years the political, social climate of South Africa has been growing viciously difficult for a non-white to write in. It requires tremendous organization of one's mental and emotional faculties before one can write a poem or a novel or a play. This has become all but impossible. When Vilakazi (in his earlier career), Mqhayi and Mphahlele wrote, oppression provided just a sufficient spur to adult creative writing. The spur is a paralysing one today. Although the short story is very demanding, it is often used as a short-cut to prose meaning. And so it has become the most common medium in African literary activity, barring the large volume of vernacular literature being produced for school use.

The appearance of *Drum* magazine on the South African scene in 1950 and the broadening of the scope of the weeklies—all produced almost exclusively for non-white readership—have excited enormous writing activity in the form of the short story and sketches through the medium of English. Again, the short story moves between escapist and protest types.

Can Themba, who is forty, took his B.A. degree at Fort Hare University College with a distinction in English. He is a restless man who has a cynical attitude towards his condition as an underdog: this consists in a belief that to worry and talk about oppression can have a corrosive effect on a man who is oppressed. So the best thing is to cover oneself with a hard crusty cynicism; suffer and endure, but not to burn oneself up. One of the ways in which he tries to protect himself against the 'whips and scorns' of oppression is to revel in a verbal felicity in his fiction. It is in his journalistic writing where, face to face with the real world, he shows how poignantly he feels oppression. And, ironically, journalism steadies and sobers him. When he turns to fiction, he is literally turning his back on life. He is now an assistant editor of the weekly, *Golden City Post*.

Themba's *Mob Passion, Remember Jane* and other pot-boilers are strictly escapist. *Mob Passion* has the Romeo-Juliet theme. The rival factions are tribal groups. After a brutal faction fight, in which the boy is killed, the girl avenges him on one of her group who had a hand in the killing. This kind of story is one of hundreds the South African underdog writes. He lives inside violence, breathes it, feeds on it, whether it be vindictive or wanton. Robbery, murder, thuggery sum up his environment, where Negro fights against his own kind as well as against whites and even turns his violence on himself. But the story itself is most often a poor Hollywood imitation, with a strong love interest or a crime-does-not-pay element, or both. The following extract from *Mob Passion*[1] typifies this violence and the sensationalism that has reduced it to cliché:

'Mapula acted. Quickly she picked up the axe whilst the mob was withdrawing from its prey, several of them bespattered with blood. With the axe in her hand, Mapula pressed through them until she reached the inner, sparser group. She saw Alpheus [one of her faction] spitting upon Linga's [her sweetheart's] battered body. He turned with a guttural cackle—He-he-he! He-he-he!—into the descending axe. It sank into his neck and down he went. She stepped on his chest and pulled out the axe. The blood gushed out all over her face and clothing. That evil-looking countenance she gradually turned to the stunned crowd, half lifting the axe and walking slowly but menacingly towards the largest group. They retreated—a hundred and twenty men and women retreated before this devil-possessed woman with the ghastly appearance. But then

[1] *Drum* (Johannesburg).

she saw the mangled body of the man she loved and her nerve snapped. The axe slipped from her hand and she dropped on Linga's body, crying piteously.'

Richard Rive's *Black and Brown Song* and *The Bench* are vigorous protest sketches. The former has a strong early Richard Wright flavour, including the element of violence. It is about gang warfare between black and Coloured. *The Bench* is about a man who summons a great deal of courage to break a segregation by-law, just to get the glorious feeling which he expects when he equates himself with the white folk whose bench it is that he is sitting on.

Rive is a young Coloured teacher in Cape Town. Between his outright protest and Themba's romanticism, stand Alex la Guma, Bloke Modisane, Arthur Maimane, Dyke Sentso, Alfred Hutchinson, Casey Motsisi and Todd Matshikiza. In these writers we see the meeting point of acceptance and rejection in the broadest terms: acceptance and protest in specific areas of black-white relations within implicit acceptance in a larger area.

La Guma was one of the 156 South Africans who were arrested and charged with high treason. He is a columnist for a weekly non-white paper in Cape Town. His excellent story, *Out of Darkness*[1] tells of a long-term convict who is in for culpable homicide. Old Cockroach, as he is nicknamed, was a teacher and in love with a very fair-complexioned girl, Cora. She started to play white and gradually drifted away. The teacher continued to love her, and pleaded with her.

' "She said I was selfish and trying to deny her the good things of life. The good things of life. I would have given anything I *could*. And she said I was denying her the good things of life.

' "In the end she turned on me. She told me to go to hell. She slapped my face and called me a black nigger. A black nigger."

' "Then you lost your head and killed her," I said quietly.

' "Oh, no," Old Cockroach answered. "I could never have done that to Cora. I did lose my head, but it was Joey whom I killed. He said I was a damn fool for going off over a damn, play-white bitch. So I hit him, and he cracked his skull on something. Ah, here's Joey now. Hullo, Joey. I hope you've brought my book. . . ." '

[1] *Africa South* (Cape Town).

Seven years in jail has undermined Old Cockroach's brain.

There is a delightful satire by Bloke Modisane, *The Dignity of Begging*,[1] which has a marked Goldsmith flavour. Modisane ran out of South Africa without a passport and, after traversing hundreds of miles through to Tanganyika, he finally landed in England in 1959. He had been a jazz critic for the Sunday paper, *Golden City Post*, in Johannesburg, for a number of years. He writes: 'I could not live with it. I knew I had to run, or lose my temper and even my sanity. . . . The situation became unbearable to me as an individual. I felt stifled, unable to express and fulfil myself as an individual man. I felt the relentless inevitability of the clash, the direct immediacy of blood. . . . ' Modisane's fiction back home was as non-political as he was, but now he is an angry nationalist of the Pan-Africanist brand, although he is outside it all.

In his satire, Nathaniel is a beggar, and he earns more money this way than he would in an honest job. He is even contemplating forming a United Beggars' Union. 'One of these days when I'm on my annual leave, I hope to write a book on begging, something like a treatise on the subject. It will be written with sensitivity and charm, brimful with sketches from life. . . .' So he says.

Nathaniel appears in the magistrate's court a few times and just manages to stay clear of the social worker's clutches, the Refuge or some other institution. One day, when he arrives at home he finds a letter from his wife asking him to come to the country because their son is ill. 'I had to wait for something like this to show me the folly of my ways,' he regrets. 'A man's place is next to his wife and family. I had hoped that some day I would be able to provide my boys with a decent education, to grow them like normal boys, not just sons of a helpless cripple . . . to find a place for them in the sun. I might be a big shot beggar but as a husband and father, I stink. . . .'

'I'll always have your room for you if you should ever want it again.' (Says the landlord.) 'Deep down I know that I will want it again. I have three hundred and thirty-five reasons why I should. . . . I have to come back. I owe it to the profession.'

One of Arthur Maimane's stories, *Just a Tsotsi*, tells of a white constable who kills an African while he is on police duty. When he

[1] *Drum* (Johannesburg).

examines the body he discovers a mark the African made with a knife on his wrist when the two were intimate playmates in their childhood. The constable himself has a similar mark which clinched the pledge of friendship. As an adult, especially as a constable, he has been hurled into the arena of race conflict. He also finds his long-missing knife on the boy, his initials still clear on it after ten years. 'He looked at the jagged scar on the inside of his left wrist and walked away, massaging it.'

Maimane was a journalist in Accra, Ghana, where he migrated from South Africa in 1958. He has been trying to restore his balance in a social climate that does not contain the same degree of general sophistication that gave a reason for, and coloured, his writing in South Africa. As a journalist there he wrote Runyonese for large urbanized communities who could understand him. Like me in Nigeria, he had to create without the kick in the back, without the agonizing physical and emotional urge to protest against immediate oppression. We now have to adjust ourselves to a situation where all life must be viewed as one huge protest. An irksome transition, but exciting: the paralysing spur is not there for us any more, and we have got to steer along on our own steam.

Todd Matshikiza, composer of the music of the famous jazz opera, *King Kong*, is now in Britain indefinitely. In South Africa, where he was born and lived until he left in 1960, he had a way of bull-dozing his way through or dodging light-footed tricky situations of black-white contact. In many of his sketches about non-white living, he shows an American slickness and a temperamental twist that is a trait of Matshikiza the man:[1]

'Me and a European lady did a Non-European thing at Crown Mines. Crown Mines is outside Joburg and out of the way, so nobody saw us. We were safe. It was broad daylight. It was in a telephone booth clearly marked *Non-Europeans Only*. We arrived at the place together. She went in first. This is how it happened. I was in a hurry to phone my boss. The European lady was in a hurry to phone her ma. She was pushing a baby in a pram.

'She said, "I don't care. I've got to phone my ma. And if you don't like it, go and tell the postmaster."

[1] *African Treasury*, ed. Langston Hughes (Crown Publishers, New York 1960).

'When she came out, I said, "Missus, you know you breaking the law?"

'She said, "Why?"

'I said, "This phone is written *Non-Europeans Only*. The police will catch you."

'She said, "Get away, you damned black Kaffir! I'm European. I can do what I damn well like."

'The baby made a *ga . . . ga . . . ga* sound. I hope it wasn't laughing.

'This ain't a laughing matter.'

The writer of *Road to Ghana*, Alfred Hutchinson, graduated in Arts at Fort Hare. He has an unpublished novel in his cupboard. In his short stories, as in *High Wind in the Valley*, it is the displaced and dispossessed non-whites he highlights: people who have to move from long-established homes to encamped locations (by Government order) where they cannot own houses. And when the decree breaks upon the community, they realize more than ever before that they are not a closely-knit whole: some want to resist, others are too scared because, heaven knows, they have been through so much already that if they stand in the way of the steam-roller it will crush them. Whom can they tell these fears and still convince him that being dispossessed and displaced corrodes a people's fibre so that things can never hold together again?

Hutchinson was in the treason trial also, and became one of the sixty who were neither acquitted nor re-indicted when the original charge was quashed. Immediately he was released he ran out of the country and travelled under another name until he reached Tanganyika. He arranged a rendezvous with his white fiancée which was to be Nyasaland. She had to leave later. Again, throughout his journey he was struck by the horrifying degree of dispossession among Rhodesians and Nyasas, and the interminable queues that Africans are made to fall into at every place where there is a Government official. And in oxlike fashion they take their places in these queues.

From Tanganyika he made his way to Ghana, and after he and his girl-friend had got married, they stayed in the country for eighteen months. They are now in Britain.

All these experiences are related in his *Road to Ghana*. Hutchinson has known the paralysing pain of fear at various times when he has been hounded by police in South Africa, and, the highly sensitive person that he is, he is always amazed when he comes out at the other end of the tunnel of fear, wondering how he could have found courage to want to survive. His sensitivity and periodic nervousness can be felt in the very texture of his language.

These South African writers are fashioning an urban literature on terms that are unacceptable to the white ruling class. They are detribalized or Coloured (of mixed blood), not accepted as an integral part of the country's culture (a culture in a chaotic state). But, like every other non-white, they keep on, digging their feet into an urban culture of their own making. This is a fugitive culture: borrowing here, incorporating there, retaining this, rejecting that. But it is a virile culture. The clamour of it is going to keep beating on the walls surrounding the already fragmented culture of the whites until they crumble.

What is the larger context in which the non-white writer operates? Briefly this. In military, political and economic terms, the conquest of South Africa by whites was brutal and complete. Migrant labour led to a wide circulation of Africans in rural areas who had come into contact with whites in the towns and on their farms. The blacks in turn influenced the rural communities to which they returned in-between labour contracts. Such new gadgets as gramophones, radio sets, concertinas, mouth-organs and others which they brought back, together with cloth and style of dress, and such industrial life as they told stories of, naturally took on a symbol of the white man's power and also of progress. The church mission was in turn equated with these conveniences. The school books the missionaries used for teaching their wards implicitly glorified the white man. The conquest of the mind was thus ensured for future generations. And that is how Christianity came to be equated with technological civilization. What is significant is that the missionaries themselves also identified the one with the other. So when the Africans began to chafe against mounting oppression, and spoke out through the press and through political organization—in the medium taught by the missionary—the church regarded this response as a sign of gross ingratitude.

Ingratitude to Christian institutions and therefore ingratitude to the whole white race, with all its gadgets and trinkets.

Now because the Government is using institutions of a fragmented and almost unrecognizable Bantu culture as an instrument of oppression, we dare not look back. We have got to wrench the tools of power from the white man's hand: one of these is literacy and the sophistication that goes with it. We have got to speak the language that all can understand—English. But the important thing always is that we daren't look back, at any rate not yet.

The West African, on the other hand, is a full citizen of a country that is wholly Negro. He does not live in the stresses that daily harass his South African counterpart. British indirect rule has left African culture more or less intact where it has been applied, except in certain Christianized communities where old-fashioned missionaries have exorcized the spiritual forces of indigenous cultures. In these areas, the educated black man has adopted Western thought.

There is no cross play of impacts between the literatures of South and West Africa. Communication between them is nil. Although the Nigerians Wole Soyinka, Chinua Achebe, Gabriel Okara, Cyprian Ekwensi are sophisticated in a way that Amos Tutuola is not, there is nothing in these four writers like the cultural cross-impacts one finds in the South. Our idioms are different. There are not, in West Africa, the anger, impatience, restlessness, moodiness, semantic violence and the self-assertive laughter which hit the various planes of South African expression. There is an overall steady pace and sedate mood in West African writing. This includes writing by the Sierra Leonian Abioseh Nicol, the best English prose writer in these parts; the Ghanaians Efua Sutherland, J. H. Kwabena Nketia, and others. Individualism in West African prose writing never reaches a pitch such as we observe in, say, Alfred Hutchinson, whose prose is full of panting rhythm, now lurching forward, now stalling, now turning round on one spot.

Because of large communities of illiterate and unsophisticated folk in West Africa, and the resultant wide gulf between the educated man and the uneducated, the clash between the old and the new is much sharper than you can ever see in the South. And the artist in West Africa is preoccupied with this clash. There is no doubt that this preoccupation is going to become more intense with the present cultural invasion by commercial radio, television and high-powered advertising. But the man of culture in countries of British influence hasn't really caught the negritude fever of the assimilated men in countries of French influence. The English-speaking African is much steadier and more confident of himself and is merely content with portraying the clash. It is only a man like Gabriel Okara, the outstanding Nigerian poet, who quite frankly says his poem *You laughed and laughed*[1] was written 'in the spirit of negritude'. He tells the white man:

> 'In your ears my song
> is motor car misfiring
> stopping with a choking cough:
> and you laughed and laughed and laughed.'

He says the white man has long laughed at the African's 'ante-natal walk', his dance and drums, his 'mystic inside'; and yet the white man's is 'ice-block/laughter and it froze your inside/froze your voice your ears', where the black man's is 'the fire

> of the eye of the sky, the fire
> Of the earth, the fire of the air . . .
> the fire of the seas and the
> rivers fishes animals trees
> and it thawed your inside
> thawed your voice, thawed your
> ears, thawed your eyes, and
> thawed your tongue'.

And when the white man wonders what is happening to him, the African answers:

> 'Because my fathers and I
> are owned by the living
> warmth of the earth
> through our naked feet.'

But the artist takes off where slogans and catchwords stop. And

[1] *Black Orpheus* (No. 6).

the true poet in Okara appears not when he is asserting his negroness, which is only a fraction of his humanness, but when he exposes himself to disparate impacts, without trying to say which is the more or most valuable; as in his *Piano and Drums*.[1] In this he has a more convincing image of himself:

When at break of day at a riverside
I hear jungle drums telegraphing
the mystic rhythm, urgent, raw
like bleeding flesh, speaking of
primal youth and the beginning,
I see the panther ready to pounce,
the leopard snarling about to leap
and the hunters crouch with spears poised;

And my blood ripples, turns torrent,
topples the years and at once I'm
in my mother's laps a suckling;
at once I'm walking simple
paths with no innovations,
rugged, fashioned with the naked
warmth of hurrying feet and groping hearts
in green leaves and wild flowers pulsing.

Then I hear a wailing piano
solo speaking of complex ways
in tear-furrowed concerto;
of far away lands
and new horizons with
coaxing diminuendo, counterpoint,
crescendo. But lost in the labyrinth
of its complexities, it ends in the middle
of a phrase at a daggerpoint.

And I lost in the morning mist
of an age at a riverside keep
wandering in the mystic rhythm
of jungle drums and the concerto.

[1] op. cit.

In the Nigerian playwright Wole Soyinka's drama, *The Swamp Dwellers*, the conflict between the old and the new is subtly portrayed in the character of Igwezu, the son of an old couple who still believe in the Kadiye, the priest of a snake cult. The play is set in the Niger delta. The Kadiye claims his dues from the delta community in order to appease the snake that often brings the floods to destroy the people's crops. Igwezu comes from the city where he lost his wife to his prosperous twin brother, a business man. He has borrowed money from the brother on the security of an expected harvest from his field. But the floods have destroyed all, and he believes the Kadiye has let him down, for all the sacrifices he has given the priest. He condemns the priest as an impostor, a corrupt man, and threatens to kill him. In despair Igwezu renounces his delta life and returns to the city, aware that he is going back to a sordid if new existence. Against this serious young man who represents the new, is the Kadiye, who appears as a caricature. Also as a symbol of new thinking is the blind Muslim beggar who now wants to be a farmer instead of begging his way through life and exploiting his religious significance as the *raison d'être* of man's philanthropic exercise.

The play was produced in London recently. Soyinka is now doing research into Nigerian drama.

Again, against a white background, the black stands out in bold outline in Wole Soyinka's poem, *The Immigrant*,[1] which shows his incisive sophistication, born no doubt of his long stay in Britain as a teacher. A black immigrant asks for a dance at Hammersmith Palace. He subconsciously wants to assert his dignity. A white girl refuses. At the suggestion of 'You? Not at any price!' in her eyes, he feels hurt.

> He felt the wound grow septic
> (Hard though he tried to close it)
> His fingers twitched
> And toyed with the idea,
> The knife that waited on the slight,
> On the sudden nerve that would join her face
> To scars identical

[1] *Black Orpheus* (No. 5).

With what he felt inside.
The blade remained
In the sweat-filled pocket.

He knows now the 'fatality of his black flattened nose'. He wants a chance to revenge, to degrade her sex and race.

Failing to find
A difference in the street-lamp faces
(He had sought the very best)
He makes his choice at random
Haggles somewhat at the price,
Then follows her, to pass
The night
In reciprocal humiliation.

In the twin poem, . . . *And the other Immigrant*, the black man is not, like the former immigrant, doing a menial job. He is evidently schooling and training for a job back home in Africa. He shuts himself up in his apartment winter and summer, making sacrifices 'like two square semolina meals a day'. What keeps up his morale in an alien country are his prospects of a Government job and house, a senior service car, and 'hordes of admiring women'.

In his own self-assertive manner, this black man tries to stay 'untouched . . ./upon the crest of an alien, white society'; his dignity is 'sewn into a lining of a three-piece suit/ Stiff, and with the whiteness which 'Out-Europes Europe'. He disdains to exchange jokes with the Cockney taxi-driver or take a public servant seriously. His victory is proof that he 'can do without them'. This immigrant keeps to his kind, because he does not like the white face. He thinks:

'Let pedants tease their pompous heads
While to my repertoire I add
(The sound, if not the spirit of)
Our new-coined intellectuals' slogan—
Negritude.'

Yes, Soyinka can laugh in a way no other West African of British influence can—with the written word.

I think the most impressionistic West Africa writer outside the negritude crowd is Ghana's Efua Theodora Sutherland (*née* Morgue). She has also reached a degree of sophistication that is exceptional in a West African context. She is married to an Afro-American civil servant working in Accra. In her poem, *It Happened*,[1] a black woman and a white man tell each other that their love can perform wonders in spite of 'the bitter thing'—race prejudice—that keeps rearing its head to poison their beautiful relationship. The uneven, halting rhythm of her line reflects the passion, impatience, and agony that so often characterizes South African non-white prose. She writes:

It happened
And promptly I was aware
Of the bitter thing.

I said it,
I saw a furious flare
Flush his kindly brow.

What difference is there
In us, he cried.
What difference, my love?
Ask those who feel not
Those who are not us.

Enough of this thrust pain!
A song within us
Lifts us all this above
And lets our joy remain.

He would make a garden,
Planting its ready earth
With palm and strawberry,
Rose and arum,
Crocus and cocoa-lily.
There, O races and empires,
Shall we live in fragrant peace
Without liaison, without pact.

[1] *Anthology of West African Verse*, ed. Olumbe Bassir, (Ibadan University Press, 1957).

But where shall you lease us
Tweed-side or Volta bank,
Coconut grove or heatherland?
We ask because we must,
Because of the bitter thing.

But enough of this thrust pain.
Our song lifts us up
And lets our joy remain.

Know you, races of earth,
Two of your colours met
And gave each other all
As earth reeled blindly past
In silence and in pain
Our fountains did mingle
Because of the bitter thing.

It can be!
How can it be?
No, it cannot be.

O, you shall be free
From the pain of me.
Go to your own
And be free
From the sting
Of the bitter thing.

But what about their plans? he asks. No, it cannot be. No use exposing themselves to the 'stubble of prejudice' and 'political burrs'.

The bitter thing
Looms large before us,
Mouthing, threatening
To crush us
Should we dare.

With a sense of futility, the two persons decide they cannot go on with the affair. But at least they have shown the world that it can be done if . . .

Children of Despair

To come back to Nigeria, Chinua Achebe, writer of two novels, is also keenly aware of the conflict between systems of living; again in a way that does not occur to the South African writer, with the exception of Africans living in a rural setting and writing in one of the three main vernacular languages. Achebe, who has been working on radio, is touring East and Central Africa, the West Indies and the United States on a Rockefeller Foundation grant to study literary trends.

The story in his powerful novel, *Things Fall Apart*, dates back to the beginning of this century when the whites were said to be 'pacifying the natives'. Okonkwo is one of the elders of an Ibo clan in Eastern Nigeria. He has earned this position by sheer hard work, spurred on by a haunting obsession to live down the poverty which he has inherited from his father who was a carefree and unambitious man. Okonkwo takes titles and as a one-time great wrestler, he is highly respected.

Ikemefuna, a boy who was given to the clan as a penalty for the killing of a woman of Okonkwo's clan by a member of the boy's, is entrusted to the care of Okonkwo. This act, the killing of Ikemefuna by the clan as a sacrifice to Agbala (Oracle), and the whole Ibo way of life, are challenged by the coming of white missionaries and the introduction of European justice. What angers Okonkwo more than anything else is the conversion of his son, Nwoye, to Christianity, which shatters all the plans he had for the boy.

The centre of the clan's life is going to pieces. The people speak with different voices. What should be done to the convert who desecrated the clan's shrine? 'It is not our custom to fight for our gods,' said one of them. 'If a man kills the sacred python in the secrecy of his hut, the matter lies between him and the god. We did not see it. If we put ourselves between the god and his victim we may receive blows intended for the offender. When a man blasphemes, what do we do? Do we go and stop his mouth? No. We put our fingers into our ears to stop us hearing.' But Okonkwo thinks this is being cowardly. 'If a man comes into my hut and defecates on the floor, what do I do?' he says. 'Do I shut my eyes? No! I take a stick and break his head.'

At another meeting, Okika, one of the speakers, tells us to what extent the new life has eaten into the new. He says:

'Are all the sons of Umuofia with us here? . . . They are not. They have broken the clan and gone their several ways. We who are here this morning have remained true to our fathers, but our brothers have deserted us and joined a stranger to soil their fatherland. If we fight the stranger we shall hit our brothers and perhaps shed the blood of a clansman. But we must do it. Our fathers never dreamt of such a thing, they never killed their brothers. But a white man never came to them. Eneke the bird was asked why he was always on the wing and he replied: "Men have learnt to shoot without missing their mark and I have learnt to shoot without perching on a twig." We must root out this evil. . . . We must bale this water now that it is only ankle-deep. . . .'

Okonkwo kills one of the white Commissioner's messengers who are carrying an order for the meeting to stop. 'Why did he do it?' he hears someone say. The crowd do not act, and he realizes that he is alone. He goes and takes his own life.

The conflict continues. At the scene of the suicide, Okonkwo's old friend tells the Commissioner it is against custom for the body of a man who has committed suicide to be taken down by his fellow-clansman or to be given a decent burial. Strangers must do it. 'It is an abomination for a man to take his own life. It is an offence against the Earth.' Turning to the white man he says fiercely: 'That man was one of the greatest men in Umuofia. You drove him to kill himself; and now he will be buried like a dog. . . .' The messengers, who represent a stranger, take the body down.

And then the sting at the tail-end: 'The Commissioner went away, taking three or four of the soldiers with him. In the many years in which he had toiled to bring civilization to different parts of Africa he had learnt a number of things. One of them was that a District Commissioner must never attend to such undignified details as cutting down a hanged man from the tree. Such attention would give the natives a poor opinion of him. In the book, which he planned to write, he would stress that point. . . .'

Achebe clearly sympathizes with Okonkwo, but throughout the story he is detached like the ancient Greek poet. Although this particular theme is no more relevant in present-day African society the clash portrayed by Achebe has a symbolic significance for all Africa. It is a symbol of that larger irony which is the meeting point between reconciliation and conflict; it has therefore important reference to the larger context of black-white contact.

In *Things Fall Apart* we see the impact of a proselytising religion on a somewhat passive tribal religion, an impact which resolves itself into a clash. In this catastrophe, Okonkwo finds himself alone, unable to incite apathetic clansmen to violence.

In a novel called *Ingqumbo Yeminyanya* (*The Wrath of the Ancestors*) written in a Bantu language by the South African, A. C. Jordan, the conflict is between persons, and it develops into one between groups. A young man goes to a mission institution for his education. He marries a schoolmate, against the wishes of his tribe whom he has to rule as chief when he goes back home. The two decide to run the gauntlet. The tribe does not accept his wife who is much too sophisticated for them and seems deliberately to go against all tribal sanctions relating to the humble position of women. He is installed chief, and his people prepare to foist a tribal girl on him.

The educated woman is literally driven mad by public censure after killing a snake—the messenger of the ancestors—which she saw moving towards her child. Her madness is considered to be a fulfilment of the wrath of the ancestors. The tribe is split into factions for and against the young chief. Here, too, 'things fall apart'. The chief lets go of himself, becomes indifferent to his official duties and in the height of distraction, takes his own life.

In Jordan's story, we witness an internal disintegration in persons torn between two forces: a process that would most probably not take place if the couple involved were not thrown into a prominent position and therefore committed to their tribal role. Achebe sees a disintegration rather in the community than in individuals. The characters in both stories are children of despair.

In a sense, Jordan's and Achebe's stories are two sides of the same theme. Achebe shows the conflict from the tribal side, and Jordan from the Christian side. In another sense, *The Wrath of the Ancestors* is a development of *Things Fall Apart*. In the former, the new values are represented by the 'Westernized' African, while in Achebe's book, the new values are represented by the 'Westerner'. But in neither is there a question of an irreconcilable clash. In certain areas of protest, Christianity is accepted and racial oppression only is attacked by the blacks; in other areas, because the white man's creed has sunk to the level of what E. M. Forster calls 'talkative Christianity', and is being used to justify injustice, it is being challenged. In other cases again, the black man's and the white man's social values are irreconcilable in varying degrees. These paradoxes, with which Africa teems, will for a long time to come constitute rich literary material for the African artist. Facile rejection and facile acceptance cannot stand 'ironic contemplation'.

Although Dr. Jordan, who is a lecturer in African studies at the University of Cape Town, is a sophisticate, he was obviously telling a story that could only take place against a rural setting. And as hereditary chieftaincy is now a thing of the past, and the Government has for the last half-century been appointing chiefs who will obey it, in the place of rebels, such a conflict is fast becoming irrelevant except as a symbol of the larger irony in black-white relations.

Epilogue

BLACK AND WHITE CAMEOS

I

Outside the concourse of London Airport a group of Europeans took a fancy to the Basotho grass hat on Bloke's head. They insisted that one girl among them take a photograph with us, the only two blacks in the place. Sylvester, one of the bunch of South Africans who had come to meet me, asked the heavy-looking lady organizer of the photographic performance what the African angle was in aid of. 'Our daughter has just arrived from abroad,' she crowed, 'and it's for luck.' It seemed Sylvester and I were never going to stop laughing. London has everything, a Nigerian friend—a 'been-to'—had told me. Maybe this was one of them.

Ivan whisked us off in his car. Sylvester was showing me some of the outstanding features as we drove through to Primrose Hill. Your Victorian and Georgian architecture; quaint-looking taxicabs; terraced residential grounds; 'underground' signs; blue plaques; Hyde Park that excites dark and dingy, brave and lusty images; bowls of greenery in the form of parks into which Londoners filtered. And even as I saw part of London for those brief moments of my first entry in England, the immensity and continuity of things couldn't escape me—and, of course, the cold impersonal exterior of things and people. I felt at once small and superior. Like the feeling a man gets when he has entered somewhere in the middle of a long long queue, sensing only the immediate pressures, knowing that those whom he finds in the queue are going to be too scared to go just round the corner to relieve themselves!

During that drive I was trying to organize every part of me so as to recognize the thrill of being in a place that had for years been a distant dream, a thought that was written with smoke across the sky and was swallowed up by the blue. Dickensian images that had piled up in my mind began to make sense.

Jenny, Sylvester's wife, stood at the gate to welcome me. Suddenly she drew her husband to one side. Something was wrong. I was apprehensive for them. Sylvester disappeared, with a tragic look on his face. Another tense moment. He left again, by which time we were in the kitchen.

'What's the tragedy?' I asked light-heartedly.

'Felicity's dog's lost,' said Jenny, and I saw part of the profile of despair in her slightly drooping attitude.

'I don't know how to tell her. . . . She'll break down. . . . It'll just kill the poor thing.'

I just couldn't work myself up into a state over the dog, not even on behalf of friends. Funny, these people are, I thought, not without a feeling of ungrateful impatience. If it isn't dogs, it's cats, it's parrots, or canaries, it's monkeys, it's rabbits, and then it's . . . dogs. I thought of South African pets on which whites lavish heaps of love, but I refused to believe that dogs were treated better than human beings here too.

I was thinking all this when Sylvester returned, with boyish glee on his face. The dog had been found, he announced. Jenny sighed and relaxed and that profile of pain dissolved. The other dog-stricken friends also settled down. I was at pains to suppress a laugh which, if released, would have blown out particles of boiled egg that was disintegrating under the vicious onslaught of my full set of natural teeth.

Bloke laughed and said: 'You wait, Zeke, till I tell you all about the English and their dogs.' I bawled out laughing. This frightened Zumbi, Sylvester's little dog; he barked so much as to say to me: If you weren't brought up in the middle-class tradition of dogs, cats and gardens, I'll have you understand that I've a right to feel concerned.

I visited Britain at the end of June 1959. At the end of my four-and-a-half months' vacation I literally ran out, in a state of near-neurotic tremor. I must say outright that I wasn't with my family (they had gone to South Africa so that our baby should be born there; otherwise it would not be regarded as a South African citizen, and might be declared a prohibited immigrant). Again, maybe it was a mistake for a hypersensitive asthmatic small-town bumpkin like me (ex Pretoria and Johannesburg) to be initiated into British life through London. Furthermore, I wasn't committed to living in Britain. Third, although I had emigrated from South Africa two years before, I had not yet learned to live with freedom. I was still quivering and bristling all over. It could also have been because I had left Nigeria almost up to boiling point with anger over the gross disregard of human life shown by the British Government in its handling of the Central African crisis and in detaining so many Africans.

I was determined to lap up as much cultural entertainment as I could. Apart from a symphony orchestra in Johannesburg which gave a few, scattered near-charitable concerts for non-whites in poor non-European halls, I had never heard a live symphony concert; nor had I ever seen big theatre, except for a single *Hamlet* performance given to only blacks in a small theatre, and student performances at the liberal University of the Witwatersrand (Johannesburg).

So I went to ten plays: Charles Laughton's *King Lear* at Stratford, one at the Royal Court, one at Regent's Park, and the rest in the West End. Then there were five Proms and a Vienna Boys' concert at Albert Hall, four musical occasions at Royal Festival Hall, including a piano recital and the concert version of *Don Giovanni* (by far the most moving musical experience I have ever had), and an open-air symphony concert outside Kenwood House. I took thirty-two films in good stride, many of which I should never have smelled in South Africa or in Nigeria: the former because of the colour bar, the latter because of an utter lack of sophistication and an enlightened cinema-going public. In South Africa Louis Armstrong would certainly be removed bodily from *Four Pennies*, as he was from *The Glenn Miller Story*, before we should see it. I needn't talk of Continental films.

Mr. Kenneth Tynan, the drama critic for the *Observer*, wrote recently on his return from a Broadway season: 'In my absence, the drama of earthy social comment, which Broadway derides as a hangover from the 'thirties, has belatedly caught on in the West End; while in New York, the citadel of materialism, there has been an increasing emphasis on fable and fantasy.' He added that the English stage has adopted some of Broadway's 'discarded aspirations', and vice versa.

Well, now, I am glad I raided the West End after the exchange. I shall prefer drama of social comment for a long long time to come. Maybe it is because I come from a continent of myth, fable, allegory, which have their own kind of 'visionary statement' and are intended to heal the 'eternal sickness of the individual soul'. What African tales we used to adapt for the stage (two of which an Old Vic group admired very much when they were visiting South Africa) were chosen because they provided excellent drama—purely for the sake of entertainment.

Even in the social comment that came from the 1959 West End stage I sensed an apologetic tone. *A Taste of Honey* appealed to me most because the story came straight from the shoulder as it were. It was as if the playwright had become aware at a certain point in the making of the play that she had a big and intricate subject on her hands and that it was threatening to get out of hand. Then she had very skilfully and sensitively nursed the drama to a neat and convincing end, without any pretence to a startling discovery in black-white relations. I liked *The Hostage* least, with its noisy clatter that makes it difficult for one to keep pace with the story. For that matter, although *Ulysses in Nighttown* is constructed on such flimsy material (from a dramatic standpoint) it was most entertaining—which the dramatist may very well have intended it primarily to be. Between Miss Delaney and Mr. Behan, I liked *a raisin in the sun* next best. I'm putting the fascinating *West Side Story* and the fabulous *My Fair Lady* in a class by themselves.

So all in all I had my fill of English culture; almost constipating. It seems this is the only thing that will save the Britisher from himself eventually; although this must depend on what fraction of the population culture is available to.

It is safe to say that in South Africa there are among non-whites two classes. These are determined by literacy: the 'educated class' and the 'illiterate'. Astringent conditions more or less level up incomes of non-whites, so that the moneyed class is negligible. In Nigeria, for instance, where people can live where they can afford to and are not herded into areas willy-nilly by their own government, class distinctions are sharp: money, occupation and education each have their role in deciding what company a man keeps.

In England it seemed quite obvious that money, education, occupation, decide a man's social status and therefore class. It was in the pubs and cheap restaurants that I realized how very similar working-class folk are to African working-class, whether in West or South Africa. The same down-to-earth language, the same circumlocution. An African will say: 'Just as I was saying, he came to see us on—what day was it? Yes, it was Sunday. Yes, Sunday—I'm sure of it, because that day I remember sending one of Petros' children—you know the clever one—to buy tea for him—remember Petros whose wife acts like white people——'

'Has she given birth already?'

'No. As I was saying, he came to see us. . . .'

We have the same them-and-us attitudes as you have in your country, but distinctions have a different basis from yours.

In a bus from Stratford-upon-Avon to Barford I was startled out of my bafflement by the chatter that continued all the way among the rest of the passengers. Something I had never heard in a London bus or tube where passengers sit with hungry-looking, funereal faces and gave one the sensation of being among so many dozen eggs; I didn't know whether one of them would crack if I so much as inched farther away from the aisle.

I soon discovered, incidentally, that a companion didn't let you pay for him in the bus and get away with it: He sooner or later paid back your 'goodwill money'. Most annoying: two streams of vanity, one overtaking the other. I am not used to this sort of thing. Are the English, after all, as close-fisted as they are reputed to be in South Africa? It doesn't tie up with the lavish manner in which they feed you when they have invited you to a meal. But then they insist that you, the guest—I hesitate to think it is because one is black—sweep the table clean. 'Oh, do finish this,' the hostess says. 'Oh no, thank you,' you say. 'I'm really full.' 'Oh come on, you *must* finish this last bit. . . .' And at the point of a gun—the gun of amiability—you shut your eyes and throw the last bit down.

I found Welsh folk quite charming and warmer when I was in North Wales. The Welshman would be the first to tell you, I think, how rotten and stuffy the English are. Said one, a stocky, round bundle of concentrated Welsh venom, to me: 'One of these days we'll stop the water they get from us, and we'll starve the lot of those English.' This was at a conference on race relations! Yet the first people with whom acquaintance went beyond a cocktail party encounter in London were a Welsh couple.

How heavy going it is to crash through even the outer layer of this mighty structure. The males are much easier than the females: the females seem to be on the defensive all the time. And you talk of the emancipation of women!

For all Mr. Harold Macmillan can say about the class war having ended in Britain, the one thing that hit me between the eyes was this gulf between classes. None of my intellectual acquaintances could direct me to a working-class home they knew intimately. One, a social worker, did know a family, but I failed to contact him again. I had to content myself with meeting working-class folk in pubs—that most fascinating of British institutions—and at work and on the cinema screen, as in *I'm All Right Jack*. This wasn't enough.

I was told that there is a continuous process of social climbing from the lower classes. Maybe middle-class people have taken Orwell's hint given twenty years ago. He was born a middle-class snob, wanted to sink his identity by affiliating as it were with the working class; but he found this only *intensified* class prejudice: the middle-class English seem to have tacitly agreed on levelling the working class *up* instead of themselves *down*: levelling the others up 'by means of hygiene, fruit-juice, birth-control, poetry, etc.,' as Orwell would put it. Furthermore, they seem to have succeeded in accommodating a dictatorship-of-the-working-class of some sort. The fact that only about 25 per cent of children who pass out of primary school enter grammar school may continue to ensure a preponderance of the number who enter secondary modern school—a substantial reservoir of the working-class potential. One must wonder how many there are of Orwell's favourites (and mine) who, having procured a higher education by means of scholarships, continue as mechanics, dock labourers and so on, not bothering to change their working-class accent and habits?

In Nigeria the moneyed man who hasn't had much of an education continues to speak pidgin English, the common medium among the working class. Nigerian professionals speak a more or less standard English, where they belong to different language groups, but interchange English and mother-tongue as between members of the same language group. Social climbing can thus be a forked process: a short cut to money, and a way to money via education. The latter direction takes in lawyers, doctors, senior government servants: some fall a little 'lower' and end up as teachers, junior government clerks, ministers of religion. The moneyed and professional classes distrust each other, but need each other badly in a country where the accumulation of capital overshadows everything else and tends to falsify the wonderful qualities of the Nigerian individual. Notice how all social services here are centralized in government, and what a rarity charitable enterprise is. Perhaps I worry myself over class in countries where it isn't made a fuss of: it's simply lived and accepted.

There in the distance Snowdon stands, and the valleys near us are grimly enchanting under an overcast sky. This is the kind of grandeur one misses in the monotonous view of tropical rain forests, where you drive miles and miles and on either side of you jungle threatens to cover you up. Driving like this one day my wife remarked: 'Gosh, it feels like we'll be seeing God walking across the road with long strides!'

The luxury bus we boarded at Bangor glides beautifully towards Bettws-y-Coed. We have been told our destination is Swallow Falls. I'm breathless with anticipation: for the first time in my life I'm going to see real waterfalls; I think to myself, maybe just what I always dreamed the Victoria Falls to be like. Here we are. We pay at the toll gate, thread our way down to the falls. Several other people are about, with eager faces that speak of some mysterious emancipation. Down there we see water pour down a stretch of very low rock that just manages to cause cascades. Disappointing. I climb up back to the gate, and stand outside.

Suddenly I notice how interesting it is to watch these holiday-makers. Absorbing: their faces always eager—over what? I wouldn't know. They swallow tons of ice cream, tripping about with what I regard an assumed gaiety. They come and go through the gate. And as they come out, their eagerness seems to have reached an orgiastic pitch. Over what? I'm still to know. Maybe the sun's being out has something to do with it.

I was puzzled by the same sort of empty eagerness among the crowds who go to see Derwent, the site of the flooded village in Castleton. I experienced almost the same thing at Brighton; although here the immensity of the crowds, the places of amusement bespattered with so much colour, the line of sea-front hotels, the spirit that came from the grotesquely beautiful Regency building at the back of us—all these were understandable reasons for gaiety. Still, so much seemed put on.

My nose leads me to Soho, still sniffing for English group behaviour. Anthony and Carol take me to the Fabulous Flamingo. The walls are a blazing red toned down by dim lights. The place is hot with modern jazz, but the atmosphere is sedate and sluggish —too much so. Then we wind our way through the night life of this busy little cosmopolitan place. Funny that one can step out of, say, Regent Street, into Soho and feel that one has traversed a number of social miles into a different world. Outside there people live so much apart; there, two persons sit apart, leaving a space in the middle for the third one, as on one of those two long seats facing each other, nearest the bus entrance. Inside here (Soho), people are so close to one another, so uninhibited. Yes, their faces are too pale, but one soon forgets to be offended in easy human conditions like these. Then I'm taken to Cy Laurie's Club. A shabby hall with a shabby jazz combo. But there's an electric, boisterous atmosphere, and there's an appearance of down-to-earth dissipation. No, no, that's not the way to jive, I'm tempted to say to the dancing couples. Don't do it as if the legs had nothing to do with the heart and the rest of the body. You see, the bosom (what there is of it) must move in rhythm with the abdomen, the waist and feet: it's not just a turning and whirling about like two tops gyrating next to each other. In fact, you *gyrate* too much and *dance* too little. You should come and see how Africans do it. . . . Yes, you English simply haven't the art of creating fun: you want to sit and watch performances, and then one or two of you go home and set up a practice as critics.

I have said much about behaviour patterns before without indicating what I mean in terms of contrast. Enough has been said of the African extended family: by other writers and news reporters. A man asks his employer for leave to go home in some reserve two hundred miles or so away, because his aunt's cousin's husband (spoken of as a direct uncle) is dead. The employer often doesn't understand why a man should travel two hundred miles to see a corpse. He doesn't know what it means to his 'boy' in terms of human relations and communal living.

I'm told the English working class and peasantry recognize some sort of extended family. What often puzzles me is the way in which English children are often allowed to come in and out of the lounge when grown-ups are conversing. Worse still, they are allowed to sit on Mummy's lap or Daddy's knee, pull his ears about, and render all conversation irrelevant. We never allow our children to do this. We don't even have to remind them to keep out. I must admit, though, that I have noticed three or four educated Nigerians allow their children to hang about when there were visitors in the house. 'Who's Daddy talking about?' one of the brood might chip in. How exasperatingly distracting this kind of behaviour can be.

You English are too cautious in your relations with one another and with foreigners. You don't seem to want to commit yourselves because you don't want to risk appearing foolish if you should fail someone else. This is how we conduct some of our relations: A visits B, a friend of mine. B brings him to me to introduce him. I spontaneously go out of my way to entertain A, never in the absence of B; it's discourteous to invite A for any occasion and leave B out. B, for his part, virtually bullies A by taking him to other friends, to a concert or to pictures. Unless A is obviously indisposed, he is never asked whether he likes to go here or there. It would be discourteous for him to look persecuted.

If I were inviting a friend to a meal or party, I shouldn't think of saying, as you English do: 'Come if you can—you know—if you can't manage—you know—don't worry!' or something to that effect. I should leave it to his discretion; but I don't want to suggest that *I* shan't bother if he doesn't turn up. So I sound unwittingly demanding: 'Come to dinner, won't you?' And by the way, if my friend should bring two or so other friends of his to a party, I shouldn't mind at all. I always prepare for such eventualities. When we send one hundred printed invitations to a wedding, we cook enough for two hundred. But I am told that you English usually buy just enough stores for just so many and no more when you have a party coming on. And yet you look so prosperous!

Once word has been received that someone is very ill or dead in a family we know in our locality, we go to the house or send someone to represent us. We should feel offended if we were not told of a severe sickness or death.

I admire the Englishwoman for the way in which she can look after herself, not like the South African white, whose whole week's programme goes out of gear if her African maid or manservant cannot turn up for work one or two days. The Englishwoman, on the whole, dresses much better than the South African white, who looks expensively dressed but does not make a good overall impression. And I think is has something to do with personality. The impression the onlooker gets is the same as that which a view gives of an unselected collection of South African whites at any place: they overplay their sophisticated manner which has an undertone of a feeling of insecurity, even in their feudal comfort. Looking at any unselected group of people in Britain, I sensed a self-confidence and an unaffected manner. I do not rule out the possibility that I look at South African whites with a decided prejudice; I remember them always as masters and as people I have watched entering a theatre or concert hall, to which I could never gain admission, with a consuming hate that now takes in all white sophisticates in South Africa who are not obviously on our side.

Proportionately, the standard of cleanliness in the home of an English couple, even where the woman is a housewife, is lower. The bedding leaves much to be desired, the sheets being changed once a fortnight at the most. The legs of the women folk I often saw in the trains needed a good scrubbing. Our non-whites in South Africa could, in much smaller rooms and shanties, put up a much better show.

I want to take a bus to Victoria Station from Vauxhall House. Not sure if I'm on the right side of the street, I ask a respectable-looking gentleman with a bowler hat on.

'I'm afraid you're on the wrong side,' he replies benignly. 'You should go to the other side.'

I move to cross the street. I hear footsteps behind me, and, looking back, see the gentleman, who says breathlessly: 'I'm awfully sorry, you were right, and I'm on the wrong side.'

I walk back to the stop.

'I wonder,' he says stopping midway. 'Let's ask this gentleman.' It turns out that my informer's first guess was right—that I was on the wrong side in the first place.

'So awfully sorry,' he apologizes. 'I was right in the first place, it appears, and you were on the wrong side.'

I walk away to cross over, baffled by the gentleman's persistent effort to be correct. In the Deep South of Africa, a white man would seldom take so much trouble. Or he wouldn't speak to me at all.

Another incident. We are at lunch at Hayward's Heath during a summer school. Sylvester wants to know whether the dessert we are eating is black strawberries or not. The waiter reckons they are currants. She disappears and reappears with the information: 'They're strawberries, sir, I was wrong—sorry.'

An admirable effort not to misinform; or, positively, to give correct information.

During my stay in Britain, because of the type of questions I was asked by interested persons about African affairs, I was being driven all the time, as I have been in Nigeria, to see both sides of each issue. For instance, I have always condemned 'indirect rule' in British possessions in Africa: categorically so. But now, short of condoning colonialism, I am able to concede one point: that at least Britain trained her administrators before sending them out to the colonies. In South Africa, the so-called native commissioners in their version of indirect rule have mostly been a thoroughly inefficient, lazy and boorish lot. The stock qualification has been a smattering of some Bantu language and some sign that a man could 'manage natives'. And in any case, it was never intended that any black man should govern himself: wouldn't have been any use either, to rule oneself within a state governed by someone else.

I began to realize that this is one of the difficulties of living with freedom. In a country like South Africa, one stands quite clearly on one side or the other. To this extent one is absolved from having to think of both sides of a question: there *are* no sides—oppression cannot be freedom, or vice versa. Once outside this groove, a number of issues confront one which *can* and *must* be approached from different angles.

On another plane the difficulty of living with freedom appears in a different form. A young man we shall call Cam has been in Britain for over a year. He came as a stowaway from South Africa. Now Cam has no educational qualifications, although he is fully literate. He is a jazz fan. But partly because he has not yet come to realize that an exile cannot live all the way on his own terms, and partly because he does not have people of his kind around with whom he would perform the jobs offering without feeling humiliated, life is miserable for him. Being an underdog in one's own country affords a measure of protection: one derives moral support from one's fellow-underdogs. He doesn't starve alone. For Cam, the price of freedom is just that kind of loneliness.

When I was called 'John' by a bus conductress one day, the world seemed to collapse before me. Does it happen here too? I thought. My companion, also a South African, told her in very strong terms that I wasn't 'John'. The conductress looked bewildered. Of course, I was told afterwards that 'John,' 'Jim', 'duck' and so on are flung about without any intention to offend.

I had had a heavy dose of the lush prose of Durrel's *Bitter*

Lemons, which I had picked up after Salinger's *To Esmé, with Love and Squalor*, in the train to Manchester. And after lunch I had gone to a small gallery to see Kathe Kollwitz's drawings, with their direct social message that comes to you like a very short-range missile. Then I went to see Romanesque and contemporary art in the City Hall galleries. An acquaintance, Mr. Edmund Dell, a town councillor, took me to a pub in the evening, where I met two aldermen, whom I shall call A and B.

A (grey-haired): How does England impress you?

I: I've been baffled most of the time.

A: Of course you know that there's a strong feeling here in England against South Africa's apartheid. Do you people know that?

I: Only as much as we read about in British newspapers.

B: What do your people expect us here to do?

I: A clear and unequivocal gesture by Britain—outlaw South Africa economically and culturally. British artists should refuse engagements in South Africa.

A: A number of us in Manchester refuse to buy South African fruit, but it's spontaneous, not an organized thing.

B: I could never live in that country.

A: For the first time in years, you know, the union of bus workers have had to discipline a West Indian conductor for bad conduct, but at the same time there's much more evident honesty among Negro conductors than whites.

Dell: No doubt Negro conductors are more popular among many passengers than European workers, because of their cheerfulness and politeness. Our white conductors are often gloomy and unwilling to help.

(*A grunt of approval from the others.*)

B: There's no colour bar here but there's prejudice all right.

A: Time will cure that.

Dell: I don't think we should leave it to time. Something must be done consciously to show strong disapproval of prejudice. Take for instance the meeting I attended where a man shouted: 'We must send the blacks out of our city!' I came forward and asked aloud what party the man belonged to. The Fascists, he said. At once there was a shout of condemnation from the audience—

directed against the Fascist. Now, you see, they didn't disapprove of what he said earlier, but simply found fault with his political affiliation. You just can't leave it to time alone.

B: You know, of course, you could walk from one part of Manchester to another and not meet a Negro. They tend to collect in one area.

A: Same thing, if I went to Africa I'd look for my kind.

B: Yes, I think we're getting somewhere in the hospitals, where they work together side by side—black and white nurses, I mean.

I: Now tell me: do the working class tend mostly to vote Labour and the middle and upper classes Conservative?

B: Well, that's a tricky question.

A: Very few of the middle class vote Labour, most of the working class vote Labour, some Tory.

B: Tradition partly explains why a worker votes Tory: my father voted Tory, so I must do the same, he thinks.

A: The Anglican church inclines people to vote Tory.

I: Is it because the church is authoritarian and this is in harmony with Tory sentiments?

A: Precisely.

Dell: It's like this: If you took the English population and asked people what denomination they belonged to, those who couldn't care less and don't think about such things at all, will say *Anglican.*

A: During the war, when you enlisted and were asked what your religion was, if you said 'Atheist' the clerk would record *Anglican.* Funny thing is, you know, I was punished for going to church. It was this way. At Shrewsbury I did everything I could to dodge church parades in the army. One week when there was no parade I went to church. I was punished for going to church!

Dell: I suppose the penalty would be to stop you from attending church for a month!

(*Laughter.*)

I: Anyway, I can tell you Manchester has a much cleaner *and* more orderly central park than Birmingham.

Dell (shaking my paw which was swallowed by his massive one): Just what I've been telling them at this evening's meeting.

(*I'm given another mug of lager, and I leave them, to proceed to Didsbury Park.*)

Arthur from South Africa, whose leave in Britain coincided with mine, asked me to lunch at Holborn Restaurant. We met in front of Holborn tube station as arranged. We looked for the restaurant, turning around in circles, but couldn't find it. We asked a Bobby and right in front of us, where he pointed, was a massive building of the Midlands Bank. That's where it was, he told us. Bombed in the war, it was. Arthur laughed at himself for that. He told me it had been his favourite haunt before the war. He is British born.

Thinking about the incident afterwards, I marvelled a lot that Arthur should have hoped Holborn Restaurant would be where he had last seen it—not less than twenty years ago. There seems to come a period in one's life when one thinks in terms of long distances in time. But again there may still be that something that is solidly British in him; something that has to do with the urge to peg things and assign to them a historical niche; there now, the British seem to say, *that* takes care of you. Never leave this place, will you—otherwise I shan't know where I come from and where I'm going. . . .

I have been alarmed to observe the effect of a bloated sense of historical retrospect in the Britisher's assessment of the present. It makes for a conservative stability, the other side of which coin is an inflexible arrogance. All so frightening. This was when I went to the House of Commons to listen to the debate on Central African Federation. What Mr. Lennox Boyd said, even in the face of the Devlin Report, seemed to me to find a concrete symbol in the very structure of Westminster, in the numerous statues, antique buildings, blue plaques and so on. And even as Mr. Boyd spoke, his words seemed to fossilize into yet another relic of colonial blunders. It's all so alarming to look at these concrete symbols and know that one is looking at Britain's huge historical backside which will not allow her to move more than a fraction of an inch at a time, while suffering continues in East and Central Africa. And when she moves an inch there are so many shuffling and puffing and wheezing noises.

I am in the Educational section of the County Council premises. I have decided to do supply teaching in Grammar school, just to get the feel of it, to know what English children are like in the classroom. My curiosity has been sharpened since two West Indian teachers and an African told me how hopeless discipline was where they were teaching in London, and how impossible it had been for them to give notes or written tasks in secondary modern schools where they had taught, because large numbers of pupils simply could not read properly or write at all.

A lady comes to me and says: 'You must produce an X-ray report and a letter from the Ministry about your qualifications. What subject would you be wanting to teach?'

'English.'

The lady visibly opens her mouth and holds it for about three seconds. Feeling embarrassed for her and wanting to break the awkward silence, I say: 'And Geography.' (Although I hate to teach that subject.)

Then, as if to imply 'Now you're talking', she says: 'All right then, do let us know when you have all the necessary things.'

I leave. A week later I deliver all the necessary things, all in order. I wait and wait, but I get no appointment. I should like to think that it is because there was no vacancy, because I know of West Indians who teach English in London. Still, I can't help thinking how naïve I felt when I left that building—to think a black man like me from Africa should hope to teach English children English!

All in all, although I eventually gravitated towards places and things and kept there: the telly, art galleries (not without enjoyment), and so on, I did meet a few very interesting persons on more or less intimate terms. William Plomer, for instance, whom I had met for the first time in Johannesburg when he was visiting in 1956, asked me to spend a day at his Sussex place. I have great admiration for him. His warmth and sincerity penetrate every fibre of his prose. For some reason I cannot explain outright, when I read William's prose, I cannot help experiencing the same exquisitely pleasurable sensation I had when I read Max Beerbohm's *Seven Men*. He told me he was compiling his verse for publication in order 'to leave things in a tidy state when I die'.

Dennis Duerden and his pretty wife, Rhoda. I spent two days

with them at Wheathampstead. Dennis is an abstract painter and works in the Nigerian section of the Overseas Service of the B.B.C. He was at the time in a conflict: whether or not he should switch over to figurative painting, feeling as he does, most dissatisfied with the social significance (or lack of it) of what he's producing. But he doesn't know how he can forsake abstract painting which he has served and justified so long? It's a glorious experience knowing Dennis and his wife. So unaffected, unconventional and profoundly human.

Then there was Mary Benson, former secretary of Africa Bureau. She is Pretoria-born, and between her, her successor, Jane Symonds, and Michael Scott, they have turned out enormously valuable work to enlighten the world on African affairs. Their journal, *Africa Digest*, is one of their most effective instruments in this task. Mary Benson is a frail-looking woman and has organized her failing health remarkably through the years by sheer will-power that runs like tough wire through her tenderness of heart.

A man of considerable depth is Accha de Lanerole, a Cingalese architect. A dark young man with pathos and wisdom in his eyes and large crop of hair.

And then there were the West Indian writers. John Hearne, who has an almost reckless passion for London life; Andrew Salkey, the bearded fellow with very kind and large eyes. At a glance, he is a mixture of Falstaff and some patriarch. He thinks the West Indian novel has been 'promising' too long now. He himself has ingeniously invented an English dialect in which he is writing up tales about that human spider in the West African and Caribbean fable, Anansi. Jan Carew, from British Guiana, is a tall fellow with a scalding tongue for those West Indians he likes to call 'intellectual buffoons', who he says are always acting superior in their relations to Africans.

And then there were the South Africans: a very very lonely crowd, both black and white.

There were a few others whom I had known before, and I must take these for granted. Need I also mention that I was fêted by the editors of Fabers and my agent until I felt almost swollen-headed?

I had been to Cambridge a week before and now I visited Oxford for the second time that summer. All so overwhelming. I kept saying to myself: how I wish I had the opportunity to go to university! In the afternoon I gave a talk to the Oxford Africa Society on African writing. Later in the afternoon my host had asked me to tea at Queen Elizabeth House where we were to meet a group of white South Africans. These were members of the South African Bureau of Racial Affairs, a body of Afrikaans 'intellectuals' supposed to correspond to the liberal Institute of Race Relations in Johannesburg.

At the sound of 'SABRA' I instinctively stiffened, my whole being revolted. But out of politeness I allowed myself to be bullied by my host. A former lecturer at Fort Hare University College in South Africa, now at Oxford, led me to one of the three Afrikaners, a mountain of a man. The Oxford man remarked that it must be interesting teaching Nigerians. I said yes, and added (rather lamely, I thought afterwards): 'There's no limit to the opportunities Nigerians have of being educated.' Suddenly I was conscious that I was groping in my mind for something I could say to hurt the Afrikaner.

My Oxford acquaintance asked if there was any relation between Nigerian and South-Bantu languages. 'Very little,' I replied. 'Except for a few stray words that have almost like sounds.'

'Has SABRA ever thought of doing research in the subject of African languages and their interrelations?' asked the lecturer.

The Afrikaner, silent as ever like a huge antheap, said curtly, 'I think we will have a konfrens ebeowt it.' He looked exasperatingly detached while I was still trying to charge up my sluggish wit.

In reply to another question, he pointed to one of his colleagues. 'Do you know him?' he asked. Who should it be but Rev. C. B. Brink, Moderator of the Dutch Reformed Church in the Transvaal. He was chairman of the Society for the Blind, in whose institution for African blind I worked for nearly five years during the last war. I did the incredible thing. Half instinctively and half deliberately, I walked up to the Dominee and extended my hand. 'Remember me?' I asked, telling him my name in the same breath. 'Worked at Ezenzeleni Blind Centre when you were chairman.'

Smiling, the Dominee said, 'What happened that drove you out of South Africa?'

'So many things.' Again, I was annoyed at my inability to hurt when I wanted so much to, incited by my loathing of the whole lot of SABRA men and the Dutch Reformed Church, who cause so much suffering among non-whites. The conversation carried on in Afrikaans. Why, why do you stand like this and talk to such people? the little voice inside me kept nagging. I left the hall in disgust with myself.

That evening the Warden asked a few people, including me, to drinks at the same place. I was just putting the glass of gin-and-tonic to my lips for a first sip, when something curious happened. I thought I saw my host and myself in the midst of a bunch of other persons, talking. The scene had nothing whatever to do with reality. I wasn't at that moment talking to my host at all. That image overlapped with yet another, again out of context. I had two sips of my gin, trying to steady my mind. I looked about for my host and some other reality to reassure me. Although not far off, he looked distant. I couldn't continue to stand there while my mind was playing tricks with me. I asked to be excused, and the Warden took me to my sleeping quarters.

Thinking back on the incident that night as I lay in bed, my mind still not cleared, I screwed up my will power to try to track down the problem. I felt physically fit, and hadn't had a late night for weeks. Then I remembered how guilty I felt while I stood talking to those Afrikaners and not able for some inexplicable reason to move away or insult them: guilty because almost unconsciously I told myself I ought not to be talking to them. I also remembered, or rather admitted to myself, that I had gone out to talk to the Dominee as an act of self-assertion—to 'prove' something, to show that I was out of reach of his government and they couldn't do me a thing, nor could he, a symbol of oppression.

The next day, after that bit of therapy, I was quite all right. Another of my failures to live with freedom? Perhaps. Three weeks late I left Britain to come back to work. I felt sick and tired of it all. The last line in my diary of the visit reads: '*I've tried to read Britain —or what part of it I've seen—letter for letter, like a child learning how to read. Each letter has been a huge impression, and the sum total has left me a bundle of agitation. How long freedom is going to intensify my hatred of those who have denied me it, I don't know.'*

II

Three years in Nigeria. Three years of adjustment, and still no solution in sight. A hard fact to live with: that once an exile, always one. And my wife and I find we are still far from accepting whites in Nigeria simply as human beings, try as we might. On the whole we find Americans in Africa a hundred times easier to make friends with than the British.

Among the Nigerians, we find Easterners and Mid-Westerners much easier to get on with. My wife and I are still trying to make friends among Westerners (mainly Yorubas). Perhaps 'make friends' is not quite what I mean. The Westerners are a closed society, and a sharply stratified one. I am doing extra-mural lecturing in the north (mainly Hausas and Fulanis, either Muslim or 'pagan'). Like communities in Yorubaland, Northerners are intensely authoritarian. It is as though things would fall apart and people would feel helpless if the centre of authority were removed. In several Nigerian homes, even educated ones, the lady of the house does not usually appear in the lounge at all to see a visitor. My wife simply has not been able to establish contact when we have been visiting. Those she finds don't, except for Easterners and Mid-Westerners, return a social call.

Our three children now attending school enjoy it very much. For them, thank goodness, adjustment is no problem.

Although I know conditions in such a free country do not keep a man on his toes all the time as in the Deep South of the continent, I keep applying the standards of an underdog to Nigerian situations. When a Nigerian smiles in gratitude at a white man's paternalistic or patronizing treatment of him, I react violently; much like the nobleman in Browning's *My Last Duchess*. Only after the event do I remind myself that the Nigerian has ceased to regard the white man's presence as a challenge. And at the time when he did, the white man was not really oppressing him. Again, my spirits go flat when Westerners here persist in creating enclaves for ethnic groups so that minority fears should be brought down to a minimum. Then I remember that a detribalized man in the south whose predicament is perpetuated largely by chiefs who are now the government's idea of the real African leaders, cannot easily appreciate that there are people elsewhere in Africa who, having the freedom of choice, feel happier under tribal heads.

And so I realize now something I was never aware of when I was in South Africa: that the white man has poisoned my life at the spring; it goes against me all the time, this anger, in my dealings with white people.

My sense of values is challenged in my relations with Nigerians themselves. Their women work much too hard. By and large, the men seem to do much less, and seem too often to consider it a right to have a good time. It is an unhappily common thing to see a man buy an expensive car while his living quarters require cleaning up or renovating or a painting of the floors so that they can be polished. In the south, blacks would rather spend the little they get to make their living quarters—even in shanty towns—comfortable, good-looking and hygienically fit for human habitation. Here again, one realizes how a people's obsession with capital tends to falsify its character. And then we are living in a state of freedom where colonial attitudes and values are still strong.

There is that other challenge that demonstrates the class thing. I have seen Africans treat their servants here in a most distressing manner that would make a white man in southern Africa look like an angel. Servants constitute a very large class, in a country where unemployment has reached alarming proportions. The main centres of labour—domestic work, driving, public works, utility services and mining—simply cannot take in any more workers. Owning a servant or servants to look after one's personal comfort is a rotten enough institution without the pain that the employer inflicts on those who work for him.

The forty South African teachers who are in Nigeria and the equal number in Ghana all find their standards challenged in the classroom. You come from a country where you were told by white authority that you were a teacher for twenty-four hours of day and night. You worked from 8.30 a.m. to 4.30 p.m. (in high school). You were bound to conduct extra-mural activities you were interested in at school at least twice a week. Your school was an overcrowded four-stream institution, and each classroom (not class) contained no fewer than sixty pupils. In West Africa, where things are lax, you are regarded by pupils as something of a slave-driver. When you offer to give the weaker pupils lessons outside school hours, they ask how much they should pay you. Some will even stay away when they find out that *free* tuition is being offered!

The dash (tip) system harasses you right and left. Those who offer you their services can even ask or remind you to 'dash' them. A short while ago three University College employees took me and the furniture to my new station by lorry, 103 miles away. After the trip, anticipating those awkward moments when one simply says, 'Thank you' and the man one thanks still hangs about, I took out 1s. 3d. for each as 'dash'. 'How much is it?' asked the driver. I showed him the amount. 'No thank you.' 'And you?' I asked the other two. 'No, tank you, sah, na we be paid by univesty, meka no-worry sah,' one of them said. I was angry with them for deflating my vanity and at the same time for twisting a mercenary attitude so that it looked like decency; angry with myself for looking Colonial and making it possible for them to respond the way they did. Oh, so many feelings that made the problem look larger than it probably is.

Two South African friends of mine had a disturbing experience recently. Now the police in Nigeria have always been respectful and courteous—with us professional men at any rate. One of my friends left an umbrella at his house when he was going away on long leave. He returned with the other countryman to fetch it. It was not there. His steward, whom he had left to lock up had already gone. They went to the police to report the matter. A search was immediately instituted with abundant zeal. The umbrella was found in the steward's possession at his favourite recreational 'joint'. His explanation was that he was going to keep it until my friend should return from leave. But the police took him to the charge office.

'Please don't take this thing any further,' my friend pleaded. 'The umbrella has been found after all.'

'The matter's in our hands now,' said the policeman gloatingly.

'But I'm not making a charge.'

'That's all right, sir, *we* are; it is in our hands now. We know these illiterates. (Here he gave the steward a menacing look.) Plenty tief-tief too-much palaver for mastah eh! Na plenty palaver be coming for you.' My friends felt a chill to think how harsh magistrates are in this country. . . .

These are some of the things we have to learn to live with as uncommitted exiles. There is this rich promise to console us: there are definite signs that after independence, old stock allegiances and affiliations, will fall away, and that new ideas will demand expression and therefore create more organs of public opinion. This way, there is bound to be a cross-breeding of ideas that will in time purge the country of unsavoury practices. Meantime, it is glorious to be able to move about uncommitted.

BIBLIOGRAPHY

ABRAHAMS, PETER. *The Path of Thunder*. New York: Harper & Brothers, 1948.

——. *Tell Freedom*. New York: Alfred A. Knopf, 1954.

——. *Wild Conquest*. London: Faber & Faber, 1951.

ACHEBE, CHINUA. *Things Fall Apart*. New York: McDowell, Obolensky, 1959.

BASSIR, OLUMBE (ed.). *An Anthology of West African Verse*. Ibadan: Ibadan University Press, 1957.

BUTLER, GUY (ed.). *A Book of South African Verse*. New York & London: Oxford University Press, 1959.

CARY, JOYCE. *Aissa Saved*. London: Michael Joseph, 1932.

——. *Mister Johnson*. New York: Harper & Brothers, 1951.

CONRAD, JOSEPH. *Three Tales*. New York: Random House, Modern Library.

COPE, JACK. *The Golden Oriole*. London: William Heinemann, 1958.

——. *The Tame Ox*. London: William Heinemann, 1960.

DHLOMO, H. I. E. *Valley of A Thousand Hills*. Durban: Knox Printing Co., 1941.

FAULKNER, WILLIAM. *Light in August*. New York: Random House, Modern Library.

FITZPATRICK, PERCY. *The Outspan*. London: William Heinemann, 1898.

FORSTER, E. M. *Aspects of the Novel*. New York: Harcourt, Brace and Co., 1956.

——. *A Passage to India*. New York: Harcourt, Brace and Co., 1949.

BIBLIOGRAPHY

Gordimer, Nadine. *Six Feet of the Country*. New York: Simon and Schuster, 1956.

——. *Soft Voice of the Serpent*. New York: Simon and Schuster, 1953.

——. *A World of Strangers*. New York: Simon and Schuster, 1958.

Huxley, Elspeth. *The Flame Trees of Thika*. New York: William Morrow and Company, 1959.

——. *Red Strangers*. London: Chatto & Windus, 1955.

——. *A Thing to Love*. London: Chatto & Windus, 1954.

Karp, David. *The Day of the Monkey*. New York: Vanguard Press, 1955.

Krige, Uys. *The Dream and the Desert*. London: Collins, 1953.

Lessing, Doris. *Five*. London: Michael Joseph, 1953.

——. *The Grass Is Singing*. London: Michael Joseph, 1950.

——. *This Was the Old Chief's Country*. London: Michael Joseph, 1952.

Lewis, Ethelreda. "Blind Justice," *Stories of Africa*. Edited by E. C. Parnwell. London: Oxford University Press, 1930.

Mannoni, O. *Prospero and Caliban*. Translated by Pamela Powesland. New York: Frederick A. Praeger, 1956.

Millin, Sarah Gertrude. *God's Stepchildren*. Johannesburg: Central News Agency, 1924.

——. *The Herr Witchdoctor*. London: William Heinemann, 1941.

Mofolo, Thomas. *Chaka*. Translated by Reverend F. H. Dutton. London: Oxford University Press, 1951.

Paton, Alan. *Cry, the Beloved Country*. New York: Charles Scribner's Sons, 1948.

Plaatje, Sol T. *Mhudi*. Lovedale: Lovedale Press, 1930.

Plomer, William. *Double Lives*. New York: Noonday Press, 1956.

——. *Four Countries*. London: Jonathan Cape, 1949.

——. *Turbott Wolfe*. London: The Hogarth Press, 1925.

Pringle, Thomas. African Sketches. London: Edward Moxon, 1834.

SCHREINER, OLIVE. *The Story of an African Farm.* New York: W. W. Norton and Company, 1959.

——. *Trooper Peter Halket.* London: T. Fisher Unwin, 1957.

SCULLY, WILLIAM CHARLES. *Kaffir Stories.* London: T. Fisher Unwin, 1895.

SEARY, E. R. *South African Short Stories.* Cape Town: Oxford University Press, 1947.

SITHOLE, NDAHANINGI. *African Nationalism.* New York & London: Oxford University Press, 1959.

SMITH, PRUDENCE (ed.). *Africa in Transition.* Chester Springs, Pa.: Dufour Editions, 1957.

STEIN, SYLVESTER. *2nd-Class Taxi.* London: Faber & Faber, 1958.

TRILLING, LIONEL. *The Liberal Imagination.* New York: Doubleday & Company, 1953.

VAN DER POST, LAURENS. *Dark Eye in Africa.* New York: William Morrow and Company, 1955.

——. *In a Province.* London: The Hogarth Press, 1955.

VENTER, FRANS. *Dark Pilgrim.* Philadelphia: Muhlenberg Press, 1959.

WILLIAMS, GRENFELL, and MAY, HENRY JOHN. *I Am Black.* London: Cassell & Co., 1936.

WRIGHT, RICHARD. *Native Son.* New York: Grosset & Dunlap, 1940.

INDEX

Note: *Book, poem, article titles are indexed in full (i.e. under 'A' or 'The' if this is part of title)*

INDEX

INDEX

INDEX

INDEX

INDEX

INDEX

INDEX

INDEX

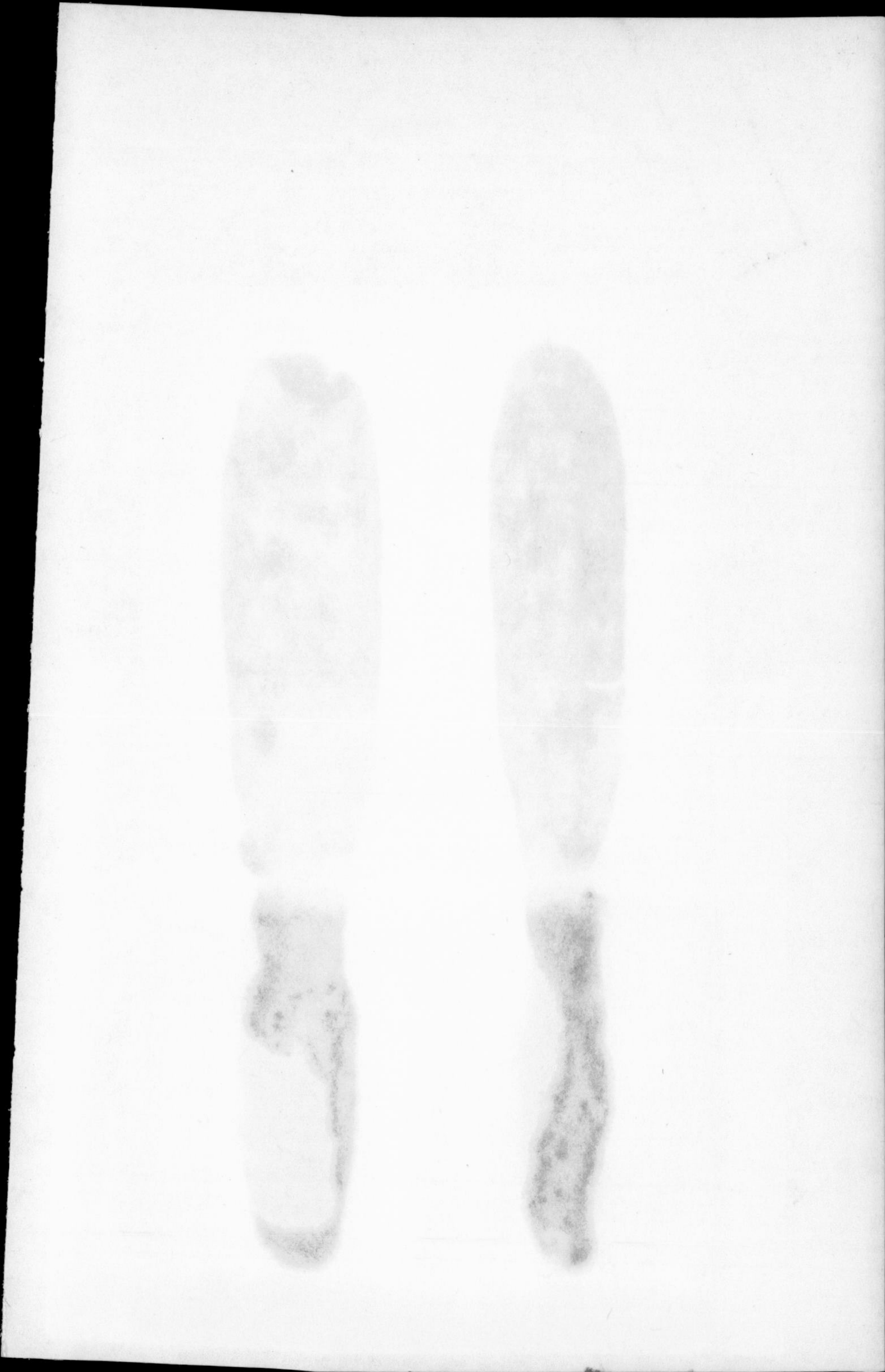